Here's what readers had to say about the first edition of *Master Your Panic and Take Back Your Life.*

"From her experience successfully treating hundreds of patients, and from her review of the voluminous literature in the area, Dr. Beckfield has distilled the essence of effective treatment into **the most readable book on the topic I have seen.**

"The information conveyed so skillfully in (the book) will also help families and friends understand the many bewildering effects of panic and agoraphobia... superb book." — John Greist, M.D.
CEO, Healthcare Technology Systems, Inc.
Clinical Prof. of Psychiatry, Univ. of Wisc. Medical School
Author, *Anxiety and Its Treatment*

"Of all the clinical self-help books on panic disorder, Master Your Panic and Take Back Your Life *is the best. I use the book as required reading for the individual and group therapy I conduct for clients with panic disorder and high anxiety. It is excellent, easily understandable and with self-help exercises that really make a difference. I recommend they read others, but I require this one."* — Tom Parsons, M.A., L.P.C.
Co-founder: The SHYNESS Institute of Colorado

"...Especially noteworthy are chapters 2, 3, and 4, helping clients to trace both the lifetime origins as well as the daily antecedents of their panic episodes.
"I haven't seen this covered so well anywhere else."
— Edmund Bourne, Ph.D.
Author, *Coping With Anxiety*

"...best book of its kind." — Albert Ellis, Ph.D., President
Albert Ellis Institute, New York

"I just turned 40 years old... I've been suffering from periodic attacks since I was 24 years old... Right now I feel 100% like my `old' self... **You have helped me tremendously..."** — A grateful reader
Memphis, TN

"Throughout the last seven years, I have hoped that someone would write a really useful self-help book... **It's fantastic to have books I can recommend without reservation...** *I am already telling others about the book..."* — Lynn Maguire
Phobia Society of Dallas

*"I was quite surprised at the impact the book had on me... This book is **just what we need!** (The book is)... user-friendly, based on sound, research-based techniques, yet also addresses emotional issues such as loss, and unresolved grief or anger (something we find hard to release)...*

"Dr. Beckfield truly understands the agony and struggle that her clients and readers experience... excellent book."
— Franci Warner, Editor, Book Review, *The Mountain Climber*

*"An excellent guide for those suffering from anxiety disorders. **Very clear descriptions of sound treatments...** an excellent discussion of the `roots of panic.' Addresses what most other books on this topic neglect: the important role of emotional factors, personality characteristics, and life experiences... This book is highly recommended."*
— John Preston, Psy.D.
Academic Vice President
Sacramento, California, Professional School of Psychology
Author, *Survivors: Stories and Strategies to Heal the Hurt*

"The minute I finished reading (Master Your Panic and Take Back Your Life), *I wanted to hop right on a plane and fly out to meet with Dr. Beckfield in person. It is **written with unbelievable understanding and compassion.** I keep a copy at home and work. It comes in handy for me and also for others who may try to understand their condition...*

"I recommend the book highly to anyone with panic and anxiety. It's a magnificent book." — M.L., a reader in Clearwater Beach, FL

*"**Straightforward, practical, and easily accessible...** (The book is) **very well-done...** bringing together lots of information and dealing with critical issues that patients face in treatment."* — Mark H. Pollack, M.D.
Director, Anxiety Disorders Program
Massachusetts General Hospital
Associate Professor of Psychiatry, Harvard Medical School
Author, *Panic Disorder & Its Treatment*

Master Your Panic and Take Back Your Life!

MASTER YOUR PANIC

AND TAKE BACK YOUR LIFE!

3RD EDITION

*Twelve Treatment Sessions
to Conquer
Panic, Anxiety and Agoraphobia*

DENISE F. BECKFIELD, PH.D.

Impact Publishers®
ATASCADERO, CALIFORNIA

First Edition, 1994
Second Edition, 1998
Copyright © 1994, 1998, 2000, 2004
by Denise Beckfield
Second Printing, September 2004

ATTENTION ORGANIZATIONS AND CORPORATIONS:
This book is available at quantity discounts on bulk purchases for educational, business, or sales promotional use. For further information, please contact Impact Publishers, P.O. Box 6016, Atascadero, California 93423-6016. Phone 805-466-5917, e-mail: info@impactpublishers.com

The "Special Helps" Summaries found on pages 103, 123, 190 and 217 were adapted with permission from columns written originally by Dr. Beckfield for the National Panic/Anxiety Disorders (NPAD) Newsletter, 1718 Burgundy Place, Suite B, Santa Rosa, CA 95403.

Library of Congress Cataloging-in-Publication Data

Beckfield, Denise F.
    Master your panic and take back your life : twelve treatment sessions to conquer panic, anxiety & agoraphobia / Denise F. Beckfield. — 3rd ed.
      p. cm.
    Includes bibliographical references and index.
    ISBN 1-886230-47-1 (alk. paper)
    1. Panic disorders.   2. Self-help techniques.   I. Title.

RC535.B43 2003
616.85'223—dc22   2003062026

Impact Publishers and colophon are registered trademarks of Impact Publishers, Inc.

Cover design by
Sharon Lea Flickinger and K.A. White Design, San Luis Obispo, California
Printed in the United States of America on acid-free paper.
Published by
Impact ℣ Publishers®
POST OFFICE BOX 6016
ATASCADERO, CALIFORNIA 93423-6016
www.impactpublishers.com

Dedicated

to Lynn Baxter MaGuire
9/22/44 — 3/02/01

&

Leila Ruth Beckfield
9/25/11 — 5/25/00

Two remarkable women
who, daily, took pleasure in the blessing of their lives;

who faced situations of pain and loss
with unwavering courage and grace;

and who, through it all,
never forgot how to laugh.

Contents

Acknowledgements

When my publisher, Bob Alberti, Ph.D., first asked me about coming out with a third edition of this book, I hesitated. I'd developed some visual and neurological problems that had made reading and writing slower and more physically arduous for me. Ultimately, though, I decided that the project might be possible "with a little help from my friends." That "little bit of help" turned out to be a whole *lot* of help, from friends, family, and former colleagues, and I welcome the chance to offer them a much deserved thanks.

While I am still equally indebted to those acknowledged in earlier editions of the book, space limitations do not permit me to re-acknowledge them here. I must make an exception, however, for Sharon Skinner, Impact's Production Manager. Given my limitations, the stack of revisions I sent her consisted of pages torn from the Second Edition with sections crossed out, additions scrawled in the margins, arrows pointing every which way and last-minute alterations tacked on at the end. Somehow, she transformed this unwieldy mess into letter-perfect, printer-ready form — and, more impressive yet, did so without once losing her patience, her encouraging tone nor her sweet temper. I am left equally in awe of her talents and her saintly temperament. Clearly, this book could not have existed without her.

Likewise, there are three professionals with expertise in the area of anxiety disorders who contributed directly to this edition of the book, and without whom it would not exist. First, my thanks to Scott Bohon, M.D., a friend and former colleague at the Dean Medical Center, for his immense help in updating and revising portions of the medications chapter. I asked Scott for his help because I knew him to be exceedingly well-read and informed in the area, experienced clinically and — having worked with him for some ten years — unfailingly compassionate. I can scarcely thank him enough for his generosity and the meticulous care he took with his many suggestions, revisions and rewrites.

Thanks also to Emily Hauck, Ph.D., who generously agreed to read the entire text to catch any needed updates I might have overlooked. Emily has been treating those with panic and agoraphobia for upwards of fifteen years, drawing on her excellent graduate and postgraduate training in the area. And, in a remarkable coincidence that I find beguiling, Dr. Hauck's major professor during graduate training was Dianne Chambless, Ph.D., a personal heroine of mine and, I feel, an unsung hero in the field, whose work alerted me to the importance of emotional factors in panic disorder and agoraphobia — a realization which has been valuable clinically, meaningful to those with panic and, I believe, often crucial in achieving a comprehensive and lasting treatment of the disorder.

Finally, this book would never have existed — not a First Edition, nor a Second, *nor* a Third — were it not for the generosity, guidance and expertise of John Greist, M.D. Dr. Greist is the first person I asked to read the manuscript of the book, back in the days before its publication when it was peppered throughout with reference notes, which ultimately were removed to a separate appendix for the ease of readers.

Dr. Greist is internationally esteemed for his expertise in the field of anxiety disorders — for his top-notch, prolific, often ground-breaking research; for his sophisticated theoretical insights; and for his sheer wealth of knowledge. What is perhaps less well-known about Dr. Greist is his well-earned reputation for kindness, warmth and boundless generosity, which gave me the courage to approach him in the first place. His comments on the book were, without exception, thoughtful, well-reasoned and informed. Because we differed somewhat with respect to one element of the book, I want to emphasize the customary caveat that any errors of omission or commission are solely my responsibility.

A classic "John Greist" incident that I recall vividly occurred during a conference on psychiatric topics I attended some time ago. John gave a talk on social anxiety, and the talk was, as usual, superb — comprehensive, cutting-edge and engaging, accompanied by charts, graphs, tables and the occasional Far Side cartoon. What's surprising in all this? John had agreed, with less than an hour's notice, to pinch-hit for the scheduled speaker who, we were told, was "trapped in Tucson by a snowstorm" — presumably the one around Chicago that had grounded all incoming flights. What's not surprising, however, is that John's talk was of such exceptional quality, despite the lack of formal preparation time. Given his intellectual prowess, his vast experience in the field and his unquenchable zest for his work, it's as though he simply leaps out of bed every morning, already prepared!

Medical twists and turns of fate in my life have slowed and, at times, interrupted work on this edition of the book, but I've been remarkably fortunate to be under the care of a number of truly gifted physicians. I'd like to thank Drs. Ossama Al-Mefty, Marc Feeley, Joseph Fok, Michael Frontiera, Thomas Hirsch, Basil Holoyda, and Mark Pyle, as well as Russ Rohrdanz, M.S., C.C.A. I found them all to be warm, empathic human beings as well as experts in their respective fields. I only hope this book shows the same blend of compassion and expertise that I've encountered in my own medical care.

Two reference librarians were an invaluable help to me in gathering the research articles on which this update also depended. Jodi Burgess, a staff member at the medical library of St. Mary's Hospital Medical Center, has been locating references for me for over fifteen years; she probably knows the literature in the field better than I do! She continues to amaze me with her skills and efficiency, her ability to anticipate what I need and her consistently good humor. And Mary Griffith, M.L.I.S., dear friend and reference librarian *extraordinaire*, was an incredible support, tirelessly available to locate whatever I needed at the oddest of hours, and to help me tie up those annoying loose ends.

Other technical help came from Kelvin Klassy, "our computer guy," who was ever-attentive, responsive and clever at devising computer solutions to allow me to work around my visual problems. My thanks to Kelvin, most of all, for his dedication to the task — puzzling over it, conferring with his colleagues and never giving up — all because of his touching belief that the book was worth the effort.

Numerous individuals important in my personal life have, likewise, been important to the completion of this book. In addition to the long-standing and loyal friends acknowledged in earlier editions, several exceptional people have come into my life and enriched it in myriad ways. When I've encountered roadblocks in the work, they've bailed me out, boosted my spirits and lent needed balance to my life.

My deepest thanks to the Lyndes — Dar, Paula, Elliot and Drew — for their abiding friendship, generosity, and acts of kindness too numerous to mention; to Janet Easley Farin, who so quickly became so dear to me; to Kathleen and Lee Olson, for their warm, engaging friendship; to Don and Krista Nelson, for their ongoing interest and kind concern for me; and, finally, to Sally Wilmeth and Terry Geurkink for their deep and valued friendship over the years.

While I see less of my former colleagues at the Dean Clinic, the fond place I hold in my heart for them is as large and warm as ever. Although I've acknowledged the staff as a whole in earlier editions, I must single out, in particular, Don Ferguson, Ph.D., and Peter Clagnaz, M.D., for their perennial kindness, support and friendship.

Thanks, too, to the many family members who so greatly eased my burdens during the preparation of the book. My mother, Romona Fisher, once again my annual nominee for Mother of the Year, checked references for me, proofread text and even agreed to type from my dictation, never an easy task. Once, she encountered the words, "Anxiety Disorders Association," and apparently couldn't quite decipher them. Finally, clearly baffled, she typed the words, "Thesaurus Association" and forged bravely ahead, betraying only by a tiny, discreetly-pencilled question mark in the margin that she had any doubt whatsoever as to what a "Thesaurus Association" could possibly have to do with panic and agoraphobia!

Thanks also to my father, Dalton Fisher, and his wife, Kris, who were always there to encourage, support and sympathize, as the occasion demanded. Further thanks to my dear Aunt Mabelle, an extra bonus of my marriage, who offers me strength and inspiration through her many cards and letters, and by her own example; and to my Aunt Betty, who, despite serious health problems of her own, remains the cheerful good sport she's always been.

Also, my thanks to the Sievers — Kay, Sherm, Ginny and Emily — for their open-door policy on family holidays, their periodic "road rescues," and their constancy in our lives; to the Kapps, who've always felt like family; and to Cousin Ken, who, quite simply, is good for the soul.

This book would not exist were it not for the contributions of the many panic sufferers I've known, who freely shared their stories and their struggles with me, and whose hard-earned wisdom appears throughout. Each of them taught me much about the caring and courage that exists in everyday life. I thank them for this book, and for all they've given me.

My love and gratitude, as always, to my dear husband, Paul, with whom I've traveled Life's ever-surprising course for some thirty years. It's heartwarming to discover, after so many years together, that someone still loves you, can still make you laugh, and still believes you when you say, "I used to be really thin."

Finally, my deepest thanks is reserved for our sons, John and Peter. The sacrifices they've made on my behalf, and on that of the book, have been nothing short of noble. Some things in life come to us because we deserve them. Others, like John, and like Peter, are simply wonderful gifts.

— Denise Beckfield
January, 2004

"First Aid" for Panic:
Sixteen "On the Spot" Strategies to Get Through a Panic Attack

1. Sit down and take several **slow, deep** breaths. Take at least four seconds to inhale, through your nose, and at least four more to exhale, through pursed lips as though you're whistling. Continue this for several minutes, trying, as you do so, to consciously relax your muscles.

2. Picture a relaxing scene using all your senses. *Now put yourself into the scene.*

3. Recall a time when you handled a similar situation well, or felt successful and in charge. Recapture the good feelings you experienced then.

4. Snap your fingers to "break the spell" and interrupt catastrophic thoughts of the disasters you imagine happening. Refocus on the concrete objects around you, making a game of noticing the details of every object you see.

5. Allow your anxious thoughts to "float on through," in the recognition that panic *can't hurt you, isn't dangerous and doesn't mean you're crazy* — no matter how it feels!

6. Picture a person you trust, someone who believes in you and cares about your well-being. Now imagine the person is with you, offering you encouragement.

7. Remember, panic is only your body's natural alarm system kicking in when it needn't. Say to yourself, "This is just a simple mistake. *There is no danger here.*"

8. Take a "time out" and **slow down. Slow** your rate of breathing, **slow** your racing thoughts, **slow** your entire body, head to toe. Then *slowly* resume your previous activities.

9. Ask yourself what you were feeling just **before** the first signs of panic. Now let yourself really "feel" those feelings. The feelings might be painful, but *recognizing* them is likely to send your panic packing.

10. Take a giant yawn and stretch your body, head to toe. Now chew a stick of gum, slowly and deliberately.

11. Occupy your mind with an absorbing task: start a complicated work project; listen to an interesting radio program; phone a friend. Focus your mind on what's happening in the **environment** rather than on your **body**; and on the **present,** rather than the **future.**

12. Get mad. Vow not to let panic win out over you. You deserve better.

13. If there are places available, take a stroll. If there are people available, talk to one of them. Better yet, do both.

14. Count backward from 20. With every number, picture a different image of someone you love, something that pleases you, something that calms you. These might be images you recall from the past or those you only imagine.

15. Take a moment to say a word of prayer or meditation, and let yourself feel calmed by your faith.

16. Remind yourself that a panic attack always ends. **Always.**

What's in Store — and Is It for Me?

If you just opened this book for the first time, you may be wondering how you can possibly overcome panic just by reading a book. The list below, of strategies found inside this one, will give you some idea:

Ten Strategies to Help You Overcome Panic

-Explore the *reasons you developed panic* in the first place (chapter two) and the *personality features that can keep you vulnerable* to outbreaks (chapter three).

-Discover your *"personal triggers" for panic,* the events and feelings that lead to repeated episodes of panic (chapter four) and those that spark individual attacks (chapter seven).

-Learn how panic spirals out of control — *and how to interrupt the spiral* before panic strikes (chapter six).

-Learn to *conquer the catastrophic thinking* that "fuels" panic (chapter eight).

-Discover how *new breathing habits* can reduce the physical symptoms of anxiety — and alter your blood chemistry to *increase your resistance* to panic (chapter five).

-Learn about *emotional traps* and sensitivities that *lower your threshold* for panic, and how to address them so panic doesn't come back (chapters two, three, four and seven).

-Increase your "comfort zone" with the *external situations* and the *internal sensations* that can trigger anxiety and panic (chapters nine and ten).

-Find out when *medication* is appropriate and when it's not, what the newest medications can do for you, and the "do's and don'ts" of medication use (chapter eleven).

-Read about how *real people* solved their problems with panic. Learn from their successes and struggles, and feel less alone.

-*Put it all together* (chapter twelve) and keep yourself calm and panic-free, for the life that's ahead of you.

The book is set up in twelve step-by-step "sessions" that parallel those of an in-person treatment program. Each session builds on the one before, and the exercises that follow will help you tailor the lessons to your own unique circumstances. And there are "troubleshooting" sections to help you solve problems you might encounter along the way. As you read *Master Your Panic and Take Back Your Life,* you'll feel a bit like you're being guided by your own personal "therapist in a book."

You'll be glad to learn that there's more and more sound evidence that self-guided methods, such as those found in this book (also called *bibliotherapy),* can be a very effective way to overcome panic attacks, and can, for a great majority of people, lead to lasting improvements large enough to make a real difference in your life.

One special feature of the book, highlighted as a particular favorite by readers of the first two editions, is its emphasis on the *emotional themes* important in panic — the sensitive issues in your life (like loss and suppressed anger) that can underlie repeated outbreaks of panic and the feelings that can spark individual attacks. The first edition pioneered those notions and the second included further refinements — for example, additional examples of the different triggers for panic, and tips on how to discover yours.

Readers familiar with the Second Edition of *Master Your Panic* will not find dramatic changes in this edition. Like the art and technique of good cooking, sound, well-proven strategies for overcoming panic have not changed substantially in the five years since the last edition was released. Research published during the past five years was evaluated, approximately thirty new references were added to

Appendix V, and several findings judged to be of particular importance to panic sufferers were incorporated into the text.

The greatest changes appear in Session Eleven, which describes first-line medications currently available for panic disorder, their typical side effects and their advantages over older medications. Some refinements of technique have been added to Session Five, which teaches a controlled breathing strategy for reducing physical arousal level and vulnerability to panic. And a new appendix on alternatives to controlled breathing was added, which includes a discussion of the increasingly popular practice of mindfulness meditation and its unique advantages for panic sufferers.

Finally, a section on Susceptibility to Panic was added to Session Twelve, which provides a concise summary of the histories, habits, thought patterns and emotional styles that contribute to the development and ongoing vulnerability to panic, and which have been addressed with the strategies presented throughout the book. These strategies should help readers to not only overcome their *current* panic attacks, but to become more resistant to *future* outbreaks as well.

No matter what brings on your panic attacks, the strategies in the book can be used to overcome them. That includes *panic disorder*, described in the first chapter of the book, and the panic attacks that are experienced quite commonly by people with *other anxiety disorders*.

If you struggle most of all with agoraphobia (that is, you avoid going to a variety of places, perhaps almost to the point that you're nearly housebound some of the time), this book is definitely for you. The method of *exposure*, described in Session Nine is the most well-proven method that exists for overcoming your symptoms and resuming life as it was before your panic and agoraphobia developed. The other sessions will be very important too, of course, giving you the strategies you need to ease the process, to feel less fearful and, of course, to overcome any current panic attacks. It will also help you to understand better how your problems developed in the first place, and how to stay free of them in the future.

Even if you don't have panic attacks, but you suffer from *anxiety in specific situations,* from *near-panic* episodes, or from more *low-level, chronic anxiety,* the methods can help you. How to apply them in your specific circumstances is discussed in a special section you'll find at the end of the book, called *Everyday Anxieties.*

Just for fun, try taking the quick quiz below to see how closely you match others with full-fledged panic disorder:

1. Do you have times when feelings of terror sweep over you, when your heart pounds or you feel weak and dizzy, and you think you're about to die or go crazy and lose control?

2. When you notice a pain or a change in your body, like an "extra" heartbeat or a tight, achy chest or a bad headache, do you worry that something might be seriously wrong?

3. Do you often think that with all the physical symptoms you have, there must be something wrong with your body that your doctors have missed?

4. Do you sometimes have trouble getting your breath, feel you're smothering, or have the frightening sensation that things around you aren't real?

5. Do you worry a lot about the safety and happiness of loved ones? About doing a good enough job? About most *everything???*

6. Are there places you avoid going because they make you nervous, even though you can't really explain your uneasy feelings, even to yourself?

7. Do you often try to sit near an exit when you go out somewhere, so you can leave, if you need to, without drawing attention to yourself?

8. When you were young, were you ever separated from an important family member because of an event like a lengthy hospitalization, or even a death?

9. As a child, did you worry a lot about new situations, or was it hard for you to be away from home; and do you still get "homesick" at times, even though you're fully grown?

10. Do you find conflicts scary or unpleasant, maybe so much so that you've gotten very good at avoiding them?

Did you discover some ways in which you resemble others with panic? For a much fuller description, why don't you continue reading and learn more, beginning with your first session, *What Is Panic?*

What Is Panic?

Carol is a genuine success story. She always *looked* like one. A competent, attractive woman in her late thirties, she was married to a successful businessman and had two bright, appealing children. She worked part-time as copy editor for a local newspaper, volunteered her time to community organizations and was involved in activities with friends and family. In short, her life looked full and fulfilling.

But beneath the composed and smiling surface, Carol was quietly drowning. She forced herself to leave the house each day, but she constantly struggled to keep going. Everything she did outside the home was carefully arranged to accommodate her fears. Though she could drive to selected locations in her own car, she could ride in someone else's only if her husband or sister were driving. If she attended any sort of event, she made certain she was accompanied by someone she trusted, and she seated herself near an exit in case she needed to leave in a hurry. When she traveled out of town, the first thing she did on her arrival was to check the locations of the hospital emergency rooms.

She often missed her children's activities at school because of her anxiety about being in crowds and felt saddened and ashamed for not being what she considered "a normal mom." When she did

Names and identifying information of those whose stories appear in the book have been changed significantly to protect their identities.

attend, she found herself concentrating mostly on getting through the event without humiliating herself or her family.

She spent as much time at home with her children as she could, but she was unable to do a whole host of things because of her fears. She couldn't even play board games with the family because she couldn't sit still for more than a few minutes without becoming extremely nervous.

She worried constantly about her children's safety and imagined all sorts of horrible tragedies that might befall them when they were out of her sight. She forced herself to let them live normal lives, but it was torture for her to see either of them walk out the front door.

At least once a day, without warning, Carol was overtaken by feelings of massive terror. In a split second, her heart began to pound, and she became faint and dizzy. She felt like she was suffocating and had to rush outside for air. Along with the physical sensations came the overwhelming feeling that something horrible was about to happen to her. After fifteen minutes of agony that seemed unending, the attack would finally ease, leaving her drained and weak, sometimes for the entire day.

Carol was deeply ashamed of her "spells" and had told only three others about them. She felt no one could truly understand the experience and was secretly convinced she was going crazy. She felt successively more alone and frightened and wondered what was to become of her. Sometimes she thought she'd be better off dead.

Carol's history. Carol's panic attacks had begun eighteen years earlier when she was only twenty years old. In the previous year, she'd married her childhood sweetheart, moved several states away from her family and had her first child, a daughter. She felt lonely being so far from her family and overwhelmed with the responsibility of caring for a baby.

One day she was outside hanging up laundry when, out of the blue, her heart began to pound so vigorously she thought it was going to explode out of her chest. She felt breathless and dizzy, her fingertips tingly and her legs rubbery. An indescribable, overpowering sense of doom engulfed her. She rushed into the house in terror to call her husband, but by the time he arrived home, the symptoms had abated. She continued to feel shaken and washed out, but her doctor could find nothing wrong with her, so he reassured her it was "probably nerves," and sent her home.

Soon after, the couple moved back to Carol's hometown, and the attacks disappeared on their own. Carol went on to have another child, a son this time, and although she had occasional minor attacks after he was born, once again they diminished fairly rapidly without treatment.

A few years after her son was born, Carol became pregnant again. She lost the child in what proved to be a tubal pregnancy and was advised to have no more children. Shortly thereafter, she began having frequent panic attacks and became unable to tolerate attending church, riding in elevators, or shopping in crowded stores for fear of an attack. If she went to a movie, she sat in an aisle seat in the back. She began to make adjustments so that if she needed to go out in the evening, a family member was able to accompany her.

About a year before Carol sought treatment, her daughter was in an auto accident and suffered minor injuries. Carol was overcome with guilt for having allowed her daughter to borrow the car, even though there was no reason to have refused. She was furious with the other driver, whom she blamed for the accident, and equally furious at her husband's refusal to take any action against him. Her panic attacks increased and she started having difficulty swallowing. She stopped eating in restaurants and lost ten pounds. She began to more vigorously avoid traveling out of town. She delayed some much-needed dental work because she felt unable to sit in the dental chair for a prolonged period.

A month or so before Carol appeared at the clinic to seek help with her difficulties, her daughter left for college. Carol's symptoms increased until she was having several attacks every day and was finding it difficult to stay at work. One day, in the midst of her worst attack ever, she called a friend who brought her to the clinic.

When Carol was seen for her initial evaluation, she described one major trauma early in her life — the sudden death of a beloved older sister from an aneurysm when Carol was nine. Aside from that, she described her childhood as normal and happy. She'd been successful in school both academically and socially. Although she'd had a few fears (storms, heights and large dogs), they hadn't interfered with her day-to-day life. Her mother was an anxious woman who was very protective of Carol, which annoyed Carol's brothers and sisters but simply made Carol feel all the more loved and secure.

Carol's condition was diagnosed as panic disorder with agoraphobia. She was greatly relieved to know that her difficulties weren't imaginary, that she wasn't the only person in the world going through this torment, and that she definitely wasn't "crazy." She was even more relieved to learn there was treatment available to help her overcome the crippling attacks.

Before we turn our attention to treatment, let's talk more about the disorder itself. The events in Carol's life may seem more dramatic than those in your own, but her story illustrates numerous features that are very typical in panic disorder.

Typical Features of Panic Disorder

Symptoms. Carol's primary symptoms during an attack were a rapid, pounding heartbeat, shortness of breath, feelings of weakness and dizziness and tingly or numb hands and feet. She also experienced blinding terror and the intense urge to flee during an attack. Sometimes she felt pains in her chest, and as her disorder progressed, she had occasional difficulty swallowing.

Other typical symptoms during a panic attack include trembling or shaking, hot flashes, chills and nausea. People often have the feeling during an attack that they're "going crazy" or that they're about to lose control. All these symptoms are normal parts of panic. They don't mean you're crazy. And they don't mean you're dying either, but you're likely to feel as though you are — and to feel it with an almost overpowering intensity.

Sometimes a panic attack is preceded or accompanied by feelings of unreality focused on yourself or the outside world, sensations termed *depersonalization* and *derealization*. You may feel as though everything around you is foggy, strange, unreal. These sensations can increase your worry that you must be "losing your mind," but in fact, they aren't at all unusual during attacks of anxiety. One study examined more than 100 people who'd been in circumstances of extreme danger, in which they thought they were about to die. The researchers found that 81 percent of the people described feelings of unreality in the situation. A majority also reported a changed perception of time (78 percent) and a sense of detachment (61 percent). Another study found that feelings of unreality were among the four most frequent symptoms experienced during a panic attack (59 percent). So whether intense anxiety comes from an external situation or from a panic attack, unusual perceptions are likely to accompany it.

The chart below lists the most common symptoms of a panic attack. If you experience at least four of these symptoms during an attack, developing abruptly and reaching a peak within ten minutes, the attack is considered an "official" panic attack. (A "limited-symptom" attack is the term for an attack involving fewer than four symptoms.)

Diagnostic Symptoms of a Panic Attack*

1. palpitations, pounding heart or accelerated heart rate (tachycardia)
2. sweating
3. trembling or shaking
4. sensations of shortness of breath or smothering
5. feeling of choking
6. chest pain or discomfort
7. nausea or abdominal distress
8. feeling dizzy, unsteady, lightheaded or faint
9. derealization (feelings of unreality) or depersonalization (being detached from oneself)
10. fear of losing control or going crazy
11. fear of dying
12. paresthesias (numbness or tingling sensation)chills or hot flushes
13. chills or hot flushes

If you have at least two unexpected panic attacks and at least one of them is followed by a month or more of persistent fear of having another, or worry about what the attack might mean, or a change in behavior due to the attack, you're likely to qualify for a diagnosis of panic disorder. (There are two other requirements for the diagnosis: The attacks are not the result of a *different* condition, for example, not provoked by a specific feared situation (as in a specific phobia) or by being the focus of others' attention (as in a social phobia); and the attacks are not the result of a specific medical condition or the ingestion of a substance.

*Reprinted with permission from *Diagnostic and Statistical Manual of Mental Disorders, Fourth Edition, Text Revision*, ©2000 by American Psychiatric Association.

Though there are similarities in the sensations that different panic sufferers experience during attacks, you may experience symptoms that seem especially unusual to you. Some people, for example, describe a "tilting" sensation during attacks — a feeling they might suddenly lose their balance and fall down. Others describe "surging" sensations in their heads. Some describe a fear that they might suddenly, impulsively do something bizarre or horrible. Most people notice the rapidity of their heartbeat, but others are more struck by its power and intensity. The sensation of "extra" or early heartbeats is common and often fuels fears of heart disease. And symptoms can shift over time, with new ones developing and old ones gradually dropping out.

Maybe you experience symptoms so bizarre it's impossible for you to believe they could result from anxiety, increasing your fear that you're suffering from a serious, undetected medical problem. Everyone experiencing unusual physical symptoms should be evaluated by a physician. But if the physician says you're suffering from panic and that you're otherwise healthy — believe it. Blurred or distorted vision, temporary blindness, sensations of numbness down one side of the body, severe headaches, chest pains — all of these have been seen at times as part of a panic disorder. When the panic disorder is successfully treated and the attacks disappear, so do the symptoms.

The unusual nature of some panic symptoms is just one aspect of the disorder that makes it so frightening and so frustrating. Another is the avoidance that often develops in the wake of the attacks.

Avoidance and Agoraphobia. A majority of panic sufferers, once they've experienced a panic attack, begin to avoid situations in which they fear they might have another attack (or at least some of the panic-like symptoms). Panic disorder *with agoraphobia* is the recognized term for someone whose panic attacks are accompanied by the avoidance of different places and situations

There are people who have panic attacks and still manage to continue participating in all their usual activities, but they typically do so with much more discomfort than previously. And there are lots of people who avoid in subtle ways, though not overtly. They may continue to work out, but they take pains to keep their exertion low so their hearts don't pound too vigorously. Or they unconsciously adjust the times at which they drive or shop to avoid crowds. Or they feel "under the weather" on the day of the big staff meeting and stay home from work that day.

The vast majority of panic sufferers experience at least some avoidance, and much of the material in this book speaks directly to them. But anyone experiencing panic attacks will find the exercises aimed at halting avoidance to be useful. They'll help you to rid yourself of panic across a whole range of settings and allow you to begin enjoying activities again rather than simply trudging through them, worrying the entire time.

So, whether you avoid overtly, covertly or not at all — whether you have panic disorder with agoraphobia or panic disorder without — this book is for you.

There are even a very small number of people who have agoraphobia *without* panic attacks. They simply avoid places and situations out of fear of having panic-like symptoms (especially those of an incapacitating or embarrassing nature) and not being able to get help, or to escape without difficulty (or embarrassment). Most clinicians believe that this disorder is so closely related to panic disorder that it represents virtually the same underlying condition. It is also treated in essentially the same manner as panic disorder. For this reason, and to avoid cumbersome language, this book generally refers to both conditions simply as "panic disorder."

Now let's get back to Carol to take a look at her avoidance. The situations Carol avoided were quite classic and are likely to ring a few bells for you. She avoided closed-in places like elevators, crowded places like malls, and any situation that might be difficult to escape from easily or without drawing attention to herself. If she were persuaded to go to a movie, a restaurant, a lecture, or a church service, she took care to position herself toward the back and near an exit. And she modified the times she attended various events to avoid large crushes of people.

Carol felt most at ease in her own home and in her home community, most ill at ease in unfamiliar places. Some sufferers report that the farther from home they are, quite literally, the less comfortable they feel; sixty miles is worse than thirty miles and thirty miles is worse than fifteen.

When Carol left her home for any reason, she felt most secure accompanied by her husband, least secure alone. Many individuals with panic find being alone the most frightening situation of all. For some, this reflects a fear of being in a situation where they might need medical care and no one is available to help. In addition, many panic sufferers have had childhood experiences of feeling frightened and alone. For them, being alone seems to evoke their earliest feelings of fear and helplessness.

Most people who develop panic attacks come to avoid situations that bring on the *physical sensations* associated with panic. Let's say your first panic attack involved a rapid heart rate, shortness of breath, and sensations of warmth. A few days later, you go to the gym to work out and begin to develop the very same symptoms. Chances are, you'll start to feel panicky. Physical sensations that weren't the least bit troubling two weeks ago suddenly have a very different and ominous meaning. And not surprisingly, your response to that new meaning is to feel intensely anxious.

Most panic sufferers who have an attack in a particular *location* come to dread that location and to avoid it just because of its association with previous feelings of panic. If you have a panic attack in a large grocery store, you might feel unable to return to that particular store; you might even begin to avoid *all* grocery stores.

We'll talk in more detail later about how avoidance develops and how to overcome it. For now, simply note that unless you take steps to halt it, avoidance tends to worsen and to "spread" to more and more situations.

Fluctuations in symptoms. Recall that during several periods in her life, Carol's panic symptoms arose, and then after a few months, diminished or disappeared on their own without any treatment. This pattern is highly typical of the disorder and, for many people, represents another frustrating aspect of it. While the disappearance of symptoms is a great relief, it's a double-edged sword. If the attacks can go away unpredictably, they can come back again just as unpredictably. Plus, the tendency for symptoms to come and go without apparent reason can add to the feeling that you're dealing with something completely incomprehensible and uncontrollable.

As Carol examined her own outbreaks more carefully, though, she realized that they were related to particular kinds of stresses in her life — separations and losses, feelings of aloneness, the changes of childbirth, and anger and conflict that left her feeling guilty and helpless. Carol also described the sorts of experiences in childhood that can predate the development of panic — in her case, a traumatic early loss and an overanxious mother.

The dual questions of who develops panic and when it arises are so important and complex that three whole sessions are devoted to them. For now, suffice it to say that Carol's increased understanding of her own vulnerabilities allowed her to do the work necessary to eliminate her panic symptoms. This book will teach you to do that, too.

Age and gender. Carol was twenty when her attacks began and thirty-eight when she sought formal treatment. Research indicates that panic disorder usually begins between late adolescence and the mid-thirties, though it can develop at any time. And women are two to three times as likely as men to develop panic.

Some experts believe that the number of men who suffer from panic has been underestimated because men are reluctant to admit difficulties with panic or to seek treatment for the disorder. Others suggest that men may be more likely than women to use alcohol to try to control their anxiety, so they more often end up in treatment for substance abuse than for their underlying panic. Whatever the case, more and more men who suffer from panic attacks are coming forward, and coming forward publicly — including individuals as prominent as NBC-TV weather forecaster Willard Scott and football Heisman Trophy winner Earl Campbell. (Among well-known women who've gone public about their panic are Country and Western singer Naomi Judd and well-known author Barbara Grizzuti Harrison.)

To all the readers of this book, men *and* women, *bravo* for taking the important step of acknowledging your panic attacks. It's never easy to admit to a problem that's so distressing, especially one that may feel like a personal weakness. In fact, panic disorder is no more reflective of personal weakness than high blood pressure or ulcers or migraine headaches.

"But why panic?" you may be thinking. "Why *not* something else, like migraines or ulcers or high blood pressure?" What is it that causes one person to develop panic and another to develop something different, or even to escape stress-related conditions altogether? That's the question we'll take up in the next session.

Exercise for Session One: What is Panic!

The following exercise will begin to provide you with an overview of your own panic disorder, what it "looks like," how it began and how it's affected you and your life.

Before you proceed, though, there's one thing you need to do to prepare for today's assignment and those to come: You need to obtain a fresh notebook — either by purchasing a new one or by locating an unused one around the house.

The notebook will serve as your place to keep track of all the different assignments you complete, to record various events that relate to your panic attacks, and simply to jot down the ideas and private thoughts that arise as you work through the program. It will provide the information you'll use along the way to detect important patterns in your panic and to help you troubleshoot when you encounter problems. And it will serve as a record of your ongoing progress, which is an important reward for all your hard work!

A notebook with lined paper is best. Select a size convenient to carry with you or buy a matched set of two — a standard size to keep at home and a mini-notebook to carry with you for on-site recording. You may also wish to buy a folder for any loose papers you might accumulate as you complete assignments.

A notebook to use throughout the program is more important than you may think. When a suggested assignment involves writing things down, it's very important to actually *do the assignment in writing,* not to simply identify responses "in your head." Writing down the words and seeing them in black and white will add to the impact and value of the assignment to you, and may spur additional thoughts that will further your understanding and progress even more. At various points in the program, you'll be instructed to refer back to an earlier assignment, so it will need to be written down in an accessible place.

One last point about your notebook. This is intended to be your private journal, for your eyes only. While it's up to you how crucial privacy is to you, it's generally useful to decide at the outset not to share the contents of your journal with anyone else. That way, you'll feel freer to be completely honest as you record your thoughts. And being completely honest with yourself will be a help in understanding and ultimately overcoming your problems with panic.

The Big Picture

There's only one formal assignment to complete for this session: Pretend you're a therapist conducting an interview to obtain a fuller picture of your panic disorder. Complete the following report on yourself by filling in the blanks. Be as specific and as detailed as you can be in your answers.

Completing the assignment may provoke new ideas about your panic. Jot down any that occur to you in your new notebook, even those that may seem unimportant to you at this stage.

My Panic Attacks

The first panic attack I recall happened (when? where?)_____

_____.

My symptoms included _____

_____.

I might have been feeling extra stressed at the time, since_____

_____.

I didn't know for sure what was happening. I thought that perhaps

_____.

After that time, my attacks (went away for a time? continued?)

_____.

The worst time in my life in terms of the panic attacks was _____

_____.

These days, my attacks happen about___times a week. They usually occur when _____

_____.

They seem to worsen when _____.

Because of the attacks, there are some things I no longer do and some places I no longer go, or go only if I absolutely must. For example, I avoid_____

_____.

Lots of activities I used to enjoy are less enjoyable because I worry about having an attack, or I have to make modifications to participate. For example, I _____

_____ .

I become especially afraid when I'm faced with _____

_____ .

I've noticed overall changes in my mood and personality, my confidence level and my physical sense of well-being since the attacks started. Some of the worst changes, for me, have included

_____

_____ .

I also feel as though having panic attacks has led to changes in some of my relationships with family and friends. Since the attacks started,_____

_____ .

I've worked very hard to cope with the attacks. These are some of the strategies that I use or have used in the past: _____

_____ .

The most useful technique I've found to manage or try to prevent attacks is _____

_____ .

I've spent a lot of time puzzling about why I have these attacks. Right now, my best guess is that _____

_____ .

When I finally get over the attacks, there are so many things I'd like to do. My greatest dream, once I solve the problem of panic attacks, is to _____ .

The Roots of Panic: Why Me?

So why did Carol develop panic disorder — and more to the point, why did you? Is it something you were born with? Was it caused by something that happened to you as a child? Is it simply a reaction to all the stresses in your life now? The answer is — probably a little bit of all three.

Chances are very good that your panic disorder results from a combination of factors. The first is a vulnerability to the disorder based on your *biological make-up*. The second is the "right" set of *circumstances in adult life* to bring it about. In between those two, the *experiences you had growing up* may have increased the likelihood of panic disorder in adulthood, though the evidence for that piece of the puzzle is more controversial.

This session looks at the contribution of biology and childhood experiences to the development of panic disorder in adult life. You'll find it interesting to read about some of the research in the field, and to compare the descriptions to your own situation.

Biology and Genetics

Let's consider your biology first. There are, without question, biological differences between people who suffer from panic disorder and those who don't. Researchers have found consistent differences in several central nervous system neurotransmitter

17

systems, the systems that transmit messages throughout our bodies. In effect, the structures and physical processes that alert us to incoming information, help us to process it, and guide our reactions to it seem to operate at a hyper-aroused level in those with panic disorder. In other words, people with panic appear to have very sensitive, highly reactive nervous systems, so that stressful events tend to produce strong physical reactions. If you suffer from panic attacks, that may be just what you suspected all along!

Genetics. Biological differences between those with panic disorder and those without don't necessarily prove there are genetic differences between the two groups. But in fact there are indications of a probable genetic contribution underlying these differences. Stated simply, some people seem to inherit a vulnerability to the disorder.

The evidence for a genetic contribution to panic comes from studies of the occurrence of panic disorder in families and also from studies of twins. For example, one early study that lends weight to the genetic hypothesis found that identical twins, who "share" 100 percent of their genes, are much more likely to "share" panic disorder than non-identical twins, who have only 50 percent of their genes in common.

It's not important to understand the intricacies of the genetics of panic disorder, but simply to realize that you may have inherited a predisposition to panic that made it "easier" to develop panic attacks compared to someone born with a different set of genes.

Probabilities. So what's the implication of this for you (and for your children, if you have any)? Just how important is the genetic contribution?

In the general population, the risk of developing panic disorder in a lifetime is nearly 10 percent, according to the most recent surveys. If you have a first-degree relative with panic disorder (a parent, a sibling, or a child — someone with whom you share half your genes), your lifetime risk increases to about 15 percent.

In other words, if you have diagnosable panic disorder, research would suggest that your daughter might have fifteen chances in 100 of one day developing it herself. By contrast, your neighbor down the street who has no first-degree relatives with the disorder might have only ten chances in 100 of developing the disorder. Clearly, then, if you have panic disorder, your children aren't doomed to develop it themselves. Their chances of not doing so are around 85 percent, after all. But they are at slightly greater risk than the general population.

If you have blood relatives who suffer from clinical depression, alcohol abuse or anxiety disorders other than panic, you also may be somewhat more susceptible to developing panic disorder, simply because of your genetic make-up. Carol, you'll recall, had an overanxious mother who might have had an undiagnosed panic disorder. Carol may have inherited a specific predisposition to panic disorder from her mother, or she may have been born with more generalized "anxious" tendencies that increased her vulnerability to panic in later life.

Temperament. Is there any reason to believe that you might have been "born anxious" and that this helps to explain your development of panic disorder? Perhaps. There's some evidence that children display different dispositions — different temperaments — from birth onward, and that one fairly stable aspect of temperament involves the way in which children respond to unfamiliar situations. Children who have been described as shy, inhibited, introverted, cautious and fearful are prone to respond to unfamiliar situations by showing distress, withdrawing from the situation, and seeking comfort and reassurance from a familiar person. In novel situations, these children also tend to display greater bodily arousal than bolder children (faster heartbeat, perspiration, shallow breathing).

There's some evidence that children who respond in this manner may develop anxiety and avoidant behaviors in later years. And researchers have found that children whose *parents* suffer from panic disorder and agoraphobia are more likely to show these traits than children of non-panic parents. In other words, being born with a temperament marked by discomfort with unfamiliar situations may increase your vulnerability to panic disorder in later life.

So whatever its exact source, some people appear more susceptible than others — from a genetic/biological standpoint — to the development of panic. That was likely the case for Carol and may well be the case for you, too.

You may be thinking, "This is discouraging information. I can't do a whole lot about my biological make-up." That's true. But all too often, persons with panic disorder accuse themselves of being somehow deficient or weak for having panic attacks. They look at the neighbor down the block and say, "Her life is just as difficult as mine, and she doesn't have panic attacks. So what's wrong with me?"

The answer is, there's nothing wrong with you; but there may be something *different* about you — and that difference may be your biological make-up.

Of course, your neighbor down the block, whose biological make-up is different from yours, may suffer from something equally distressing. Just as your genetic make-up may have propelled you in the direction of panic disorder, hers may have endowed her with a vulnerability to depression or migraine headaches or alcohol abuse or high blood pressure. In other words, she may also have problems at stressful times, but they may express themselves in different forms.

Then again, your neighbor down the block may have panic attacks that you just don't know about. After all, does she know about yours?

Early Experiences: Loss and Separation

There's something else about Carol that may have increased her susceptibility to panic. Recall that her sister died of an aneurysm when Carol was only nine years old. Experts are not in complete agreement, but it appears that people who've suffered losses or traumatic separations as children may be more susceptible to panic disorder as adults than those who haven't.

This may be particularly true for individuals who develop agoraphobia (avoidance) in the wake of panic attacks. One study, for example, compared the early histories of agoraphobic adults to nonagoraphobic adults and found that, as children, the agoraphobics had experienced significantly more separation from their mothers, separation from both parents, and divorce between their parents.

A high percentage of people who come to a clinic for treatment for panic attacks report losses or traumatic separations in their early lives. Joe, for example, developed a life-threatening illness that resulted in a three-week hospitalization when he was only five — an experience that was physically painful, terrifying and totally incomprehensible to a small child. When Joe returned home, he suffered terrible nightmares for years. As an adult, he developed panic disorder. While he didn't remember much about the hospitalization, it clearly had an important impact on him.

A death in the immediate family is probably the most dramatic example of loss and may bring about the special vulnerability to loss that often seems to go along with panic. In a treatment group of panic disorder sufferers led by the author, six of the eight participants had experienced traumatic losses, five as youngsters and the sixth as a young adult. Most of the losses were of a parent or sibling.

Carol would have had much in common with that group. Perhaps you would have, too.

Separation Anxieties and Fears of Loss. Loss or separation needn't actually occur for people to develop fears about loss — fears that may underlie panic.

Diane was raised in a dysfunctional family with a distant, uninvolved and quietly alcoholic father. Her mother controlled Diane's behavior with explicit threats of abandonment. Diane recalls her mother telling her, for example, that if she didn't behave properly, Mother would leave the house and never return. To a five-year-old child, that's a terrifying threat. And Diane's mother was so angry when she made the threat, and made it so often, there was no doubt in the little girl's mind that it was true. While Diane was able to overcome her panic symptoms quite rapidly, it took much longer in therapy to gradually overcome her intense fears of being abandoned and to begin to feel safe both within relationships and on her own.

Such "separation anxiety" is often found in children who develop panic disorder as adults. This connection has led some researchers to suggest that individuals who develop panic disorder have a lifelong vulnerability to separation. How might such a vulnerability come about? One possibility is through biological differences; as you know already, some children are simply born with temperaments more likely to respond with anxiety to unfamiliar situations, including even minor separations.

Alternatively, growing up in a family environment that doesn't foster a sense of security might lead a child to respond to separations with greater anxiety. After all, if you don't feel secure yourself, being left alone is likely to be extra scary for you. If your parents were anxious about separations themselves, for example, it may have been hard for them to help you feel comfortable going off on your own, or being away from them. And of course, an actual loss or traumatic separation in childhood offers one more potential route to an enduring vulnerability to separations from loved ones.

The individual question. Obviously not everyone who develops panic has suffered an early loss — and not everyone who survives a painful loss in childhood goes on to develop panic as an adult. Yet the issue of loss seems to arise again and again in treating people with panic.

Whatever the findings of research on large numbers of people with panic, the crucial question is this: Is loss or separation a touchy issue *for you?* Do *you* feel alarm or distress when you pause to consider experiences with separation or prospects of loss? If so, realizing that it's a dilemma *for you* can be an important first step in tackling it.

Early Experiences: Family Environment

There's considerable interest in the question of whether particular upbringings may contribute to the later development of panic. Theories about this come from both clinical observation and from research on the early family experiences of panic sufferers.

"Underprotection." Children who grow up in circumstances that force them to fend for themselves (emotionally, physically or both) before they're equipped to do so may be vulnerable to panic disorder in adulthood.

A whole variety of unfortunate situations might lead to this result. A parent may be severely depressed, for example, or unavailable due to a chronic illness, or alcohol abuse, or even extreme preoccupation with a very demanding job or family situation. Children can be left on their own at crucial times in unfortunate, even disastrous ways. And even though the circumstances (and your abilities to manage them) have changed, the feelings you developed from those early experiences can hang on pretty tenaciously.

June had to care for three younger siblings from the time she was quite small. Her father was a caring man, but he worked three jobs to support the family and was rarely at home. When he was, he seemed overwhelmed by his cares, and June, an exquisitely sensitive little girl, tried her best not to burden him further by seeking his help. June's mother had chronic mental problems and spent much of her time isolated in her bedroom or, at best, attending to her latest baby, leaving June to take care of the household tasks.

June was a very competent little girl — a little adult, really — who managed to do an adult job exceedingly well. But inside, she felt constantly anxious — that her mother's state would worsen, that the family's finances would deteriorate, that her father would get sick, that the chores wouldn't get done, that something would crack in her tenuous family structure.

There was no one on whom she could rely or give over her burdens, no opportunity to be a child. Some therapists might describe June as having "unmet dependency needs;" she needed someone to depend on but no one was there. June's sense of aloneness and lack of safety persisted into adulthood when she developed panic attacks at the age of twenty-one after finishing college and starting her first job.

Chronically chaotic or abusive family circumstances can put children in situations similar to June's — unable to rely on anyone for security and nurturance, forced to fend for themselves at an inappropriately young age, forced, further, into a position of vulnerability and fear. It doesn't seem surprising that such circumstances might place someone at greater risk for panic. In fact, one study of individuals with panic disorder found that one-quarter of those studied had experienced a chaotic childhood and one-fifth had suffered abuse during their early lives.

Any family situation that leaves you feeling the world is a dangerous, uncertain and hurtful place, or that leaves you feeling inadequate to protect yourself or to cope alone could conceivably place you at risk for the later development of panic.

But these situations sound pretty extreme. Most panic sufferers come from families they'd describe as pretty "normal." In fact, there are hints of some fairly subtle differences among families that may help to explain the later development of panic, especially when they're combined with biological vulnerability.

Overprotection. Some experts believe that being raised in a very overprotective home can contribute to panic in adult life. While this may seem like a contradiction, perhaps you can see how overprotection (though seemingly the opposite of under- protection), could also lead you to believe that the world is full of risk, and that you're not equipped to cope with it. Research does not support this notion strongly, but in clinical settings, there are occasionally times when people's overprotective upbringings seem to have contributed to their eventual struggles with anxiety and panic.

Marilyn was the only child of an older couple who'd feared they'd never succeed in having a child. Her parents were overjoyed at her birth and ferociously determined to protect her from harm at any cost. Throughout her childhood, whenever she expressed anxieties or encountered obstacles, they rushed in to soothe her and to smooth her path. When Marilyn was in the fourth grade, she began having frequent stomachaches. Her doctor encouraged a matter-of-fact approach to them, but instead, her parents began to keep her home from school, nursing her solicitously and sharing freely their expressions of worried concern.

In her early twenties, Marilyn married but stayed in close contact with her family, phoning her mother daily and visiting several times a week. Five months into the marriage, Marilyn and her husband began to have increasing conflicts over her excessive closeness with her parents. Soon after her husband refused to consider a joint vacation with Marilyn's parents, insisting instead that the young couple go alone, Marilyn had her first panic attack.

Marilyn's situation illustrates the potential drawbacks of a parenting style that's intended to be helpful and nurturing but instead can serve to discourage independence and diminish confidence. Overprotective parents like Marilyn's can, by their very protectiveness, inadvertently convey the message that the world is a dangerous place in which a child isn't safe without the protection of someone older and wiser. The overprotective parent may be an anxious one as well. That anxiety may be passed along to the child through genetics or by example. A child growing up in this situation may become fearful and reluctant to venture out on her own. This tendency in turn lessens her opportunities to practice the skills needed to build confidence and increase her independence.

When the child reaches adulthood, she may continue to rely heavily on others — perhaps her parents, still, or a new spouse. This reliance puts her in a vulnerable position. She worries about losing the people on whom she depends not only because of her attachment to them, but also because she feels so unable to survive alone. When the individual is put into the position of having to give up her source of security, panic can result.

Excessive messages of risk. Some families communicate very directly to their children that the world is a risky, dangerous place. One woman from a very protective home, for example, described having been warned by her mother to be extremely careful when crossing railroad tracks, lest she catch her shoe in the tracks and be hit by an oncoming train. Another reported that when her family went shopping in a nearby large city, her mother insisted she shield her eyes when meeting other shoppers, "to keep out the germs," should the strangers happen to cough just as she was passing by. You may be able to offer some examples of "risk messages" from your own family.

Critical, controlling parents. Several researchers have noted, in addition, that many panic sufferers experienced their parents as critical and controlling. One woman with anxiety problems described having written letters home from college — only to have them returned to her by her father the following day with every grammatical error corrected in red ink!

Unfortunately, in their genuine efforts to ensure their children's safety and success, or perhaps in reaction to their own problems or their own experiences as children, parents can become overly intrusive and excessively critical. And though you realize that they didn't intend for their parenting style to have negative effects on you, you can still be left with inaccurate beliefs about yourself and with difficulties in adulthood — possibly, difficulties with panic.

Difficulty dealing with feelings. In the next session, you'll learn that discomfort with feelings — especially "negative" feelings like anger — is fairly common among panic sufferers. If this is true for you, you may suspect that this developed during your formative years, as a result of experiences in your family. This can happen in a couple of ways. Certainly if feelings were painful to you as a child because of a very troubled family situation, you may have learned to avoid and suppress them. But there's also some indication that many families of panic sufferers simply have difficulty dealing with feelings comfortably, and that they communicate this discomfort to their children. They may convey the message that some feelings are "bad," or maybe that any feelings at all are somehow dangerous — dangerous to express, maybe even to feel.

In short, a whole variety of family characteristics, from quite dramatic to very mild, can contribute to differences and problems in adulthood — to feelings of vulnerability, to insecurities about your ability to manage life in a world that may feel dangerous and uncertain — possibly to problems of panic.

Why Me?

Now that you've read about possible early-life contributors to later panic, which factors seem most likely to fit your particular situation? Are you aware of blood relatives with panic, excessive anxiety, alcohol problems, or clinical depression (that is, depression that's more than the occasional "blues" we all feel at times)? You may have inherited a biological predisposition to panic anxiety.

Did you experience early losses, traumatic separations, or marked anxiety about separation as a child? These, too, may have "loaded" the deck toward your development of panic as an adult.

Was your family unusually protective of you or, conversely, unable to protect you at an early age from a world that was scary or hurtful? Did you feel unsupported in your early years because a parent simply wasn't very available to provide the nurturance you needed — for example, because he or she was dealing with chronic illness or personal difficulties? Was someone very critical of you in ways that left you feeling anxious or inadequate, or constantly questioning yourself and your capabilities? Or was your family markedly uncomfortable with the expression of feelings, perhaps even with the whole notion of really feeling them?

If you didn't encounter any descriptions that seemed to fit your family, don't be dismayed. Every family is unique, after all. Or you may be one of those people for whom there really *are* no identifiable factors to explain why you developed panic — no known biological predisposition, and no clear-cut explanation based on early events or circumstances. They do exist, you know!

But if you're someone whose early life may have contributed to your vulnerability to panic disorder by influencing your feelings about yourself and your reactions to the world, it's worth spending some time on the topic — because it can help you to ultimately master your panic, and that's a goal well worth pursuing.

The exercises that follow this session will help you to explore these questions systematically. As you complete them, you may find that another question comes up — the question of personality.

Do people who develop panic disorder have a particular sort of personality? We'll take a look in the next chapter.

Do the exercises below first; then give yourself a short break. Take a deep breath, take the dog for a walk, take a moment for yourself. When you return — in a few minutes or a few days — you'll be ready to dive into the topic of your own personality.

Exercises for Session Two

The following set of exercises will help you to look formally at possible "sources" of your panic disorder. As you complete them, be sure to include all the examples or possibilities you think of, even those that may seem minor to you.

I. Biological/Genetic/Temperamental Contributions

The following items are designed to elicit information about your degree of "match" with those who appear most prone to develop panic disorder, i.e., those who may have been "born anxious."

A. (1) List all of your blood relatives whom you think might have had difficulties with anxiety or panic. You might have been told directly of their problems. You might have heard that they saw a doctor or took medicine "for their nerves." Maybe you know they suffered from medical problems that were considered anxiety- or stress-related, like ulcers. Or perhaps they simply avoided family gatherings or activities without explaining why, and you now suspect they struggled with panic and/or agoraphobia.

(2) Now make a list of all your blood relatives whom you suspect or know to have had problems with alcohol use.

(3) Finally, list those who appear to have had problems with depression. (The different lists might include the same individuals, of course.)

B. Read through the following list of descriptors. Now consider what you were like as a youngster, both what you recall of yourself at that time and what you've been told by others. Place a check mark next to the descriptors that portray you accurately.

As a child, I probably would have been described as:

$\sqrt{}$ shy.

_____ introverted.

$\sqrt{}$ quiet.

___timid.

___cautious.

___fearful or easily frightened.

___nervous in new situations.

___not comfortable with changes.

__✓_more likely to have one or two close friends than a large collection of playmates.

__✓_not liking to be away from my mother (or mother figure).

__✓_having difficulty starting kindergarten because of anxiety about being away from home.

__✓_likely to become homesick when on overnights away from family.

__✓_preferring safety over excitement, and familiar over new situations.

__✓_having nervous habits at times, such as twisting my hair or chewing my nails.

C. Answer the following questions about yourself:

- Have you ever had the thought that your body is particularly responsive to your emotions? _✓_

- When you're under stress, are you prone to getting a stomachache or headache, or to experience some other specific and recurrent physical reaction? _✓_

- Has a health professional ever told you that you display a medical condition or physical symptoms that appear to be stress-related? _✓_

- Aside from actual panic attacks, do you tend to have a physical reaction when you're upset or worried or even badly startled — like breaking out in a sweat or feeling your heart start to pound or becoming queasy or developing butterflies? _✓_

- When you go through a period of worry, do you find it seems to throw your body off, making it difficult to sleep well, affecting your appetite, or causing you to feel exhausted? _✓_

- Do you often notice that your reaction to an upsetting event is more intense than that of your partner or friends or siblings? ___

- Has anyone ever told you "don't get so upset" or "relax" or "take it easy" because of your strong reaction to an event? _✓_

II. Early Events and Influences

The following exercise will help you to consider the potential impact of early events and influences on your eventual development of panic disorder.

A. Make a list of all the losses, traumas and disruptions in relationships that you experienced as a child and as a young adult, putting them in chronological order.

Include deaths of family members, friends, beloved pets, teachers, co-workers — anyone who's been important to you in your life.

Include divorces, moves or job changes that separated you from loved ones or from familiar surroundings.

Finally, include accidental events that, at the time they occurred, were traumatic for you — being lost in a theater, being left by your parents at a birthday party and fearing you'd been forgotten or abandoned — any event at all that you still recall as having been frightening to you.

B. Now take a ruler and draw a timeline in your notebook. Give yourself lots of space — you might draw it across two pages. Place the events from your list on the timeline. It's not important that the line be evenly divided into years, simply that the events be lined up in the correct order.

One person's time-line might look like this:

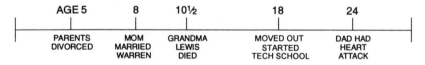

C. Now create a second list of any circumstances in your life of a more ongoing nature that have been difficult for you (whether short-term or long-term): serious financial problems in the family, heavy drinking by a parent, abuse you may have suffered, tensions between you and a stepparent, fear your parents were going to split up, and anything else that caused you worry or unhappiness.

Consider, for example, whether there are ways in which you were treated in your family that had a negative impact on you — even if the person involved had only the best of intentions. (For example, did you ever, as a child, vow, "I'll never treat a child of mine the way I was treated"?)

Also, consider your exposure to important people in your life who may have demonstrated a great deal of anxiety or in some other way "taught" you that certain situations were much to be feared.

As before, include all the situations that come to mind. If it pops into your head, trust that it did so for good reason. Even events or circumstances that you might now describe to another as "trivial" may have had a powerful impact on you at the time, and it's that impact that's important, not how a situation might be judged by an outsider — particularly an adult outsider.

D. Now add these circumstances to your timeline by creating a second row beneath the events. Use as much space as you need and again, don't worry about making the line represent time "evenly."

When you finish, your line might look something like this:

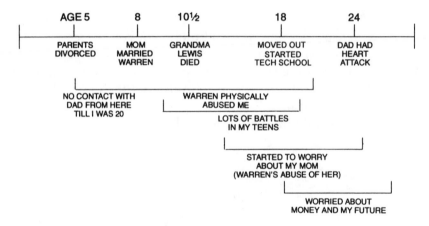

III. Stresses in Adulthood

This portion of the exercise asks you to examine events in your adult life. This will provide the "raw data" to be used in another assignment at a later point, so be sure, as with all the exercises, to complete it in writing and to keep a copy of it in your notebook or folder.

A. Consider the time when your panic first erupted noticeably. Now list all the sources of grief, pain, worry and stress that occurred within the six months prior to that time. Pay particular attention to circumstances that occurred right around the same time as the first attack. Again, include everything you think of, even if "it seems like nothing."

To spur your thinking, consider the following possibilities — and, by all means, add to them if you can:
- Financial setbacks
- A move
- A change in your primary love relationship
- Acquiring a new supervisor or new duties at work
- A recent incident that you found terribly humiliating
- A separation from a loved one — even when it's for a "positive" reason like marriage or college or a job promotion
- Having a child leave for kindergarten or college or reaching some other milestone that's meaningful to you
- Coming to some realization that isn't easy for you — e.g., that a child is having problems in school, that a parent's health is failing, that your parenting style isn't what you'd wish it to be
- The death or loss of anyone in your circle of acquaintances, friends or family
- Hearing of someone's serious illness — even if the sufferer isn't someone central in your own life
- Strong feelings of regret or sadness in your life, even if you aren't sure what initiated them
- Something that occurred in your life today that led you to think more about a difficult time in your past
- Too much to do and not enough time for all of it
- An illness that sapped your strength and energy

B. If your difficulties with panic have ebbed and flowed substantially (e.g., your attacks disappeared or lessened significantly for a time, then resurfaced recently in full force), create a second list, this time for the six months prior to the most recent outbreak.

IV. Precursors of Panic: Putting It All Together

To complete this exercise, simply spend a few minutes scanning the work you just finished, thinking about the following questions and, if you wish, jotting down reactions and ideas in your notebook. (This is one assignment that can be done completely "in your head" if you prefer.)

A. Do you think you may have inherited a predisposition to anxiety, based on what you know about your blood relatives?

B. Based on what you know of your childhood temperament, does it seem likely to you that you were born with a tendency toward anxiety?

C. Do you seem to have an ultrasensitive arousal system?

D. Are there ways in which your early life (through one-time, traumatic events or ongoing difficult circumstances) may have "sensitized" you, making you extra vulnerable to particular experiences, worries or feelings later in your life?

E. If your answer to D is "yes," how did your beliefs about yourself and the world change as a result of those early, sensitizing experiences?

F. Were you "taught" — by a frightening event or a difficult loss or a nonsecure family situation or even by observing someone else's reactions — that the world is a dangerous place or perhaps that you aren't very good at coping with it?

G. Are there sources of anxiety in your adult life that may have mounted sufficiently to bring on panic, even if you aren't someone who was somehow predisposed to develop panic disorder?

V. Taking Care of Yourself

Take a moment to ask yourself how you're feeling right now. You've just been examining — perhaps even reexperiencing — what may have been some difficult, painful times in your life. If so, you might be feeling sad, distressed, even overwhelmed.

Or you might feel relieved about having a greater understanding of your situation, but even that new awareness may throw you off balance a bit — you might need some time to digest it all.

If you're having strong feelings of any sort at this point, select at least two of the following three strategies to "decompress" before moving on to the next session.

1. Give yourself a physical and emotional break from self-examination. Take a brisk walk, a bubble bath, or a nap. Work out for half an hour. Work on a craft, read a favorite book or magazine, go see a movie.

2. Find someone you trust to talk with, a friend or partner or perhaps a therapist or religious counselor — even a crisis line if you feel the need. Let yourself share the powerful feelings you're having. Shared with the right person, pain becomes more bearable, confusion more comprehensible, joy and relief more real.

3. Remind yourself that the work you're doing, though it can be wrenching, is part of your path out of panic. It's doing something ultimately healthy and positive for your life, a means of turning the tide and transforming a life filled with some very difficult times into one filled with more and more positive ones.

Pat yourself on the back for your courage thus far and for taking the important step of tackling *all* the dimensions of your panic.

Panic and Personality

You know that panic is "in the genes" and in the experiences of childhood. That is, it's related to a probable biological predisposition, and most likely to early experiences, whether specific events or more ongoing family circumstances. But you may have wondered something else about panic: Is panic related to a particular personality profile?

The answer to that question is — perhaps. In this chapter, we'll take a look at some of the personal qualities that seem to go along with panic, starting with traits having to do with attachment and fears of loss. As you consider the descriptions that follow, you may notice some overlap between the descriptions and the discussion of early experiences of panic sufferers. Not surprising, if you think about it, since early experiences are one important contributor to personality.

As always, when you read about the features of panic sufferers, ask yourself which ones accurately describe you. Some of the descriptions might not fit you at all. But others will, and those may be especially important in understanding and overcoming *your* panic.

Attachment and Loss

Are you the person who's a "marshmallow" when it comes to seeing someone you love suffer? Would you do anything to protect your loved ones from harm or distress? Do you long for your family to be physically near you so you can be absolutely certain that they're safe? Do you worry about their well-being when they're not?

If you answered "yes" to any of these questions, you've got lots of company. Panic sufferers are frequently people who attach deeply to others, who are extrasensitive to separation and who experience intense fears of losing the loved ones who are so important to them.

In the previous chapter, you learned that separation anxiety may be more common in the histories of those who develop panic than those who don't. One study, in fact, found that over half the people who developed severe panic disorder and agoraphobia as adults had suffered from separation anxiety as children. These were the youngsters who fretted about going off to school and leaving Mom behind, who became homesick on overnights with friends, who dreaded going off to camp, and who couldn't bring themselves to move out of the house after high school.

For many with panic disorder, separations continue to be worrisome and upsetting in adult life. One might even argue that some adult panic sufferers experience an adult version of separation anxiety — only now the worries are less often focused on themselves, more often on the loved ones from whom they're separated.

Frequent, serious worries about death and disaster. All of us have some anxieties about death. In surveys of the general public, in fact, only one fear (the fear of public speaking) is more common. But for panic sufferers, fears of death are especially prominent.

Louise says, "I never had anyone close to me die before. I guess I'm lucky that way. But I still worry constantly about death — about my parents dying, about my children dying, about me dying. When I'm having a panic attack, I'm sure it's happening: This is it. Even when I'm not, the thought of death is always in the back of my mind, keeping me just a little bit uneasy all the time."

Why would panic sufferers worry so much about death? Perhaps because the experience of a panic attack feels so much like imminent death. It's awfully hard to feel again and again as though you're dying and not start believing it. And some panic sufferers already may have had a special sensitivity to death and loss at the time their panic developed. For them, the first panic attack only heightened a fear that was already lurking beneath the surface.

You're aware of the history of early loss that some panic sufferers report. Perhaps, as a youngster, you experienced the traumatic death of someone close to you — a parent, a grandparent, a childhood friend, a beloved pet. If so, you may struggle especially hard with a fear of death. And if you experienced firsthand the anguish that death causes, the fact that sudden death is a rare event isn't very reassuring. Maybe it isn't likely to happen, but if your world crashes in around you as a result, it's something to worry about. And worry you do.

Other panic sufferers, as you know, grew up in homes where an overanxious, overprotective parent transmitted a strong message that the world was a dangerous place, with death just around the corner waiting to pounce. Catastrophe never actually occurred in these children's lives, but according to their parents, this was only because of the most amazing luck! If you grew up in a household like this, you're likely to overestimate the chances of disaster and expend a lot of energy worrying about how you'll survive when it finally strikes.

In short, if at a young age, you lost someone beloved to you, or if you lived with the ever-present notion that you might — perhaps helped along by an overanxious parent — you may have developed intense fears of death early in life. Even if that wasn't the case for you, repeated panic attacks can bring about vivid fears of sudden death. And if you attach deeply to others, as so many panic sufferers do, the notion of death — yours or someone else's — is likely to be all the more distressing.

Excessive concerns about illness. If you worry about death, you worry about illness. (After all, illness is one pathway to death.) In addition, concerns about illness can readily arise out of the experience of panic; the physical symptoms of an attack feel convincingly like those of a catastrophic illness.

One survey of sixty people with panic disorder tabulated the individuals' guesses about the cause of their panic symptoms. More than three-quarters believed the attack represented a potentially life-threatening physical event. Of these, a majority believed they were having a heart attack; a slightly lesser number believed they were "going crazy"; and the remainder believed their attacks were caused by a brain tumor, a stroke, an infection or some unidentifiable physical illness. Only about one-quarter of those surveyed realized during their first attack that the episode might be related to some form of anxiety. In other words, if you believed your first panic attack meant medical disaster, you had a lot of company!

For most of us, the experience of our bodies is much more compelling than something we "know" only intellectually. Even though your doctor, or your therapist, or this book tells you that you needn't fear your physical symptoms — that the symptoms don't mean anything ominous about your health — those same symptoms are mighty difficult to deny when you feel them so intensely. The information from your senses contradicts the information from your intellect, and for most people, the senses win out every time. Later in the book, you'll learn some methods to convince your *senses* that you needn't be frightened by your symptoms.

Need for control. Most of us prefer to be in control of our fates, but this preference is often especially striking in those who have panic attacks. Wanting to have control may be partly an effect of panic attacks, which can make you feel so very out of control. Or the need for control may be related to your fears of tragedy and loss: If you're in control, by definition, you can prevent bad things from happening to yourself and to those you love. If your early world felt especially out of control and unsafe (physically or emotionally), and left you with core feelings of vulnerability, this quality may be especially strong. Being in control, quite simply, means being safe.

To review, panic sufferers often describe themselves as characterized by *deep attachment to others* and *extrasensitivity to separation and loss; frequent, serious worries about death and disaster; excessive concerns about illness;* and *need for control.* Perhaps all four qualities could be summed up by saying that panic sufferers seem to struggle to feel secure from loss. It's as though they have *little confidence in the world as a safe place.* Panic sufferers also report oftentimes that they have *little confidence in themselves and their own capabilities.*

Self-Confidence
Panic attacks in and of themselves are powerful agents for eroding confidence. Suddenly, you feel unable to do all sorts of things you used to do, all sorts of things "normal" people do. On top of that,

you feel as though you've lost control of your own body, something so basic to your sense of self that you probably never even gave it a second thought before the attacks hit.

In addition to losing confidence as a *result* of panic disorder, many panic sufferers say they struggled with feelings of inadequacy before their attacks first began (and sometimes with a need to rely too much on others as a result). If you're someone who's battled with a lack of confidence in the past, it's worth spending a few minutes to consider the sources of those feelings, so you can fight back more effectively. Try asking yourself these questions:

1. Were you constantly criticized, treated coldly, ignored, or abused during your early years? (Remember, people learn to treat themselves in the same way they were treated by the important people in their lives.)

2. Could you have drawn some mistaken conclusions over the years about yourself and your abilities because you overlooked or misunderstood important information? (For example, did you compare yourself negatively to an older sibling, feeling small and inadequate as a result, yet completely overlooking the age difference between you, or your own unique talents?)

3. Did you grow up in a family that cared for you so well, you never had the opportunity to care for yourself? (If so, perhaps you never developed that core feeling of competence that comes from mastering tasks independently and that provides the resilience to bounce back when you run into the inevitable obstacles of life.)

4. Did you have to fend for yourself, physically or emotionally, at a very young age — perhaps because a parent was incapacitated or unavailable to you due to a chronic illness, alcohol problems, or emotional struggles? (If so, you may have simply not had the predictability or the bonding experiences that allowed you to feel safe and secure. You may have been left feeling unimportant or unloved; and feelings learned at a young age have a way of enduring even after circumstances have changed.)

5. Finally, did your family experience difficult or unhappy circumstances, such as a divorce or severe financial hardship? (Sometimes children can feel at fault and "bad" inside when misfortunes occur, simply because of the way children think. And those bad feelings can persist well beyond the time of their origin.)

Consider, in general, how a young child might react to the kinds of events you experienced early in your life. Put yourself in

that child's shoes. Now consider beginning to trea
the same compassion and understanding you'd sho

In session eight, you'll learn a formal method for tackling any lack of confidence you experience by directly challenging your critical and undermining self-talk. Research also shows quite consistently that once people overcome their panic attacks, many of them automatically become more confident and independent. For now, one of the best ways to improve your confidence is to continue working through the program — and to take pride in your accomplishments along the way.

Lack of assertiveness. Panic sufferers often describe themselves as "people-pleasers" who find it extremely painful to risk others' dislike or disapproval. They may agree to others' requests, suppress their own opinions, and put the needs of others before their own — sometimes to the point that they almost lose touch with their own wishes and feelings. As one woman put it, "I'll turn myself inside out for you if it will get you to say just one nice thing about me."

There are many reasons people find it difficult to assert themselves. One important reason relates to fears of loss; you may feel you'll put a relationship at risk if you assert yourself too forcefully. Or you may lack the confidence and self-esteem to express your own wishes, perhaps seeing them as unimportant.

Maybe you're so tender-hearted that you can't bear to refuse anyone anything. Or you may have become so accustomed to the role of "giver" in your family of origin that it scarcely occurs to you to refuse.

Many panic sufferers describe themselves as perfectionists who feel it's a sign of "laziness" or "weakness" or "selfishness" to refuse another's request. And still others hold strong religious beliefs about the importance of giving that makes it hard to know where to draw the line. In short, for any number of reasons, you feel obligated to give and give and give some more — even when you feel there's nothing left, even if it leads to resentment inside.

There's one more reason you might be less assertive than you'd like: You may be especially uncomfortable with conflict and strong emotion. If so, you've got lots of company.

Conflict and Negative Emotion

Lynn, who developed panic disorder in her mid-thirties, described herself as "a born peacemaker." Even as a child, she seemed to have a unique talent for sensing tensions and smoothing them over before they could erupt. Over time, she realized that perhaps her parents deserved some of the credit for her diplomatic skills, for her entire family placed a considerable premium on peace and harmony. Negative emotions were rarely expressed, disagreement was discouraged, and open confrontation was avoided at all costs.

Many panic sufferers describe a similar style. Though they may or may not feel frank dismay at the prospect of conflict, oftentimes they've become so skilled at sensing others' moods and responding to others' wishes that conflict simply doesn't arise. And many do, in fact, freely admit that the idea of confrontation is distressing to them, even frightening (a tendency that research studies confirm).

You may be thinking, "So what's wrong with harmony?" Nothing, of course, in and of itself. But not everyone is going to agree all the time, in a family, in a workplace, or in a friendship. Avoiding conflict can result in disagreements being "swept under the rug" and never being resolved. And in your efforts to keep the peace, you may find yourself going along when you really don't want to, acting agreeable when you really don't feel that way. Bad feelings can develop. And you may not even be aware of the process occurring, especially if you're uncomfortable with painful, unpleasant emotions, as so many panic sufferers are.

Avoidance of Emotion. Imagine that your boss overlooks an important contribution you made, giving credit instead to her "pet" in the office. Are you likely to storm around at night and tell your family how angry you are, or to get a stomachache instead? Do you sometimes insist to a friend who inquires that you're "just fine except for a headache," then realize later that you've been worried all day about your aunt's upcoming surgery? People with panic disorder often don't seem to give themselves a lot of latitude for experiencing feelings. They can be exquisitely tuned in to internal *physical* sensations but somehow overlook the *emotional* reactions that underlie them — perhaps because emotions are even scarier. In fact, there are some clinicians who consider discomfort with emotion to be one of the hallmark features of panic disorder.

Sometimes individuals with panic deliberately try to avoid experiencing emotions because they fear that powerful feelings may lead to panic, or to sensations that feel awfully close. Laughter, anger, grief, sexual arousal — any strong reaction can cause a heightened heart rate or more rapid breathing or a surge of sensation. And that can feel a lot like the beginning of a panic attack. The result is that many panic sufferers come to avoid emotions in much the same way they come to avoid the supermarket or a crowded football game.

Others have a history of suppressing feelings long before the onset of their panic. Terry Ann was only six years old when her mother was diagnosed with a terminal illness. She learned about her mother's illness when she overheard her father tell one of her aunts about it. No one ever talked directly with her about her mother's condition or gave her the opportunity to talk about her own fears and feelings. For her, blocking out her emotions was the only way to deal with the almost unbearable fear and loneliness of her situation. As an adult, Terry Ann finds that "turning off" painful feelings is an almost automatic reaction.

Sometimes people learned from their families that certain feelings were not "OK," and came to restrict their experience of emotion accordingly. Or they minimize their feelings because it simply doesn't occur to them that their feelings are important. And people in crisis may ignore their feelings because of the need to "get through it in one piece." You're familiar with this phenomenon if you've ever had the experience of handling a stressful emergency with cool efficiency, then once the crisis was over, "going all to pieces."

Beyond that, there's an increasing realization that ignoring or suppressing feelings, especially the so-called "negative" feelings such as anger, may relate to panic attacks in important ways. Many people find, as they examine their attacks more closely, that their panic often arises when they suppress anger and other strong feelings — a process that can happen so rapidly and automatically they're not even aware of it. It's almost as though they experience the feeling not as an emotion, but rather as a physical sensation, which then prompts panic.

They often discover, in fact, that once they can allow those feelings to arise instead of pushing them down, the feelings are less likely to result in panic. In other words, recognizing a feeling for what it is, as it occurs, keeps the feeling at a "feelings" level, and seems to reduce the likelihood of panic.

What About Me? If you think you inhibit yourself from fully experiencing your emotions, take a few minutes to think about what's behind the inhibition. Is this how you learned to handle grief or pain at an early age? Was it a family style? Or have you made a conscious effort to avoid strong feelings in the belief you can prevent a panic attack this way?

There's nothing wrong with deliberately setting aside your feelings for a time to allow you to get through a rough situation. The trick is to be sure it's a *temporary* solution to an *emergency* situation, because ignoring and denying your feelings can become an unfortunate habit. You can find yourself insisting you have no feelings about a matter, and sincerely believing it, when deep down, you do have feelings — and they're mighty strong ones at that.

And the problem with *that* is that the feelings you push down don't just go away. They stay with you, out of awareness, and then, sometimes when you least expect it, they burst out — often in the form of panic attacks.

The Total Picture

So there it is, an overview of the qualities that seem to be typical of people who develop panic disorder, especially panic disorder with agoraphobia (avoidance). Let's summarize the traits and relate them to one another (realizing of course that these are generalizations that won't describe anyone perfectly).

One could say that people with panic disorder don't feel totally secure physically or emotionally. They attach deeply to others and have intense fears of losing their loved ones to death or other catastrophes. And they fear dying themselves and leaving loved ones behind. These fears lead to attempts to control the world to ensure that things are safe, and to marked concerns about illness and accidents which, after all, can lead to death. Separations are difficult since they take loved ones into arenas where harm could come to them. Besides, a separation can feel like a death.

Panic sufferers worry about losing relationships in other ways, too. Anger and conflict are frightening because of the threat they pose to important relationships. To keep conflict at bay, panic sufferers may spend their lives doing things for others, setting aside their own needs and choosing not to express their own feelings. Also, they may be people who've learned early on to suppress their feelings, sometimes without even being fully aware of it. In fact, sometimes they may experience feelings more as *physical sensations* than as pure *emotions*. They then may come to focus on the physical sensations exclusively, and completely overlook the underlying feelings that brought about the physical reaction in the first place.

Finally, they may lack confidence in themselves and their own abilities. They may perceive the world as a dangerous, unpredictable place, and themselves as inadequate to cope with it. This can lead, in turn, to feelings of overreliance on others and to even greater feelings of vulnerability.

What About You?

What about you? Did you see yourself in any of these descriptions? Try making a list of the qualities you've noticed in yourself and consider how you may have developed each one.

In the next week, try to notice how the various traits express themselves in your daily decisions. Do you agree to chair the PTA, or do you decline because you're already as busy as you want to be? Do you allow your son to go on an overnight camping trip with the Scouts, or do you say no because you'd worry about him too much? Do you allow yourself to feel sad when you see how your father is failing in his old age, or do you bury yourself in activity and try not to think about it? Do you tell your spouse or children you need some time for yourself, or do you jump up to wait on them whenever they express any wish? Notice the choices you make automatically, without question. That's the sum total of your task for now — simply observe yourself and become more aware of how you operate from day to day.

You've been doing a lot of thinking about yourself and your life, about your personality style and about the possible origins of your panic. Before moving on to strategies to halt panic attacks, there's one more question to ask yourself. Why did your panic develop at the particular time it did? Was the onset completely random or is there a way to make sense out of it?

The next session will help you look at the timing of your panic attacks and, in so doing, will offer one more perspective on the meaning of your attacks.

'riting — An Important Habit

begin to use your journal every day. The aim of the journal writing at this point in your program is simply to get to know yourself and your panic.

• Simply record the date at the top of a fresh page each morning and jot down the following:

-thoughts about your panic

-observations about yourself and your anxiety

-feelings you experience as you go through the program

-your successes in dealing with feelings of anxiety or discomfort

• Each evening, take a few moments to consider your day and add any other ideas that come to mind.

Whatever your feelings are, write them down. Let writing in your journal be like having a conversation with your best friend — a place to pour out all that's going on inside you.

(Note that in future sessions, you'll use your journal to record some very specific information following a particular format; but for now, the assignment is simply to get into the habit of using your journal every day for general thoughts, feelings and observations in any format you choose.)

II. Personality Features — Increased Awareness

The only other assignment for this session is to return to page 43 and, if you haven't already done so, carry out the suggestions to help you increase your awareness of your own personality style found in the section, "What About You?"

III. Personality Features — A Closer Look

The following is an optional exercise to help you consider your personality features more systematically.

First, make a list of all the qualities that you really like in yourself. Next, post the list in a prominent place in your home and review it whenever you think of it, to remind yourself of your many fine qualities and to counteract any tendency to focus on the negative.

Now think of one quality that you criticize in yourself and that negatively affects your self-image. Ask yourself the following:

-What conditions contributed to the development of this trait originally?

-Do the same conditions still hold or has the situation changed, making what was once an adaptive trait now an obstacle or a source of pain?

-What are some of the positives of this trait? That is, what would you give up if you modified the trait?

-What are the negative consequences of the trait? What would you gain if you modified it?

-If you could modify the trait, how would you like to be instead? What would "the new you" look like?

-Can you think of any consequences of this trait that might relate to your panic attacks? (Just make your best guess.)

-In the coming week, when you "catch" yourself behaving in your usual fashion with respect to this disliked trait, note it mentally and consider how you might have handled the situation differently.

Don't try deliberately to change how you handle situations at this stage; simply ponder the alternatives. Your journal is a good place to record your thoughts about this.

The Timing of Panic: Why Now?

Think back to your first panic attack. What was going on in your life just then? Was someone ill? Had you recently lost someone dear to you? Was an important relationship in trouble or on the brink of major change? The times in a person's life that panic strikes are not random or meaningless. Certain kinds of events are particularly likely to bring on panic attacks in individuals who are predisposed.

Times of Separation or Loss
First, and perhaps most strikingly, a time of loss or separation or of threatened loss or separation is a common time for panic symptoms to first arise. People report the onset of attacks after someone's death, after an aging parent is hospitalized, following a serious accident in which a friend is injured, upon hearing of a loved one's ominous medical diagnosis. One man who had a mild heart condition (and secret fears of heart disease) had his first attack while watching a television show depicting the medical consequences of a heart attack.

Some people start having attacks after a move or a divorce or a difficult job change. Any circumstance that results in a separation from people you're familiar with and care for can bring about an outbreak of panic. Many women report having developed panic when they were moving out on their own for the first time, particularly if the move was to an unfamiliar and challenging environment like college or a first "real" job. And mothers sometimes have their first outbreak of panic when a son or daughter is moving out of the house.

Reactivation of Earlier Losses

You might be thinking, "My attacks may have started right after my great aunt Josephine died, but that can't be the reason; I got through the death of my sister three years ago with no trouble at all. And I hardly even knew my aunt."

In fact, it's not unusual to survive a devastating loss without developing panic symptoms and years later, develop them following a relatively mild experience of it.

Helena's father died when she was twenty-four. An only child, she'd always been especially close to him (in contrast to her mother, whom she described as "impossibly demanding"). To everyone's amazement, though, she shed only a few tears at her father's death and quietly went on about her business unaffected. Three years later, a cousin she saw perhaps twice a year was killed in an auto accident, and Helena, by her own account, "fell to pieces." She began to have severe panic attacks along with symptoms of depression and had to take a leave of absence from her job at a prestigious law firm.

Her frustration and puzzlement over the timing of her symptoms compounded her dismay. Why, she wondered, would she have so much trouble now, after losing a cousin she didn't even particularly like, when she'd coped with her beloved father's death with such striking calm? Had she simply become, to quote her words, "weak and unstable in three years' time"?

Quite the contrary. What happened to Helena is neither a sign of weakness nor instability. In fact, her tale is in many ways a testament to her adaptability and capacity to survive tragedy. When Helena lost her father, she felt she'd lost the most important person in her life, the one person she trusted absolutely, the only one who adored her and supported her completely. She somehow sensed that if she allowed herself to feel the full impact of the loss, the pain would be unendurable. So she let a tiny corner of her grief into her consciousness and rapidly moved ahead with her life. But underneath the exterior of calm and competence lay an immense well of grief. The loss of her cousin three years later tapped into that well and brought to the surface all the powerful feelings that had been submerged. The reaction after her cousin's death may have been in small part a response to that loss, but more than that, it was a delayed reaction to her father's death — released by the similar experience three years later.

Liz's experience in many ways resembles Helena's. Liz gave up a child for adoption when she herself was only sixteen. She never doubted she was making the best choice for her child, and she didn't allow herself to grieve much, partly because she knew the decision was a positive one (which, to her, meant she shouldn't cry over it), and perhaps, too, because the loss was so painful.

When Liz was in her early thirties, she began having panic attacks. The attacks were a complete mystery to her since everything in her life was going "swimmingly." As she reviewed the timing of the attacks, though, she realized that her daughter's eighteenth birthday was approaching and that she'd been thinking and wondering more and more about her daughter: How had she turned out? Did she have Liz's blond hair, her father's deep blue eyes? Did she ever wonder about her mother? Was she well? Should Liz take steps to locate her? Liz came to realize in therapy that she was grieving anew for the baby she'd surrendered eighteen years earlier, and for the many milestones in her daughter's life that were forever lost to Liz.

Even though you may not have experienced a recent loss (or threatened loss) that seems powerful enough to explain your symptoms, recent events may have disturbed some strong feelings from the past. Perhaps you arrived at the anniversary date of a painful event in your life and reacted without consciously noticing the connection. Perhaps a recent experience, similar in some way to an unhappy episode in your past, re-ignited the earlier feelings and panic was the result.

For Carol, outbreaks of panic occurred after a move that took her far from family and friends, after a son's departure for college, and after two illness-related episodes — her own miscarriage and her daughter's auto accident. The last two events, in particular, represented losses themselves, re-aroused chronic fears of loss and reactivated feelings about the earlier loss of her sister.

And remember Terry Ann, only six when she learned that her mother was going to die soon (and did die just ten months later)?

Said Terry Ann, "From that point on, every separation felt like a death to me. When someone leaves, even for a short time, I never feel sure they're really coming back." When someone does leave, Terry Ann often reacts with a fresh bout of panic attacks.

Wait a minute. Is all this talk about separation and loss getting confusing by now? Let's review how loss or separation might relate to panic: First, there's some indication that traumatic loss (or separation, its first cousin) may be more frequent in the early histories of those who go on to develop panic. Second, people who develop panic as adults are somewhat more likely, as children, to be anxious about losses or separations (whether or not they actually experienced serious instances of it in their early lives). Third, adults with panic seem, in their adult lives, to be more sensitive to issues of loss and separation. And fourth, the time in adulthood that panic first strikes is often related to a recent (or upcoming) loss or separation.

Perhaps you're taking inventory of your own situation and finding no hints of loss or separation, nothing even suggestive of it: no deaths, no medical worries, no departures, no important anniversaries, no ruptures in a relationship with friend or partner or family member. Perhaps there've been multiple stresses, but none that seems to connect with loss in any conceivable way. That takes us to the second class of events that can precipitate panic — overwhelming stress.

Stress

Panic outbreaks can occur in response to stress of great magnitude, whatever the nature of the stress. Jim came in for treatment after his panic attacks had continued without relief for about three months. In the several months just prior to the first attack, he'd been under increasing pressure from his bosses at work, who had responded to understaffing in the agency where Jim worked by routing more and more projects to Jim's desk.

Jim's wife had been laid off from her clerical position shortly before, so it was all the more essential that he keep his job. In fact, even with his income, there was some question about whether they'd be able to keep up their mortgage payments. Then Jim's alcoholic brother moved back to town and began showing up intermittently at Jim's house. The last straw came when a teacher from school called Jim to report that his eleven-year-old son was having trouble in school, the result, she thought, of an undiagnosed learning disability. Jim described feeling as though he were "in a pressure-cooker, boiling and about to blow."

The stressfulness of Jim's situation would surely be apparent to any observer. Sometimes, though, stresses can be less obvious on the surface — but just as powerful in their impact. Patricia developed panic attacks soon after her twenty-ninth birthday. When she was asked about stresses in her life, she protested that there were none "outside the usual." It soon became clear, though, that she was underestimating her feelings about a whole series of events.

In the previous year, Patricia had changed jobs, helped her favorite sister through a bitter divorce, and seen her mother die a painful death from lung cancer. Because these had all happened eight to ten months earlier, she felt she ought to be "over" them. Then her landlord announced that he was selling the duplex where she lived, and she'd have to move out in thirty days.

Over the next few days, she began suffering several panic attacks a day, "for no reason at all." As she took a closer look, though, she came to realize that losing her home was a greater trauma than she'd appreciated. Through all the losses and disruptions in her life, the one stable element for her had been her home. When everything else around her was changing, her home had been her unchanging retreat. Now she was going to lose that, too.

It's easy to minimize the impact of events when you're caught up in the midst of them. Sometimes totaling them up at someone else's request is necessary to help you appreciate their number and magnitude. And Patricia was a person who tended to discount her emotions in the first place. Once she learned to recognize and acknowledge the feelings she had, and to grieve the many losses in her life, her panic attacks were rapidly brought under control.

Hormones, Pregnancy and Medical Events

Hormonal events can play a role in panic disorder. Some women — close to a third in one study — experience initial outbreaks of panic following the birth of a child, a miscarriage, or a hysterectomy. A few others report their first episodes of panic during menopause. These outbreaks could have more to do with the emotional aspects of these experiences than with physiological processes per se. However, among women with panic disorder, a high percentage report an increased frequency and intensity of attacks during the week or two before their menstrual periods, suggesting that hormones play at least some role. (Recall that Carol developed attacks after the births of her two children and after a miscarriage.)

You may be wondering about the effects of pregnancy on panic attacks. The impact varies widely, not only from one woman to the next, but even for the same woman during different pregnancies. However, many women report improvement in symptoms during pregnancy, from 30 percent in some studies to 60 percent in others.

Finally, some people develop panic attacks following a major physiological upheaval unrelated to pregnancy, including major illness, surgery, endocrinological disturbances such as thyroid disease, and withdrawal from some medications like sedatives or pain medications. In cases where the medical event is not combined with any preexisting vulnerabilities to panic disorder, a resolution of the medical event will often mean an end to the panic.

Perhaps this is the best place to mention that ongoing medical conditions which produce or mimic panic all by themselves, in people with no preexisting vulnerabilities, are fairly uncommon, and easy for your physician to rule out. At the close of chapter six, the question of overcoming panic attacks in the face of complicating medical conditions is discussed in more detail.

Anger

One last class of events that relates to the timing of panic attacks encompasses a variety of events connected with anger. Several studies have found an increase in the onset of panic during times of interpersonal conflict, which typically involve anger. There's also evidence that panic attacks often follow a period in people's lives marked by frustration and resentment. And, finally, a number of clinicians have described an apparent connection between the eruption of panic and the suppression of angry feelings.

These clinicians note that panic sufferers often have difficulty expressing anger. In an anger-producing situation, they may be prone to experience panic instead of more fundamental feelings of anger (a notion you heard something about in session three). They may not even be fully aware of their anger, or they may feel unable to express it for a variety of reasons.

If you're angry at your husband but feel totally reliant on him; if you despise your boss but need the job; if you feel put-upon by your best friend but grew up in a household where anger was viewed as a mortal sin, you may feel trapped, stuck "between a rock and a hard place." You may push your anger down rather than express it and risk the possibility of making a bad situation worse.

Or perhaps even the experience of feeling angry is so unacceptable to you that your psyche — which can be mighty clever at times — manages to repress the feelings before you're even aware of them.

Ask yourself if your panic first arose at a time when you were in a frustrating situation — perhaps chronically fuming but unable for some good reasons to speak up about it; or if you were in a situation that *most* people would find infuriating, even if *you* didn't feel it. Carol, you'll recall, had greater difficulties with panic at a time when she was angry at the driver involved in her daughter's accident — and when she felt she couldn't have any influence over the situation because of her husband's position on the matter.

Leaf mentally through the events in your life before and around the time your panic erupted, not forgetting to count the "small" incidents. Look for losses, actual or threatened or re-ignited. Look for evidence that stress was mounting and threatening to overwhelm your capacity to cope. Consider the possibility of hormonal or physiological changes. Look closely at conflicts with others (resolved or unresolved) and about the possibility of anger — expressed, unexpressed, maybe even unrecognized. Perhaps you'll discover that your outbreak of panic isn't so mysterious after all.

Why This Exact Moment?

By now, you've considered why you might have developed panic compared, say, to your neighbor down the street. You know about genetic influences, the possible effects of early loss, and the potential impact of family environment. You've also considered, in a general way, why it may have hit when it did, perhaps at a time of loss or separation, or of mounting stress.

There's one final question to consider: Why does a panic attack hit at the *specific* time it does? Why Monday and not Tuesday? Why 3:00 and not 1:00? Why precisely now and not fifteen minutes earlier or later?

Initially, you're likely to say that your attacks come out of the blue, that there's absolutely no rhyme or reason to the timing of them. You realize that they happen more in certain situations or locations, of course, like crowds or closed-in places, but they have nothing to do with what's happening inside you on the day and the hour and the moment they hit. *Or do they?*

Perhaps your attacks come without regard to internal emotional events. After all, everyone is different. But — and this is a significant point — *most* people, once they start to monitor closely and to ponder the timing of their attacks, begin to discover their attacks are sparked in the moments they experience certain thoughts or feelings. Let's consider a couple of examples.

Monica was only eight years old when her mother was hospitalized for several months. Monica was unable to visit her mother in the hospital and worried the entire time that her mother might not live to return home. Although her mother did survive and return, Monica was left with massive fears of abandonment and difficulty being alone. Her first episode of panic attacks, like Carol's, occurred when she married and moved away from her family of origin.

The attacks subsided on their own for a time but reappeared when her youngest child went off to school, leaving her alone in the house every day. This time, Monica sought treatment for her attacks and began keeping a diary of when her attacks occurred — and of what else was happening at the time. To her amazement, she discovered that an attack almost always erupted when feelings of aloneness were stirred up inside.

This was true not only in the obvious circumstances — when her husband was out of town on business, for example — but in subtler instances as well. One day, she was reading the newspaper and began to hyperventilate and become panicky. When she later examined the steps leading to that attack, she realized she'd seen a headline about women outliving their husbands, and an image had flashed through her head of being all alone in her old age.

Another time, she was describing her intermittent discomfort when she drove her child to school in the morning, puzzling about why it happened only part of the time. Suddenly she realized that the only time she had difficulties were the mornings when she knew she'd be returning "to a cold, empty house."

It's important to stress that the emotional events which can initiate an attack are only one part of the picture. What happens next is a spiraling of anxiety and physical symptoms based on fears about the meaning of the physical symptoms themselves.

This spiraling is of crucial importance in paving the way for a full-blown attack. And learning to interrupt the spiraling is crucial to recovery from panic. But the *very first* step in the sequence is often the moment some emotion or uneasy thought flits through your consciousness and evokes the first blip of physical arousal.

Discovering the emotional reactions that spark the first stages of your attacks won't happen overnight. The whole notion that emotions underlie your attacks may be a new one to you, a notion you don't readily accept. But if you can accept that there may be an element of reason to your attacks, and you examine them carefully, you can usually discover what sets off many of them.

Think back to the attack Monica had while reading the newspaper. Initially, she experienced the attack as coming out of the blue. In fact, she insisted at first that, if anything, she was more relaxed than usual while sitting in the easy chair perusing the evening paper. It was only when she carefully examined the experience minute by minute that she recalled the sudden image of herself all alone — so fleeting she almost missed it, but enough to spark the first flash of anxiety.

Similar examples abound in the experiences of those who overcame their panic. Lois entered treatment for panic attacks in her mid-thirties. At the outset she insisted, like Monica, that there were no particular precipitants of any of her attacks — the timing of each one was as random and as puzzling as the next. Later on, though, she discovered a curious pattern to them.

Both Lois and her husband Steve came from large families. Because of Lois's considerable cooking talents and generous nature, relatives on both sides of the family frequently called on her to cook for them. It didn't matter that Lois had her own job, her own family and her own activities. If someone needed a cheesecake for an office party or a spectacular dish for a potluck, they called on Lois, who always obliged.

After keeping a journal of her panic attacks for several weeks and discussing its entries in therapy sessions, Lois announced that, to her own amazement, she had learned to predict "almost perfectly" what brought on her attacks: Any time she was asked by one of her relatives to prepare something in her kitchen as a favor, she felt she "couldn't say no," began to feel resentful and exploited, and experienced the beginnings of an attack (which, before treatment, often progressed rapidly to a full-blown one).

Sometimes just thinking about the requests — or hearing that a sister and brother-in-law were out boating while she was laboring over a tray of h'ors d'oeuvres for a post-boating party — could cause her heart rate to shoot up and initiate an attack.

Once the pattern became clear, Lois could accompany her efforts to interrupt the attacks with parallel efforts to become more assertive. It wasn't easy. She had to risk some unhappy relatives, and to resolve in her own mind that it was "OK to say no." But now she's glad she did, because her combined efforts both ended her attacks and decreased the circumstances that evoked them in the first place. And now that she's not spending all her spare time in the kitchen, Lois has more opportunities to enjoy her newfound freedom from panic.

The main issue for Monica was feeling abandoned and alone. For Lois, it was feeling exploited. Other panic sufferers find that heightened feelings of inferiority, feelings of pressure to conform, or the momentary awareness of grief, dismay or anger, quickly suppressed, can initiate an attack at a given moment.

You may have noticed that some days you wake up in the morning feeling more vulnerable, and that on those days, attacks are more frequent. Here, too, it's likely you can become more skillful at identifying underlying reasons for your extra vulnerability. Maybe it's anxiety about an upcoming interchange with your difficult father-in-law, or leftover distress from a battle with your adolescent son, or the lingering sadness of a dream you had about a friend who died two years ago.

Whatever the source, when you start to look for the feelings beneath the attacks, you'll find them. Maybe not right away, maybe not for every attack, but eventually, and enough to make a difference.

All this talk about underlying feelings and underlying issues may leave you feeling a little dismayed. You may be thinking, "Does this mean I have serious emotional problems, problems I have to solve before I can get over my panic attacks?"

Not at all. Everyone who's honest admits to areas in which they're extra-sensitive, tendencies to react with greater distress to certain kinds of situations than others. The fact that you have "underlying issues" isn't something that distinguishes you from anyone else. What distinguishes you is that your underlying feelings can evolve into panic attacks, thanks to biology and to the spiraling process that quickly follows the initial emotional reaction.

Paying attention to the feelings that underlie your attacks can lend extra power to your efforts to overcome panic. But that's only one of the reasons this book talks so much about feelings. The other is that paying attention to feelings can enhance and enrich your life — as it does for all those who explore their inner experiences in an effort to improve their outer lives.

Your efforts to pay increased attention to your feelings should occur in parallel with your *direct attack on panic.* Let's turn now to that.

Exercises for Session Four

The exercises for this session are a combination of specific assignments you've already begun on a daily basis (recording spontaneous observations in your journal) and new exercises you should add to your daily routine. To make your task simpler, the instructions following each session will provide you with a complete list of the daily practices you should be engaged in — both the previous exercises to continue using and the new exercises to add.

I. Daily Journal Writing

Continue to use your journal on a daily basis to spontaneously record your experiences with panic, thoughts about fear-producing situations, feelings about yourself and your life, and positive steps you're taking to overcome anxiety.

II. Logging Panic Episodes

The following exercise is one you'll continue throughout your work in the treatment program, and is an especially important one. The records you'll keep following these instructions will be used for several purposes: to identify important precipitants of your panic (a process you'll fine-tune as you go through the program); to monitor your progress ("Are the attacks diminishing?"); to troubleshoot when problems arise ("Why did I do terrifically well for an entire week and then have a very difficult two days?"); and, at times, to provide needed reassurance ("Today may have been rough, but look how far I've come in just three weeks!").

Beginning today and continuing throughout the program, whenever you experience feelings of panic or near-panic (whether or not the feelings progress to a full-blown attack), record the following:

a) *When* and *where* the episode occurred and *who* else was present.

b) The *severity* of the episode at its worst, on a scale of 1 to 10 (where 1 indicates no noticeable anxiety at all and 10 indicates the worst level of anxiety you've ever experienced in your life).

c) The very *first sensation* of anxiety you noticed (whether a physical sensation, a thought, a visual image, or simply an ill-defined feeling of uneasiness or fear).

d) *What you were doing* and what thoughts and feelings you were having just *before* you noticed the first sensations of anxiety.

e) Any additional ideas you have about *what may have brought on the episode,* or lowered your resistance to anxiety, or otherwise explained the timing of this particular attack (e.g., "I was extra tired that day from being up in the night with my two-year- old," or "I've never been in this particular store before and I felt disoriented and uneasy because it was unfamiliar"). Include substances you consumed that might have affected your resistance to anxiety — caffeine, alcohol, nicotine, or others.

f) If this is the first episode of the day, the *main activities and events of the day* (e.g., "Went to work all day; went to Bob's surprise party in the evening"); and the *overall mood of the day* along with any known explanations for that (e.g., "Felt kind of cranky for no particular reason").

g) *How you handled the episode* and the impact of your efforts. If you averted an attack altogether, this is where you'll indicate what you did, or what allowed that to happed (e.g., "I knew that it wouldn't hurt me and it just went away.")

For recording your panic episodes, you may want to copy the handy format below into your notebook, referring back to the more detailed description periodically to refresh your memory as needed. Or you can use the form provided in Appendix VI, which can be copied in quantity and carried with you.

Time/place/companions present during attack:

Severity of attack from 1 to 10:

First signs (e.g., racing heart, uneasy feeling):

Activities/thoughts/feelings just before attack:

Other ideas re: precipitants of attack:

Major activities/overall mood of the day:

Coping strategies used and their impact:

Here are a few more instructions about the recording of panic episodes:

• If panic starts to emerge but diminishes due to coping strategies you used, be sure to record the episode in any case. The main purpose of your log at this stage is to illuminate what can bring on panic in the first place — whether or not it progresses to a full-blown attack.

• At times, you'll experience anxiety that's clearly "anticipatory anxiety" — that is, the anxiety that precedes an experience you expect to be difficult (whether or not it proves to be), anxiety brought on by your fears of an *upcoming* situation, anxiety that mounts as the situation *approaches*. Anticipatory anxiety is usually quite distinguishable from a panic episode, in which your anxiety comes on suddenly, rapidly becomes severe (peaking within seconds to minutes), and subsides within a few minutes to an hour or two.

If you experience anxiety that you clearly judge to be anticipatory, record the episode in your log, but label it AA and note what situation you were feeling anxious about entering. You should make brief notes for those episodes, too, of time/place/ companions; severity; main activities and mood of the day; and coping strategies used, since this will help you to identify the factors that increase your vulnerability and to monitor your progress.

• If you have no panic attacks or near-panic episodes to record at the end of the day, note only the main activities and overall mood of the day. Later, this record will help you to determine what factors reduce the likelihood of panic in your life.

• Similarly, if you experience mild anxiety that progresses no further, not even reaching a point of near panic, you may want to note your experience briefly, to help you better understand how anxiety is sometimes kept in the "normal" range, whereas other times it progresses to panic — and to reinforce yourself for the former.

III. Global Precipitants of Panic
A. If you've experienced fluctuations in your panic disorder, as most people have, construct a list of all the times you've had

outbreaks or worsening of attacks. Then try to identify at least one situation in your life that may have contributed. Place the times of worsening along the left-hand side of the page and indicate the associated event(s) to the right. When you finish, your list might look something like this:

Attacks started/increased	Associated Events
Senior year in high school	Worried about leaving home
Two years after graduation	Broke up with girlfriend
When I was twenty-seven	Started new job and Dad diagnosed with cancer

This exercise is very similar to the one you completed following session two *(III. Stresses in Adulthood)*, in which you listed events related to your initial and most recent outbreaks of panic, and that list may provide a good starting point for you. But be sure to make a new list now, including all the times you've had eruptions of panic. You'll probably find you've had new realizations as you've read this chapter and that those will be reflected in your new list.

Scan the list you've just created. Do you see any themes or common threads among the items on the list? Look in particular for issues of loss or separation, evidence of overwhelming stress, indications of conflict or anger (expressed or unexpressed), and situations that may have altered your physical state significantly.

B. What conclusions do you draw about the situations — internal and external — that make panic more likely to erupt in your life? (e.g., "When I have an experience that erodes my confidence badly, like losing my job, I'm likely to develop panic attacks till I regain my confidence.") Write down your theories in your journal under the heading, "Circumstances that make panic eruptions more likely to occur."

IV. Specific Factors That Lead to Panic

After you've recorded at least six panic attacks or near attacks, excluding those you labeled as anticipatory anxiety (AA), skim over your record and look for common threads among the feelings and thoughts that can lead to panic.

(Note: Knowing the places where attacks occur isn't terribly useful just now, but you should still record place since you'll use this information at a later point in treatment.)

This task is much like looking for themes in your list of adult stressors, but here you're looking for feelings, thoughts, and events related to specific attacks, rather than those factors in your history which may underlie your outbreaks of attacks in general.

As you know, the two can often be related, so you may want to review your ideas, recorded above, about global issues related to panic to see if they help you identify feelings relevant to individual attacks.

Write down in your journal all of your ideas about the factors that trigger individual attacks (there will generally be several).

If you don't have much success figuring out underlying feelings that lead to attacks, don't worry about it. Realizations often come later in treatment when you have more experience tuning into certain aspects of your attacks. Plus underlying feelings are more important in some people's panic attacks than in others. It's useful to understand them, where they exist for you, but it's not necessary in order to overcome your attacks.

Session Five

Take a Deep Breath...

When you become anxious — whether you have an anxiety disorder or not — you automatically breathe more rapidly and shallowly. This is a natural *consequence* of anxiety, but it also *contributes* to the problem by producing a variety of physical symptoms that can both trigger and intensify panic attacks.

This session will explain some of the relationships between anxiety and breathing style. More important, it will teach you a simple, effective breathing technique to reduce the physical symptoms you experience when you become anxious.

It's a powerful technique to use by itself and will gain even more power in the next session, when it becomes one step in a three-step process to halt panic in its tracks. And it can be used on a regular basis to decrease your overall arousal level, making panic less likely to arise in the first place.

To start things off, try this simple test: Position yourself near a clock with a second hand and time yourself for one minute, counting the number of times you inhale during that minute. Try not to alter your breathing, simply time it.

What sort of number did you get? If the number was higher than twelve or thirteen, you're probably breathing too rapidly for your own good. Even if the number you counted just now was below twelve, chances are very good that when anxiety strikes,

61

your breathing becomes more rapid at that time. Along with rapid breathing comes a tendency to breathe into the upper portion of your lungs — *shallow breathing* — rather than into the lower portion — *diaphragmatic or abdominal* breathing. An anxious breathing style, then, is typically both rapid and shallow.

This rapid, shallow breathing, or *overbreathing*, results in several physical changes of special significance to panic sufferers: The proportion of carbon dioxide to oxygen in the blood is decreased, which alters the acidity of the blood. This in turn causes a rush of calcium into muscles and nerves, heightening their sensitivity and leaving you feeling shaky, tense and nervous.

Overbreathing also leads to a slight constriction or tightening in the blood vessels leading to the brain and to the extremities. This tightening, along with the change in acidity, can lead to dizziness, lightheadedness, blurred vision, confusion, feelings of unreality, numbness and tingling in the hands and feet, cold, clammy hands and stiff, aching muscles.

In other words, *many of the symptoms of panic attacks can be a direct result of the overbreathing* that accompanies anxiety. You might want to scan the list again and note just how many of the symptoms of overbreathing occur during your own panic attacks.

The symptoms that result from overbreathing frequently can be produced in less than a minute's time. More important, *they can be reversed equally rapidly by altering your breathing pattern.* That's one reason controlled breathing techniques can be so effective in overcoming the symptoms that arise during panic attacks.

Anxiety leads to other physical changes as well: an increase in the rate and strength of the heartbeat, a release of adrenaline and noradrenaline into the system, increased sweating, decreased salivation, nausea and increased muscle tension. All these changes result from the actions of the autonomic nervous system. That means the changes happen automatically, without your conscious control. You don't command your body to increase your heart rate or to release adrenaline; it just happens. In fact, if someone asked you to alter your heart rate or your adrenaline release this very minute, chances are, you couldn't — at least not directly.

But if you were asked to alter your pattern of respiration, you could do so voluntarily. And that's a crucial point, because *changing your pattern of respiration will have indirect effects on the other systems that "kick in" when you become anxious.* If you lower your rate of breathing, your heart rate will gradually diminish, blood flow will return to normal, and all the other systems will slowly "settle back to normal." That's the other reason that learning controlled breathing techniques is so useful for eliminating anxiety symptoms.

Controlled Breathing Can Help During Anxious Times

In other words, altering your respiration pattern when you become anxious will operate in two important ways to help you overcome panic symptoms: It will eliminate many unpleasant physical symptoms that result directly from the overbreathing that accompanies anxiety (e.g., the dizziness and feelings of unreality). And it will help to eliminate additional physical symptoms of anxiety that arise through the actions of the autonomic nervous system (e.g., the pounding heart and dry mouth).

Controlled Breathing Can Also Lower Susceptibility to Panic

There's another way in which breathing techniques can be used to eliminate panic episodes, a use that's far less dramatic in the short term but that in the long term may have an even greater impact on your overall success: You can use controlled breathing methods on a daily basis to decrease your overall arousal level, making panic less likely to strike in the first place.

You may be thinking, "Wait a minute. Can anything as simple as a more adaptive breathing style, even practiced regularly, really diminish the likelihood of panic occurring altogether?" It can, and in a couple of ways.

Staying Below Your Panic Threshold

To understand one of the ways, let's invent an imaginary level-of-tension scale that runs from 1 to 10, where 1 represents extreme relaxation and 10 represents extreme anxiety. Let's further imagine that once your anxiety reaches a level of 7 on your individual scale, you're likely to start panicking.

If you go into a situation operating at a tension level of 5 or 6, you don't have far to go before you hit your panic threshold. A stressor that increases your anxiety only two points on the scale, for example, will be enough to push you over the threshold.

But if, instead, you enter a situation with a tension level of only 2 or 3, it will take a much larger increase in anxiety level to put you into your panic attack zone. In straightforward language, when you're already tense, it doesn't take much additional anxiety to bring you to the point of panic. You've probably witnessed this phenomenon in your own life. On certain "vulnerable" days when your underlying anxiety level is already high, you're more susceptible to panic attacks than you are on "stronger" days when you're feeling calmer from the start.

Clearly, then, any strategy you can use to lower your overall level of anxiety is likely to decrease your frequency of panic attacks. An improved breathing style is one of those strategies.

Reversing the Effects of Chronic Overbreathing

There's yet another way in which the daily practice of controlled breathing can decrease your susceptibility to panic attacks. Many people who are chronically anxious — including many who suffer from panic attacks — *chronically overbreathe.* They're rarely aware of it, but if they were to measure their respiration pattern at any time of the day, they'd likely discover that they were breathing more rapidly than necessary. Studies have suggested that chronic overbreathing can lead to persistent changes in blood chemistry, which actually *heighten* the body's sensitivity to anxiety by reducing its ability to "buffer" the changes in respiration that come with sudden increases in anxiety.

You can read about the process in greater detail in some of the annotated references for this session, which appear in Appendix V. All you really need to know is that if you're a chronic overbreather, your body might react to a stressful situation with a more intense *physical* reaction than it would if you weren't an overbreather, simply because of the ongoing effects of chronic overbreathing. And since physical reactions often trigger alarm in panic sufferers, this more intense physical reaction could translate into an increased number of panic attacks.

Fortunately, learning and practicing controlled breathing *on a daily basis* can begin the process of normalizing your respiration and your blood chemistry and in that way can further reduce your body's oversensitivity to stressful events. Studies have shown that this normalization occurs, on average, in about two weeks' time, and that nearly everyone achieves normalization after about six weeks of regular practice.

A Summary of the Four Ways Controlled Breathing Can Help You
Before launching into the breathing technique itself, let's review the ways in which the learning and regular practice of a more adaptive breathing style can help you in your efforts to eliminate panic.

1. When anxiety strikes (or when you notice the physical symptoms that herald the onset of a panic attack), *using controlled breathing can reverse the direct effects of overbreathing,* like dizziness and the feeling that things around you are unreal or dream-like.

2. When anxiety strikes, *controlled breathing can reduce additional physical effects of anxiety,* such as an increased heart rate, by exerting an indirect effect on the functions of the autonomic nervous system.

3. Practiced on a daily basis, *controlled breathing can lower your general level of arousal* and thereby increase the "distance" your anxiety has to rise before you cross the threshold into the panic zone.

4. Practiced on a daily basis, *controlled breathing can normalize your blood chemistry* so you're less susceptible physically to minor increases in anxiety.

These all come together to make controlled breathing (sometimes called respiratory retraining) a powerful weapon against panic. In fact, studies have shown that for some people, controlled breathing alone can reduce the physical symptoms of panic, full-blown panic attacks, and *also the avoidance and catastrophic thinking that go along with panic.*

One recent study, referenced in Appendix V, questions the value of respiratory retraining in a therapist-led treatment program for overcoming panic disorder. For this reason, an increasing number of therapists are beginning to omit controlled breathing strategies from programs for treating panic. However, controlled breathing plays a somewhat more important role in self-guided than in therapist-led treatment. Thus, for the reasons just described (and those offered in the Reference Appendix) it's important that you learn the method before you proceed. You'll continue to find it of help to you throughout the program.

How to Achieve Controlled Breathing
If altering respiration is such a useful strategy, what's the best way to achieve this alteration?

There are several adaptive breathing methods available. While all of them are effective if used properly, this program employs a quick, simple method that most people can use effectively right from the start. This method has the further advantage of being inconspicuous enough to use any time and any place.

The two critical aspects of the breathing method are its timing and its manner. Controlled breathing is *deep (abdominal)* and *slow*.

Deep (Abdominal) Breathing. Have you ever watched toddlers breathe? If so, you've probably noticed that as they breathe in, their little bellies swell outward and as they breathe out, their bellies flatten again. That's the way nature meant for us to breathe, and it's surely the way we all breathed early in life. Unfortunately, as we grew up, many of us lost that natural, effective style of breathing and instead developed "backwards" breathing habits. This was especially likely to happen to women who were taught to suck in their stomachs in the name of fashion and appearance. And as you're now aware, years of anxiety can take their toll in the form of chronically poor breathing habits.

The technique of controlled breathing proposed in this treatment program uses a simple method to ensure that you're breathing abdominally: Remain in a sitting position but lean back and straighten your body so you're not hunched over; loosen any constricting clothing. Lace your fingers together as though you're about to say a prayer, open your palms and rest your hands gently over your stomach, palms down. Your thumbs should fall about an inch above your navel.

Imagine that your stomach is a balloon and that you want to inflate that balloon as fully as possible. (Of course no one actually breathes air into the stomach, but the imagery is useful in achieving the effect you want.)

Take a long, slow breath through your nose till the balloon is fully inflated. *As you inflate the balloon, you ought to see your hands move outward, away from your body.* This outward movement serves as your "check" that you're really getting air all the way to the bottom of your lungs and is an important aspect of the method. Try not to hunch up your shoulders as you inhale. Now exhale slowly and gently through pursed lips, as though whistling, and watch your hands move back inward, toward your body.

How did that work for you? Try it again, and once again, use the "hand check" to be sure you're really using abdominal or diaphragmatic breathing — the sort that pushes out your stomach and has the desired arousal-reducing physiological effects.

What if you try this and you don't see your hands actually moving outward, or you're not sure you're doing the breathing properly? In that case, lie down on your back and repeat the exercise. In this position, you should see your hands rise upwards. Once that's clearly happening, try it again in a sitting position and check for the outward movement.

Alternatively, some people find they achieve the best results by standing tall and placing their forearms, bent at the elbow, on a ledge about chest-high, then inhaling slowly and deeply. Try both methods and use whatever works best for you. Once you're well-practiced in the method, you won't need to take extra measures to ensure a full, deep breath anyway, so don't fret too much about it at this stage.

Slow breathing. Now that you're able to draw your breath into the right *location*, it's time to add a more formal *timing* element to your breathing. Your goal is to take a full four seconds to inhale and another four seconds or more to exhale.

Perhaps when you were young, you were taught to measure seconds by counting slowly, "one one-thousand, two one-thousand, three one-thousand, four one-thousand," and so forth. The insertion of "one-thousand" between the numbers slows the counting to a rate of about one number per second. That same method is a useful way to time your breathing.

As you start to inhale (through the nose), mentally count in a slow, regular fashion, "one one-thousand, two one-thousand, three one-thousand, four one-thousand." You'll probably be forced to inhale more slowly than usual from the outset in order to continue inhaling all the way to "four one-thousand." In fact, it's fine to inhale for more than four seconds, but not less.

When you finish the count, "four one-thousand," begin to exhale gently (through pursed lips) and again count slowly as you do so, "one one-thousand, two one-thousand, three one-thousand, four one-thousand." Once again, exhale in a very gradual fashion so that you're able to continue exhaling for at least a full four seconds, and even longer is ideal according to many therapists.

Now repeat this several times till you find that you're inhaling for four full seconds and exhaling for four full seconds without difficulty. Remember to breathe in through your nose and out through pursed lips. Research has shown that this is most effective, possibly because it serves to effectively slow down your breathing. Your hands should still be laced over your navel as an ongoing "location check."

Once you feel you're able to use the method smoothly, try it while watching a clock to ensure that you're in fact counting at a slow enough rate. It's easy to misjudge time when you're anxious, and accurate timing is crucial to the method.

In fact, it's for this very reason that the formal counting is recommended, even though some readers may think that it feels artificial and unnatural. Once you are well-practiced in the method and find that it reduces your anxiety and physical symptoms, you may wish to drop the counting and simply "slide" into slower, deeper breathing. And ultimately, it may not be necessary to think about your breathing at all, since calmer, more relaxed breathing will simply be your normal style, and panic, a thing of the past. But for now, use the counting to be certain to breathe slowly enough to achieve the desired effect.

Continue this for at least four minutes. You may find that after three or four cycles, you feel calm and are tempted to stop, but it's important to continue a full four minutes to get the full benefit of the method.

Putting the Method of Controlled Breathing into PRACTICE
That's all there is to the method itself. Now, how do you best put the method to use to lower your anxiety level consistently and effectively? Simple: You practice it every day, several times a day.

You already know that practicing controlled breathing regularly and frequently can help you operate at a consistently lower level of anxiety, making you less susceptible to panic arising in the first place. That's one good reason to practice the method on a daily basis.

But there's another: You may have noticed that anxiety disrupts your concentration and makes it harder to think straight. In fact, everything becomes more difficult when you're anxious — and that includes a skill like controlled breathing.

If you develop a minimal amount of skill using the method, it may work just fine for you when you're calm. But for the method to be effective when you're anxious, you need to *overlearn* it, so that you can use it without a second thought at the times you need it most.

Start by selecting at least two specific practice times a day. It's important to select them in advance and to stick to the same times every day so that your practice becomes a regular habit, as normal a part of your daily routine as brushing your teeth or combing your hair.

At your preselected times, find a comfortable position in an easy chair (or standing, if that's your preference early on). Then simply breathe in a slow, controlled fashion following these summary guidelines:

1. Take at least four seconds (counting mentally) to inhale, and inhale through the nose.

2. Keep your shoulders relaxed and inhale into the very deepest ("lowest") portion of your lungs, by placing your hands over your belly and by "filling the balloon" formed beneath your fingers.

3. Take at least four seconds to exhale, and exhale through "whistling lips."

4. Continue for a full four minutes.

Enhancing the Value of the Method

Once you've practiced controlled breathing for a few days and feel completely confident with it, there are two simple additions you may wish to make during your home practice sessions to further enhance its value.

Use Imagery. As you breathe, picture yourself in a relaxing situation, say, lying in the warm sun on a beach. Use all your senses to increase the vividness of the image. Include imagery associated with the physical feelings of relaxation — feel yourself floating, imagine a spring uncoiling, picture yourself as a limp rag doll. Now consciously focus on your muscles and allow them to become relaxed and tension-free.

Use a Cue Word. After you become adept at achieving relaxation with controlled breathing, with or without imagery, add one more element: Each time you exhale during the breathing practice, mentally think the word "relax" or "calm."

This is a particularly effective addition to the method since, over time, the word becomes a "cue" or signal associated with relaxation: At a later time, when you say the word "relax" to yourself, it will bring a measure of extra calm to your mind and body.

But to repeat, the critical elements of the method are to breathe: a) *slowly* (use the counting); b) *abdominally* (use your laced hands over your belly to check); c) *for a long enough time period* (four minutes or more); and d) *frequently enough* for the method to have an impact on daily level of arousal, and to be truly useful at times of high anxiety.

Extending Your Skills to Real-Life Conditions

Okay, you're practicing controlled breathing twice daily, you're practicing correctly, and you've added soothing imagery, conscious muscle relaxation, and a calming word every time you exhale. You're now able to use controlled breathing quite well to lower your level of arousal in the *practice* situation, seated in an easy chair at home with loosened clothing and no outside distractions. Great! But how often do you find that your panic hits in precisely that situation?

The next important step is to extend your flexibility with the method so it's useful to you in real-life situations. You can do this by varying the practice conditions to more closely match those real-life conditions.

From here on out, once a day, continue to practice as before, sitting comfortably in your easy chair. This not only gives you ongoing practice in controlled breathing, it also provides a four-minute time period every day to truly relax, a valuable strategy in and of itself.

Then, for your second practice of the day, try controlled breathing in a different position, perhaps standing or sitting upright at a desk.

After you feel you can comfortably accomplish controlled breathing in different *positions,* which will likely require only a few days, begin to conduct the second practice while performing different *activities* — while walking, brushing your teeth, talking on the phone, or driving to work.

Next try using it when other people are around and with various distractions present. The goal at this point is not to conduct your second practice during a stressful situation, simply to increase your flexibility to use controlled breathing across a wide range of situations.

Extending Your Practices to Situations of Opportunity and Situations of Need

You have now mastered the controlled breathing technique. Your final step is to use it in your day-to-day life as frequently as possible and whenever you need it. Specifically, in addition to the two formal practices each day, you should use controlled breathing: a) any time you notice some tension in your body, and b) any time you happen to think of it. If you're sitting at your desk at work, for example, and you notice your neck feels tight, take four minutes to use controlled breathing and release the tension. If you're driving to school to pick up your child and your hands are gripping the steering wheel, use controlled breathing to relax yourself. If you're walking wearily into your house after a long day and your forehead feels tight, think about using controlled breathing to ease those feelings. Clearly, this practice will help you to maintain a more consistently lowered level of arousal and reduce any symptoms of anxiety that may be present. But the extra instances of use will also increase your skill even further, so you can use the method when you need it, to better and better effect.

There's one last way you can extend your use of controlled breathing if you choose to: Select a neutral behavior you perform frequently, like glancing at your watch or opening the refrigerator — some behavior that occurs reliably several times a day and isn't associated with anxiety. Then try to take several slow, abdominal breaths *every time you perform that behavior.* Some therapists suggest putting a piece of colored tape on your watch or on the refrigerator door as a reminder.

As you can guess, this strategy provides even more opportunities throughout the day to relax, but more important, eventually the feelings connected with the controlled breathing will become *associated* with the neutral behavior, helping you maintain a more continuous state of relaxation. And while this isn't a necessary component of the method either, it's one more way to increase the value of the technique and it's fairly simple to do — so why not?

What About Relaxation Training?

Many programs for panic used to teach relaxation training as a part of their treatment. It has become abundantly clear, though, that for the average panic sufferer, relaxation training offers no advantage over a breathing retraining technique for overcoming panic attacks, and it may even impede the ultimate elimination of panic. For those suffering from high levels of day-to-day tension who may be wishing to pursue a more comprehensive strategy for physical stress reduction, however, the increasingly popular practice known as mindfulness meditation is recommended. This option, and the special advantages it may offer a panic sufferer, are discussed in Appendix II, where you'll also find references for pursuing this path. For now, however, do learn controlled breathing, as it is important on its own, and forms an important part of the SRB method for interrupting panic attacks which you'll learn in the next chapter.

Troubleshooting

While controlled breathing is typically a straightforward, beneficial method for decreasing physical symptoms of anxiety, sometimes people encounter difficulties using the technique effectively. At times, in fact, some of the very factors that heighten anxiety can create obstacles to using the method easily and effectively.

For some people, the problem is simply one of altering long-time habits; for these people, rapid shallow breathing is such an entrenched habit that it's not easy to slow down or to get air into that lower 25 percent of their lungs. Others experience excessively high levels of muscle tension that seem to interfere with the calming effect of controlled breathing even when it's used appropriately.

Other people find they actually become more anxious when they first try controlled breathing. This increase in anxiety may occur for some panic sufferers when they "tune into" their bodies during controlled breathing practice and find that internal events are more noticeable to them, causing alarm. Others become fearful of somehow "losing control" when they begin to relax during practice sessions. This feeling of fear is particularly true for individuals who've suffered abuse in the past, and for whom relaxation raises frightening images of vulnerability. Still others, when they relax, experience increased anxiety they can't explain; they simply feel a surge of emotion, often sadness, when they become quiet and still.

Appendix I offers help for anyone who's having trouble with controlled breathing. It describes the various difficulties you might encounter when using the technique, offers strategies to address them, and describes the experiences of those who've overcome such difficulties.

Even if you're quite confident in your use of controlled breathing and perhaps are already experiencing positive benefits from it, the appendix is important to read since it addresses common pitfalls in using the method, offers useful modifications for different circumstances and includes various ideas to enhance your use of the method.

Now it's time to move to the exercises to help you perfect your controlled breathing skills. Once you've mastered and refined the technique, you'll proceed to the session you've been waiting for — a prescription for what to do when panic strikes.

Exercises for Session Five

With this session, even more than the last, it's crucial that you complete certain practice sessions and recording tasks on a daily basis because the newest exercises involve mastering skills that can only be mastered successfully through frequent, regular practice.

In fact, beginning with this session, it's recommended that you take approximately one week to cover each chapter of the book (with the exception of chapter 11, on medications) to ensure that you've mastered one set of strategies before you're introduced to the next. You may be tempted to rush, to learn everything as rapidly as possible. This is understandable; after all, you're eager to rid yourself of panic as quickly as you can! But in the long run, the way to achieve the most rapid, lasting and powerful results is to take the time needed to *thoroughly master each new skill* before proceeding to the next.

Daily practices may seem difficult at first, but they should soon become a natural part of your daily routine, much like brushing your teeth or packing a lunch for work. And with practice, the exercises will become easier and require somewhat less time to complete.

I. Logging Panic Episodes

Continue to record all panic and near-panic episodes as you learned to do after the last session.

II. Daily Journal Writing

Continue to use your journal to record any pertinent thoughts, feelings, observations and experiences.

III. Planned Practice of Controlled Breathing

Select two times during the day when you'll practice controlled breathing in the manner described on pages 65-68.

Once you feel confident of your technique in an "easy" position, begin to conduct your second practice in a different position and at a new activity level as described on page 70.

IV. Spontaneous Use of Controlled Breathing

In addition to your formal practice sessions, try to use controlled breathing (adding relaxation imagery and a cue word if you wish) whenever you think of it and certainly, whenever you feel tension. If you've chosen to "pair" controlled breathing with a neutral behavior as described on page 71, use breathing at these times as well.

V. Recording of Controlled Breathing Experiences

Each evening, use your journal to note your two formal practices and any other opportunities you found to use the breathing. Also record any effects of controlled breathing that you noticed.

When Panic Hits

You're now familiar with controlled breathing, one specific method to reduce anxiety. If you've been practicing it regularly for the past week, you've probably become fairly adept at it and have had a chance to experience the way in which it can reverse some of the physical symptoms of anxiety. In this session, controlled breathing will become part of a more comprehensive method to employ whenever panic strikes.

Before launching into the method, let's review what happens physiologically during a panic attack. In the briefest explanation possible, your brain interprets a situation as one of danger and your body responds appropriately to that danger signal. Specifically, the message of danger is translated, through a series of physiological processes, into the release of adrenaline and noradrenaline, which in turn cause the physical sensations and emotional experiences typical of panic attacks.

Adrenaline release leads to an increased heart rate, increased sweating, and decreased salivation. It also causes changes in blood flow (with more blood being routed to the large muscles and away from the hands and feet), which can cause numbness and tingling in the extremities. And adrenaline causes increased respiration with all the attendant unpleasant symptoms of overbreathing — dizziness, lightheadedness, confusion and all the rest.

The noradrenaline release leads to the cognitive and emotional components of the attack — the blinding terror, the intense urge to flee, and the disruption of thinking, concentration, memory and new learning.

Panic Attack? Or Something Else?

How would a group of observers describe this cluster of symptoms? Depending on their knowledge of panic disorder, they might identify it as a panic attack, and if they did, they'd be one hundred percent correct. On the other hand, they might describe it as the so-called "fight or flight" reaction — the body's built-in emergency response to danger. And they'd be equally correct.

The point is, if you were to witness all the physical and emotional and behavioral reactions that occur during a panic attack without knowing the context in which they arose, there'd be no way to distinguish a panic attack from a fight or flight reaction. The fight or flight reaction is the body's normal physiological response to a situation of danger. And panic attacks are the result of those same normal physiological processes.

The Basic "Error" in Panic: Misinterpretation of Danger

So what's the essential difference between a panic attack and an emergency response to danger? In a panic attack, the system reacts to an interpretation of danger at a time *when there's no objective danger.* A panic attack is the body's emergency response to a situation that *feels* dangerous but isn't.

This, then, is the essential "error" in the system — the initial misreading of an event, usually a physical event, as dangerous. Several aspects of panic disorder contribute to and amplify this primary error. People with panic disorder are biologically predisposed to respond to challenges with physical overarousal. Panic often arises against a backdrop of stress when the system is already operating on overload capacity. And panic sufferers often have a history and personality that promote excessive anxiety about illness and danger. All these features make it "easy" for the body to react to a small provocation with a full-scale emergency response.

There's a second difference between a panic attack and the emergency response that occurs in the face of real danger, a process known as *spiraling*. Once the initial error occurs (the misreading of a situation as dangerous) and your body kicks into emergency mode, the physical sensations and your reactions of alarm begin to spiral upward. You react to the increased physical sensations (the pounding heart and the chest pains, say) with thoughts of alarm ("I'm having a heart attack!"). The thoughts prompt further physical reactions, which seem to confirm your initial fears of disaster and thus heighten your body's physical responses. The bodily responses then add further fuel to your belief that you're in the midst of a heart attack. In other words, physical sensations trigger catastrophic thoughts trigger stronger physical sensations trigger stronger thoughts, and the process continues, in a spiraling of thoughts and physical symptoms that ultimately ends in a panic attack — if the process isn't interrupted.

Ironically, the symptoms of a panic attack indicate that your body is working just as it should to protect you from danger, *when real danger arises*. In a situation of genuine threat, all the events and changes that develop are adaptive and protective: If someone jumps out at you in a dark alley, you *want* your heart rate and respiration to increase so that your body can operate at maximal capacity. You want your blood flow to favor the large muscles you need to run away from danger. The urge to flee in this situation is a healthy one; it may even save your life.

But the same symptoms arising in the same manner when you're standing in a check-out line at the grocery store or sitting quietly in church or driving to work in the morning can wreak full-scale havoc in your life. You want to preserve the body's alarm system, but you want to eliminate it from kicking in at the wrong times, and to interrupt the spiraling process that leads to a panic attack.

The Stages of a Panic Attack
To interrupt a panic attack, you need to understand how a panic attack develops, step by step. This model is often referred to as the panic cycle. Figure 1 summarizes the steps, or stages in this cycle.

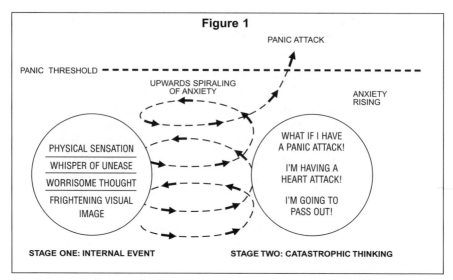

Figure 1

PANIC ATTACK

PANIC THRESHOLD ▬

UPWARDS SPIRALING
OF ANXIETY

ANXIETY
RISING

PHYSICAL SENSATION

WHISPER OF UNEASE

WORRISOME THOUGHT

FRIGHTENING VISUAL
IMAGE

WHAT IF I HAVE
A PANIC ATTACK!

I'M HAVING A
HEART ATTACK!

I'M GOING TO
PASS OUT!

STAGE ONE: INTERNAL EVENT

STAGE TWO: CATASTROPHIC THINKING

In Stage One, whether or not you consciously make note of it, you experience an internal event. This is almost always the perception of some change in physical sensation, like a "flutter" in your heart, or a sensation of warmth; but it could be a vague sense of unease, or a troubling visual image, or just a faint whisper of anxiety.

This leads almost instantaneously to Stage Two, a catastrophic thought. You instantly think to yourself,

"Oh, no, what if I'm having a heart attack!" or,

"What if I have a panic attack!" or,

"What if I pass out!" or,

"What if I need help? I'm all alone here!" or,

"What if I crash the car!" or,

"What if I lose control!" or,

"What if I'm going crazy!"

Or any other alarmed thought about the disaster that's about to happen. You surely have your own personal favorite.

What's the result of this stage? Anxiety shoots upward — understandably in light of the "What if...!" After all, if you're having a heart attack or you're about to crash your car, anxiety is a highly appropriate response.

Further spiraling then ensues, though it happens so rapidly and automatically, you're unlikely to be aware of it: The catastrophic thinking of Stage Two increases your physical symptoms dramatically, the increased physical symptoms prompt further catastrophic thoughts, which further increase the symptoms and so on — *spiraling.*

Fairly quickly, within ten minutes or less, your anxiety has risen so high that you've probably crossed the threshold and are having a full-blown panic attack. Or you may have fled the situation and experienced temporary relief from the anxiety, but now you're even more reluctant to go back into the situation for fear of what might happen. Or maybe you got your anxiety under control, but you're left feeling drained and shaken, helpless and dismayed.

Halting a Panic Attack

What can you do to interrupt the process? What you most want to do, quite desperately in fact, is to eliminate the event in Stage One — but you can't. Anxiety is a normal part of life, physical sensation of one sort or another is a normal part of life, and you can't eliminate either.

To eliminate panic, *the event that absolutely must be eliminated is the catastrophic thinking.* This point can't be emphasized too strongly. Eliminate Stage Two, your body's misreading of a benign event as dangerous, the "what-if" thinking, the catastrophic "I'm in danger!" thoughts, and the normal physical sensations and normal feelings of anxiety remain just that — normal and manageable.

And how do you halt that catastrophic thinking that brings on a panic attack? You apply three steps: *Stop-Refocus-Breathe.*

The SRB Method: Stop-Refocus-Breathe

1. Stop. The very instant you experience the slightest hint of discomfort or uneasiness, the smallest physical sensation of any sort, the first whisper that something is amiss or different in your body, immediately perform step one: Say STOP IT. Say it to yourself silently, but emphatically, or shout it out loud. Stop the "what if" thinking. Don't allow yourself to progress to Stage Two.

You're probably saying to yourself, "Sure, sounds good, but it's not that simple." True. It's only the first step. Now move to the second.

2. Refocus. To give your mind something to focus on instead of your catastrophic beliefs, perform step two: Refocus your attention on the present.

Focus furiously on anything present-centered. Use all your senses to focus concretely on what you can see, hear, smell, touch or taste in your immediate environment. Notice the temperature in the room. Try to identify all the sounds, even the faintest of them. Pick out the best-looking man in the room and analyze his features or notice his manner. If you're at work or listening to a lecture, focus your complete attention as intensely as you can on the task at hand, on the lecturer's three main points, on the application of the information to a specific problem — anything to occupy your mind so there's no room left for the "what-if" thinking.

If you happen to be in a restaurant, ask yourself, "Is the house salad dressing as good as my own? What are the three main ingredients in the pasta special? What's the best way to respond to my friend who's telling me about her difficult mother-in-law? Would the dress on the woman across the room look good on me?" You get the idea.

3. *Breathe.* Finally, perform step three: Begin controlled breathing. That will further occupy your concentration, preventing your mind from having the chance to sneak back to the "what-if's." And as you know, it will initiate the all-important physiological processes that will counteract the physiology of anxiety.

That's the method: *Stop-Refocus-Breathe,* SRB for short.

Will SRB Really Work?

Follow the three steps in sequence the instant you feel the slightest unease in a situation and focus all of your concentration on performing them as powerfully as you can: Stop-Refocus-Breathe. *To the extent you perform these three steps, your anxiety will diminish.*

You may be skeptical. That's a pretty strong promise to make to someone who's been struggling desperately hard for years to overcome panic and who's probably tried countless strategies already. It may seem too easy. Well, it is and it isn't. The first part of the promise is crucial: *"To the extent you perform these three steps."* It's straightforward, but it's not easy.

When you're experiencing the physical symptoms and sensations of anxiety, the three steps are not simple to perform. Years of panic attacks have essentially "trained" you to focus on the physical symptoms, making it tough to resist that tendency and focus on something different. The mechanism of conditioning has added its "help" in moving you along the pathway toward panic. As you know, anxiety disrupts your ability to think clearly, making any task more difficult. And the physiology of anxiety is truly compelling, especially when it's amplified by spiraling and by a highly responsive arousal system. Add to that a history that may lend special power to your fears of physical disaster and you have a forceful adversary.

But the three steps, to the extent you use them, can knock it out. And with practice, you'll develop greater and greater capacity to use the SRB method, which in turn will offer you more and more power to limit the progression to full-blown panic.

Will I Need to Use SRB Forever?

The SRB method isn't something you'll use indefinitely, but it's a very important "first step." It will offer you "on the spot" relief and will teach you important things about your panic that will, in turn, help you succeed in the later stages of treatment. In essence, it's a short-term strategy that will help you to master the long-term skills — the ones that will help you overcome panic for good.

How will it do this? First, it will give you an effective coping strategy and boost your confidence and comfort, so you won't be as likely to panic in the first place. (Remember, the *fear* of a panic attack is often what brings one about in the first place, through spiraling and by lowering your overall threshold for panic.) There's nothing quite so powerful as realizing that you can bring down your own symptoms to give you confidence. That increased confidence will also help you to face the situations where you've had panic attacks in the past, and to master the exposure methods presented in Sessions nine and ten.

Using SRB helps you to see — over and over again — how your catastrophic thinking is central to panic, and how you can influence your anxiety by changing your thinking, a skill you'll begin learning in earnest in Session eight. SRB will help you, over time, become more and more sensitive to "first stirrings" of anxiety (your cue to initiate SRB). This pinpointing of earlier and earlier triggers of panic symptoms will help you become more attuned to emotional underpinnings of your panic, a topic you'll hear more about in the next session. And understanding emotional issues related to your panic will ultimately help you to master your panic and improve your sense of overall emotional well-being.

Perhaps most important of all, SRB can start to reverse your feelings of helplessness and demoralization. It starts to give you back your life.

How Can I Maximize the Effects of SRB?

Clearly, practice is an absolutely crucial element in learning the method so completely that you can use it rapidly and reliably under the most difficult circumstances, when you're in the throes of anxiety. The exercises at the end of this session will instruct you to practice the method twice daily at home and whenever you experience anxiety "out in the world."

The other important element in maximizing the power of SRB lies in implementing it as early in the sequence as possible, the very instant you sense the beginnings of anxiety or notice the tiniest physical change. There's a strong correlation between how early in Stage One you can "catch" the developing attack to implement the technique, and how effective it will be for you. Fortunately, the more you practice and use the method, the more alert you'll become to early cues and the more able you'll be to intervene at the earliest moment.

Variations in SRB

After some experience with the SRB technique, some people modify the second step. Instead of focusing on something in their present environment, they elect to repeat a reassuring phrase to themselves, such as, "I know this isn't dangerous; it's only anxiety and I know how to handle it. I'm going to breathe it away." Or, "I'm not going to give in to these symptoms. They've controlled my life long enough. I'm going to stay right here and deep breathe till they go away." Others find that focusing on a specific memory that is both absorbing and that captures certain feelings contrary to anxiety (carefree feelings or feelings of strength, for example) works best for them.

If you've already been using a cognitive strategy you find helpful, you may want to continue using it, being careful to interrupt the cycle as early as possible and to use controlled breathing along with it.

However, if you try too many different strategies and ideas at once, it can be confusing — you find yourself faced with too many choices at the time you're anxious. So unless you've been using a strategy that works well for you, keep it simple. Start with a very specific, concrete method like SRB and use it consistently till you feel more comfortable with it.

Later in treatment, you'll learn to address underlying beliefs about physical symptoms that will have a less immediate, but ultimately more powerful effect on Stage Two. (That's the stage where you *interpret* the initial physical symptoms or feelings of unease, the stage where your thoughts can lead to more intense anxiety *symptoms.)*

You'll also learn about exposure and begin a program of gradually, deliberately "exposing" yourself to feared situations and sensations. Over time, the exposure techniques, too, will diminish your symptoms quite dramatically, in a manner that will be explained further in those sessions.

But for right now, *at the moment anxiety hits,* this is the method to use.

What if I'm Not Having Success with the SRB Method?

Keep practicing. Some people experience immediate success with the technique, finding that their physical symptoms rapidly decline and their attendant fears diminish quite dramatically. For others, it goes more slowly. Chances are, you've been having attacks for several years; it can take some time to "undo" that history. And while the technique is simple and straightforward in concept, putting it into practice when you're most anxious, at a time when thinking and remembering is more difficult, can be tricky. Realize, too, that the spiral of panic has become almost automatic. But have patience and continue using the technique. It will become more effective for you.

A common experience when first using SRB is to find that it works very well sometimes but is less successful on other occasions. That's frustrating; you've probably already "had it up to here" with unpredictability. Others report that they "can't remember to use it when I'm really anxious." The solution to both dilemmas is the same: Practice the method faithfully at least twice daily at home. In addition, review the method mentally whenever you can. Write out the three steps on a little card and post it by your phone or on your bathroom mirror. Carry the card with you and glance at it now and again, reviewing the three steps in your head.

Use the method whenever you notice signs of anxiety. And also *use it when any physical sensation occurs,* even when you don't believe that anxiety is related to the sensation. The last point is especially important since it ensures that you'll catch a potential attack early in the sequence when you can halt it most effectively, or perhaps even circumvent the attack altogether.

If you continue to find the technique unsuccessful, review the manner in which you're using it. There are several points of possible slippage, which of course are different for different people. Some people find the controlled breathing easy for them, but don't find "controlled thinking" quite so straightforward. They may be breathing properly, but find their minds straying back anxiously to the prospect of a panic attack, a heart attack — whatever their worst fear. If this is your situation, again, practicing the method, in time, will improve your ability to focus your attention effectively. It's the old familiar motto that by now you may be thoroughly sick of hearing, but one that's still true: Practice does make perfect.

Intervene as Early as Possible. Some panic sufferers utilize the technique well once they realize what's happening, but by the time they initiate SRB, find that it's almost too late. If you've been through a childbirth experience using Lamaze techniques to cope with contractions, you may recall that if you began your breathing when you were just on the verge of a contraction, you were able to "get on top of it." But if a contraction was well-established before you implemented the breathing, it was much more difficult to manage.

Similarly, if you take a pain reliever at the first signs of a headache, the headache often disappears. But if you wait till the headache is full-blown before taking something for it, bringing the headache under control can take much longer, and it may not be possible at all.

Using SRB to manage symptoms is much the same. If you start SRB early in Stage One, before the catastrophic thoughts have a chance to really take hold, oftentimes you can circumvent them altogether: The Stage One symptoms decline, anxiety rises no further, and ultimately, both the original sensations and the anxiety disappear. But if you miss the early signs, and catastrophic thinking gets established before you intervene, it can be much more difficult to stop the thinking, refocus your attention, and "bring down" the symptoms.

In fact, intervening early in the process can be the most central aspect to using SRB to halt panic successfully. Session seven, the next chapter, is devoted entirely to the topic of early signs of panic — how to "catch" attacks earlier and earlier in the process. This skill will not only increase the power of SRB to stop attacks before they get off the ground, it will help you further understand the underpinnings of your attacks, increasingly preventing them altogether so that, in the end, you won't need SRB at all.

Complicating Medical Conditions

Some readers raise questions at this time about medical conditions that can cause panic symptoms; how can they hope to halt their panic symptoms with a method like SRB if the symptoms are caused by something physical?

Indeed, everyone who develops panic symptoms should be evaluated by a physician. There are medical conditions that can mimic panic symptoms, though they're not common and are fairly easily identified in a thorough medical exam. Other medical conditions can *contribute* to anxiety. And certain medications, as well as excessive caffeine or alcohol use, can do so as well.

Let's assume that you've consulted your physician and, indeed, have some condition or must take some medication that exacerbates symptoms of anxiety. That fact does present an additional challenge to you. Your physician will surely discuss with you any available options for managing the symptoms associated with your medical problems, or in the case of anxiety-producing medications, discuss the possibility of alternative medications. And the various strategies in this book can still help you to anticipate, manage, and reduce your symptoms, though achieving success may be a somewhat slower, more challenging process.

But the fact remains that the core problem for panic sufferers is *not* the Stage One symptoms — the physical sensations — *whatever* brings them about. The core problem is the catastrophic thinking that arises almost instantaneously in *response* to those sensations. And the SRB technique remains an effective antidote to that.

Before proceeding to the exercises, it's a good idea to review this session, rereading in particular pages 79-80, which describe in detail how to employ the method of SRB.

One Final Note

When you are ready to begin the exercises for this session, you'll find it helpful to read through them rapidly first. When you get to exercise IV, you'll see — very likely with great dismay — that it instructs you to sit down and deliberately produce a feeling of anxiety, then to reduce or eliminate it with SRB. Many people with panic are horrified at the very thought! They're afraid that once anxiety begins, it will never stop.

That's just what makes this exercise so very valuable to you. The "fear of fear" is one important foundation of panic attacks. Any time you experience a mild blip of anxiety (which you can't avoid if you're a live human being!), your resulting terror about what comes next shoots your physiology upward and, through spiralling, can bring about the very thing you fear.

Regularly practicing SRB will help you learn to keep small blips of anxiety small and give you more and more confidence, showing you that you don't have to fear those blips any more. In that way, the practice can actually make panic less likely to happen. The deliberate production and elimination of anxiety can dramatically increase the power of the technique and can simply help you to reach your goal that much more rapidly, hopefully for good.

Exercises for Session Six

I. Controlled Breathing Practice

Continue to practice controlled breathing twice daily, once in an "easy" position and a second time in varying positions during various activities.

Also practice the controlled breathing whenever the opportunity presents itself. This will help you both to maintain a comfortably lowered level of arousal and to increase your skill in applying the method. Record your experiences with controlled breathing, planned and spontaneous, in your journal.

II. Logging Panic Episodes

Continue to record episodes of panic or near-panic as they occur, along with accompanying features.

Because this record will increase your awareness of the earliest signs of anxiety, it can improve your ability to "catch" Stage One events and to intervene in the cycle as early as possible.

III. Daily Journal Writing

Continue to use your journal for spontaneous recording of anything that's on your mind.

IV. Planned Practice of SRB

Twice daily, you should complete SRB practice sessions. Sit down and close your eyes. Pretend you're in a situation that arouses your anxiety. Let yourself imagine a physical sensation, or think an anxiety-producing thought, or recall the feeling of discomfort or unease that, for you, characteristically gives rise to anxiety.

Allow yourself to experience only one sensation, thought or image that elicits anxiety and then immediately use SRB — stop-refocus-breathe.

Continue till you feel comfortable, then record the practice and how it went for you in your journal.

V. Spontaneous Use of SRB

Any time you become aware of sensations of anxiety, or sensations that might be "precursors" to anxiety, use SRB to interrupt the process.

Record your efforts in your journal: Note how successful you were at "catching" the impending anxiety at the earliest possible moment, at focusing on the present, and at using controlled breathing.

Also note the effects of SRB on your anxiety, and any other thoughts you have.

The Triggers of Panic:
How to "Catch" a Panic Attack
Before it Catches You

During the past week, you've been using the SRB method, Stop-Refocus-Breathe, at every opportunity — practicing at home at least twice daily, reviewing the three steps mentally, and using them whenever you become aware of early signs of anxiety. You know from the previous session, and perhaps from your own experiences, that one key to the power of SRB is intervening in an impending panic attack at the earliest point possible.

But the notion of intervening early in panic raises the whole question of exactly "where" panic attacks begin. The initial whisper of anxiety that in the last session was labeled Stage One (whether it's physical, emotional, visual or cognitive in nature) is the best place to intervene, but that may be easier said than done. Stage One can be tricky to identify; "catching" the early signs of anxiety, whatever form they take, can be a challenge.

A Panic Attack Is Triggered — but by What?

You may even be thinking, "My attacks come totally out of the blue. There's no "early-warning" sensation (Stage One), and there's no catastrophic thinking (Stage Two). I'm just walking through the mall minding my own business, feeling fine and wham, I get blind-sided."

That's certainly a common, perhaps even classic experience in panic disorder. In fact, there are several processes that explain the out-of-the-blue nature of the attacks, processes that contribute to the almost instant onset and rapid increase of your symptoms. Let's consider them one at a time.

Mild Uneasiness Can Be More Important than It Seems

First, many panic sufferers report that they're aware of some mild uneasiness before an attack, but it seems so minimal to them that it hardly even qualifies as anxiety, and certainly doesn't seem enough to account for the onset of full-fledged panic. In fact, because it is so mild, it's easy to discount the uneasiness altogether and to feel that the attack that follows is unprovoked.

But because panic sufferers often have lowered anxiety thresholds, extremely responsive nervous systems and chronically stressful lives, even mild increases in anxiety can often provoke a panic attack. Let's take a closer look at how these processes might operate.

Chronic stress over an extended period of time, especially stress of the sort particularly important in panic (loss and separation), can place you very close to the threshold of panic so that only a slight increase is enough to "tip the scales." Imagine that you're an empty bowl. Now imagine that with every stressor, a teaspoon of water is poured into the bowl. The day comes when the last teaspoon is poured in — and the bowl overflows. The latest stressor wasn't necessarily any greater than any of the earlier ones, but it was the one responsible for the overflow — and the subsequent panic attack. If you then tried to analyze what led to the panic attack, you might think that the latest stressor wasn't "important" enough to cause panic. But if you considered all the stresses you'd experienced recently, you might discover that the sum total was indeed enough to explain the onset of panic. The latest stressor was simply "the last straw."

In addition, you know from the chapter on controlled breathing (Session five) that ongoing stress can lead to chronic overbreathing, which can heighten your susceptibility to minor increases in anxiety. Chronic stress also can result in chronically increased levels of adrenaline and noradrenaline, with similar effects. And chronic, unremitting stress can deplete your spirit and your psychological resilience so that you eventually reach a point where you feel unable to take on even one more stressor without panicking.

Intermittent circumstances, too, can lower your resistance so that a smaller stress than usual puts you over the "panic threshold." You've probably noticed that sometimes you go to the mall and have no trouble whatsoever, yet at other times, you hardly make it to the door before panic strikes. The specific circumstances that lower your personal threshold, making you more susceptible to panic at some times than at others, are to some extent unique to you. Sometimes physical factors are important — too little sleep; drinking too much alcohol the night before; too much caffeine; for some women, an upcoming menstrual period. Some people believe that too much artificial sweetener increases their vulnerability, though there's no clear evidence and it may be that excessive caffeine in many diet sodas is the culprit. Perhaps most often, though, it's an emotional event or ongoing emotional situation that makes you more vulnerable to an apparently small amount of added anxiety.

And, of course, don't forget that most panic sufferers tend to respond to physical sensation with catastrophic thinking, which leads to a spiraling of anxiety and physical symptoms. So a small amount of input can "kick off" the entire sequence which, if not interrupted first, can culminate in full-blown panic. In short, even your mild uneasiness can be enough, under the right circumstances, to explain a full-blown panic attack.

Emotions Leading to Panic Sometimes Get Overlooked

What if you're not aware of any anxiety at all — not even the mildest uneasiness — before panic hits full-strength? It's still possible that anxiety started the process, but "below the surface." Remember, you don't have to be aware of your anxiety for it to be translated into adrenaline and noradrenaline release; the very experience of anxiety can be the body's "danger signal" that initiates the appropriate physical response. And for you, that physical response can be the first step leading to panic.

It's often the case for panic sufferers that some other emotion leads to anxiety, often because of early history, but both the underlying emotion and the anxiety it gives rise to can go unrecognized. Suppose, for example, that when you were a child, every time you became angry you sensed your parents' tense reactions and ended up feeling you'd done something wrong. Or what if one of your parents expressed anger in a very scary way?

In either case, as an adult you might find yourself feeling anxious whenever you got angry without ever understanding why. That anxiety could prompt physical sensation, like rapid breathing and "butterflies" in your stomach, and that could easily initiate a panic attack — "out of the blue."

Remember Lois, from Session four? She's the woman who cooked for every occasion, at everyone's request, no matter what her own feelings or the demands of her own life. At the beginning of treatment, she, too, insisted that her attacks came totally out of the blue. Her perception changed, though, as she began to examine more closely the timing of her attacks and their relationship to other events in her life. By keeping a careful journal, Lois soon discovered that whenever a situation left her feeling exploited and resentful, she almost always had a panic attack, even though she'd been only dimly (if at all) aware of those feelings, or of overt anxiety, at the time panic was sparked. Lois also came to realize that her anger could produce the same physical sensations as pure anxiety (like feelings of warmth and increased heart rate), which could lead to catastrophic thoughts, spiraling and eventual panic. For Lois, then, half-recognized feelings of anger could cause anxiety; and anger could cause physical symptoms that led to anxiety. The final result of both these, for Lois, was oftentimes a panic attack.

Any sort of emotion under the surface can result in anxiety, especially if the feeling is one that frightens you due to its intensity or the pain it brings. Anger and grief are high on the list of emotions that can translate into anxiety before you're even consciously aware of them. The result can be a puzzling, seemingly out-of-the-blue panic experience.

Conditioning

There's another process that explains the out-of-the-blue nature of many panic attacks: *conditioning*. Remember Pavlov's dogs? A Russian psychologist at the turn of the century performed a now-famous series of experiments in which he rang a bell and then presented food to dogs. Presenting the food caused the dogs to salivate — which is no surprise to any of you who know dogs.

But after a number of pairings of the bell with the food, the sound of the ringing bell alone led to salivation, even when no food was presented. In other words, a *signal* present at the time of feeding (the bell) could prompt the response to feeding (salivation)

all by itself; the salivation response had become conditioned to —
associated with — the bell.

Now let's consider a case of human conditioning. Imagine
yourself entering a bright green room that smells like lilacs. When
you enter the room, a large, black dog attacks you. Your heart races,
you begin to sweat, your mouth gets dry, you hyperventilate, and
you experience terror and an intense urge to flee. After several
repetitions — in fact, perhaps after only one experience, since it was
a traumatic one — it's likely that simply walking into the same room
(or any green room), or smelling lilacs, or seeing a large, black dog
would produce some of the same physical symptoms and sensations
of terror. Signals present at the time of the frightening experience are
now able to produce the fear responses all by themselves; your
feelings of terror have become conditioned to (linked with) the room,
the smell of lilacs, the mere sight of a large, black dog.

In the same manner, once you've had many panic attacks in
your car, for example, it's likely that simply getting behind the
wheel of the car elicits the physical and emotional sensations of
anxiety. Your body's alarm system has become conditioned to your
car and all the cues — the sights and smells and sounds —
associated with the car.

Conditioning can occur to a situation, such as driving a car or
walking into a particular room. It can also develop to *internal
sensation*, and frequently does in the case of panic: An internal
sensation or set of sensations has been followed many times by
panic and soon, the internal sensations alone can produce the panic.

Ellyn developed panic attacks during a time in her life when she
was under greatly increased job stress, the result of major changes
in the company that employed her, including the hiring of a new
supervisor who was harsh, argumentative and demeaning. Ellyn
soon dubbed her "Dragon Lady" and began to dread going to
work each day. When Dragon Lady approached Ellyn's desk or
called her into the office, Ellyn experienced elevated heart rate,
shortness of breath, and sensations of warmth, often culminating
in a full-blown attack.

One day, soon after the attacks had begun, Ellyn went to her
health club to work out, thinking exercise would relieve her
tensions as it had in the past. She climbed onto an exercise bike
and, two or three minutes into her warm-up, experienced
increased heart rate, shortness of breath, and sensations of warmth

— the natural result of her increased exertion. She responded with increased anxiety, the conscious fear that a panic attack was on the way and, within minutes, indeed had an attack. Cues that were previously linked to panic attacks — cues like an increased heart rate — could now bring on attacks all by themselves, simply because of their previous connection with attacks.

For you, too, conditioning alone may bring on attacks in the presence of the cues, external and internal, that have been associated with previous attacks. And of course, since you're a human being, higher-level thought processes add to the phenomenon. Because you've learned, as Ellyn did, that panic often follows a sensation of warmth or a feeling of unease or a flutter in the chest, that sensation alone can lead instantly to catastrophic thinking and propel you rapidly into a state of panic.

The Special Meanings of Symptoms
There's one more way in which attacks can arise and seem "out of the blue," even though, once you come to understand their triggers, you realize they're not really out of the blue at all. Sometimes you don't realize the connection between the triggering event and the panic attack that follows for emotional reasons. That is, sometimes a particular sensation leads to anxiety because of its special significance to someone, yet to recognize that special significance would lead you to feel pain or grief, so the connection is kept out of conscious awareness.

Tom came to a clinic after experiencing panic attacks on the road in his job as a trucker. There'd been slightly more stress than usual in his life, but not enough to explain his attacks. And he wasn't aware of specific triggers for his attacks beyond a general feeling of "uneasiness." With help from his therapist at the clinic, however, Tom examined a couple of attacks in fine detail, breaking each one down into small segments and recalling the thoughts and sensations he'd had at every point in the attack.

This analysis made Tom aware that he usually experienced mild stomach pains early on in his attacks. When Tom noted that his father's death (when Tom was in his early twenties) had been from stomach cancer, the links became clear. Tom realized that, to him, stomach pains meant two things: a renewal of grief over his father's long and painful death, and heightened fears about his own mortality.

Tom gradually came to understand that there were, in fact, triggers for his attacks: his occasional stomach pains (probably food-related) and the fears and feelings tied to them. Because the feelings involved were so painful, Tom had failed to see the connection between stomach pains and anxiety till he looked very closely. It took great courage on his part, and a willingness to consider the emotions linked to a physical response before he could figure out how his attacks arose. Once he did so, he could tackle his panic attacks far more effectively.

Young Caroline had a similar experience. She often felt "woozy" during attacks. After carefully listing all the internal events she could remember occurring during an attack, she realized that as soon as she experienced any sensation suggesting "wooziness," she instantly flashed onto a picture of herself lying on the floor. It was this visual image, without her awareness of any intervening thoughts, that caused her anxiety to shoot up to panic level.

It's likely that, for Caroline, the particular image she saw had some relationship to the death, years earlier, of her beloved grandmother who was found lying on the floor of Caroline's home after a fatal heart attack. Caroline had trouble putting her fears into words — often the case with a strong emotion, especially if it developed at an early age. But all that was necessary to help Caroline stop her attacks was her recognition of the power of the visual cue: She was able to learn to use SRB the moment the image surfaced and her attacks didn't progress beyond that point.

People with panic disorder tend as a group to be more alarmed by physical sensations, more likely to interpret them as indications of physical danger. There are probably several reasons for this, including the fact that panic attacks are so overwhelming physically. A history of previous attacks is one more reason the physical symptoms are so frightening; symptoms that used to be benign, that didn't signal anything in particular, are now an indication that a panic attack could be coming.

A physical symptom may also carry special meaning for someone, as it did for Tom and Caroline, because of that person's own unique history. That, too, can explain some "out of the blue" attacks. This isn't as uncommon as you might expect. For example, it's been found that when panic sufferers are asked what they initially believe is causing their panic symptoms, those who believe their symptoms are the result of a heart condition have oftentimes lost a loved one to a heart attack in the year prior to their first panic outbreak.

If certain physical symptoms carry special significance for you, ask yourself why that may be so: Do your symptoms parallel those of someone close to you for whom the symptoms spelled true disaster? It's worth asking, because once you become aware of an important connection between a particular symptom or physical sensation and an emotional event, you can tackle that connection directly, and gain one more weapon against your panic.

In short, out-of-the-blue attacks are rarely, if ever, truly out of the blue. Such an attack may have been initiated by anxiety "under the surface." Anxiety that lies "under the surface" where it's not noticed can still translate into the physical symptoms associated with anxiety. Emotions like anger or grief, recognized or not, can cause anxiety and panic; or they can "confuse" your body by producing similar physical effects. Anxiety can seem too mild to lead to an attack but can do so anyway because of a highly reactive nervous system, or a threshold lowered by chronic stress or a temporary condition like fatigue.

Anxiety can be provoked by a seemingly innocuous situation or sensation because that situation has been linked in the past with an unpleasant panic attack. And finally, an attack might be brought on by a sensation that holds profoundly important meaning for you because of a loss or tragic event in your own history.

Two Types of Triggers for Panic Attacks

You'll notice that the term, "triggers of panic," actually encompasses two categories of conditions related to an attack. First, there are the circumstances that *precede* and prompt the first "blip" of physical sensation (which then leads to panic) — the situations that unnerve you and that you may have overlooked. You might think of those as "first triggers." Nearly everyone who experiences panic will eventually be able to identify first triggers for many attacks. And over time, you'll become more and more skilled at catching them *as they're happening*, which will help you reduce the frequency of your attacks. (More about that in a moment.)

Second, there may be specific catastrophic thoughts related to the *meaning* of particular sensations, which *follow* the sensations almost instantaneously, and which then trigger further panic through the spiraling process you learned about in session six. Such thoughts may have to do with your own unique history (as they did for Tom and Caroline), or they may result from conditioning (as they did for Ellyn). Specific "post-sensation" or "second-stage" triggers don't always exist (though most panic sufferers feel some general anxiety when they experience a physical sensation), but where they do, they're equally important to understand. Later in this chapter, we'll talk in some detail about how to do the needed "emotional detective work" to identify those. First, though, what about your first panic attack?

The Initial Panic Attack

Do you remember your very first panic attack? How do you think it came about?

Suppose your physical symptoms have become alarming to you mainly because you've learned *from previous attacks* that the symptoms mean panic is on its way. Wait a minute, though. In that case, how did your alarm and catastrophic thinking ("Oh, my God, my heart's pounding. I'm going to have a panic attack!") arise in the first place?

Think back to your first panic attack. What *did* you think was happening when you felt those flutters in your chest? Perhaps you wondered if something was wrong with your heart. (You may have been doubly sensitized to that possibility if, for example, your father or another close relative died of a heart attack.) That almost-subconscious thought then increased your anxiety slightly and, through a spiraling of thoughts and sensations, led to a full-blown attack. In other words, there *was* a specific fear engendered by the initial symptoms of the first attack (a fear of something physically wrong based on the symptoms you were having). Eventually, you came to fear the panic attacks that often followed those symptoms. Then, over time, the original fear got "lost," overshadowed by fears of having a panic attack.

Or you may have feared a serious medical disaster from the beginning, leading to your first attack, simply because you're someone who becomes very anxious about physical events and what they "might mean." A headache "might mean" a brain tumor; tightness in your chest "might mean" a heart attack. So in your case, too, specific physical symptoms triggered your anxiety about a possible disaster leading to your initial attack.

A first attack can arise in other ways as well. As you know, unease that seems too mild to account for an attack can result in one when all the conditions are "right." Following that attack, you may have become "tuned in" to internal stimuli that now carried extra meaning for you ("I might have an attack").

Also, let's face it, the physical sensations that ultimately lead to an attack can be truly unpleasant even when they're fairly mild. No one enjoys those feelings. If you're predisposed to have a marked physical reaction to stress and to worry a lot about your body and your health, it's really not so surprising that the initial, unpleasant sensations could arouse your anxiety further, leading to even more intense and frightening symptoms.

Finally, it may be that your first attack resulted from a genuine medical problem that was extremely upsetting or traumatic for you. Then the next time you had a similar sensation (though this time not because of the medical condition), you became anxious as a result, initiating the panic cycle.

Sherrill described the onset of her panic attacks following an event that had happened five years earlier, when she was still in high school. She'd gone to school that day with a touch of the flu and, during class, became dizzy and lightheaded. As a result, she tumbled out of her desk, to her intense embarrassment. From that day forward, any time she felt the slightest hint of any unusual sensation, particularly lightheadedness or a change in her sense of balance, her anxiety shot upward till she was having panic attacks regularly — the result of the catastrophic fear that something horrible would happen to her as it had years earlier, and probably the result, as well, of her automatic linkage of dizzy sensations with disaster.

In a similar process, Francesca experienced her first episode of symptoms during withdrawal from a pain medication she'd been taking for some months. Her initial symptoms, including the anxiety, were probably a physical result of the withdrawal, but from that point onward, any time she experienced some of the same sensations, she became very anxious, which brought about full-blown panic.

Chances are good that after hearing these examples, you have some new ideas about your own situation — about how your attacks were triggered in the first place and perhaps about what triggers continue to be important. Identifying current triggers of your own panic attacks can be extremely important (see box), so we'll take you through step-by-step instructions for detecting the triggers of your own panic attacks. First, though, a quick note about night-time panic attacks.

The Three Best Reasons to Identify Triggers of Panic Attacks

1. The sooner you detect a trigger, the *sooner you can interrupt* the panic cycle — *possibly even prevent* the attack.

2. If you know what *did* trigger a "panic-prompting" sensation (e.g., exertion), you also know what *didn't* trigger it (e.g., a heart attack). As a result, you'll *catastrophize* less.

3. When triggers are related to emotional issues, as they often are (for example, feeling stupid around your older sister), you can *address the underlying feelings*, which reduces panic *and* improves your mental health.

Night-Time Panic Attacks

You may find that a panic attack sometimes wakes you up in the middle of the night, and you might think, "How could I be feeling anxious while I'm sleeping?" In fact, research indicates that people with panic disorder do show irregular breathing patterns during sleep, including occasional brief pauses in their breathing, compared to those without panic disorders. You know that physical sensations creep into your awareness during sleep at times. After all, have you ever awakened feeling cold, and realized you forgot to close the window when you went to bed?

In a similar manner, you can respond during sleep to sensations such as breathing irregularities which have come to signal "danger" to you. The result can be a panic attack at the moment you awaken. Fortunately, many people find as they reduce their overarousal and panic during the day that their nighttime attacks disappear as well. Now, back to triggers.

How to Identify the Earliest Triggers of Your Out-of-the-Blue Attacks

You know what to do when you notice any signs of anxiety, or physical sensations connected to anxiety: *Stop-Refocus-Breathe.* You also know it's important to initiate management strategies — to start SRB — as early as possible in the sequence. You now know that there are often events and feelings that precede, and trigger, the physical changes. But how can you become more alert to those "earliest triggers" in the first place?

Begin by assuming that early triggers do exist, and deciding to look for them. Consider your most recent attack. Go back and replay the attack slowly in your mind and try to recall what sensations occurred first. Now try to recall what *preceded* the sensations you just identified. Consider what events occurred around the time of the physical sensations. Consider whether those events may have had emotional significance to you even if you weren't aware of any feelings about them at the time.

Phillip insisted that his symptoms of panic developed in response to nausea and diarrhea. The nausea and diarrhea generated fears that something was wrong with him and also fears of embarrassment — both of which of course resulted in more physical symptoms and then more anxiety, often to the point of panic. During countless therapy sessions, he would recount this sequence. Each time, though, as he reviewed the episode in detail, he could identify a situation which had raised his anxiety before the onset of the nausea and diarrhea.

Phillip, like many people, had learned from an early age to tune into physical problems, but he'd never really learned to identify *emotional events*. In fact, Phillip probably learned to actively ignore them, since during his own early years, emotional events were synonymous with pain and humiliation.

After a large number of repetitions, however, Phillip began to notice the emotional events that preceded his bouts of nausea *as they happened*. The events were somewhat different each time; the crucial issue for Phillip was that when he pushed emotions aside or tried to gloss over them, he developed stomach and bowel symptoms — which led to the spiraling panic.

Phillip discovered eventually that addressing his feelings, once he'd identified them, often prevented the nausea from arising in the first place. But even before tackling the feelings, simply "catching" them and identifying them as early warning signs of impending anxiety — as Stage One events — allowed him to use SRB successfully to interrupt the sequence.

People typically are most aware of a physical sensation as the first event in the panic sequence (if they're aware of any event at all, prior to full-blown panic). But there's very often a thought or feeling that precedes this blip in physical arousal. You might push the thought down so quickly, you don't even realize anything occurred before the physical symptom. And you can still intervene with SRB when the symptom occurs. But if you can start tuning into these "pre-sensation" thoughts and feelings more rapidly, you'll be able to interrupt the sequence sooner and more easily, and will gradually decrease the frequency of your attacks.

Discovering what comes before the actual physical sensations that lead to panic is oftentimes not easy. Janine, who was raised in a family with an alcoholic father, reported that her attacks often occurred when she and her husband had just returned home from a visit with her parents and now-grown siblings. She initially described these visits as "going by all in a blur and then I just feel lousy." But as she explored the visits further, she began to see just how her family functioned and treated one another, and to define more precisely how she felt in response. Through these explorations — which began with an exploration of the early triggers of her attacks — Janine began to see a decline in her panic and a gradual increase in her feelings of peace and self-esteem. This was not achieved without some emotional pain in the process, but for Janine, it was worth it.

How to Identify "Second-Stage" Triggers for Panic

Now you can catch the events and feelings that often trigger sensation (and subsequent panic). But what about the catastrophic thoughts that occur in response to sensation, the events we've called "second-stage" triggers of attacks? Certainly the thought, "I'm going to have a panic attack," can be enough to cause the rapid spiraling of thoughts and sensations that ends in full-blown panic. But even when you're not aware of it, you usually have fears of something even more disastrous happening to you, some catastrophe you envision *beyond* the prospect of a panic attack that scares you even more. As one woman said, "When I'm not having a panic attack, I feel like having one is the worst thing that could happen to me. I mean, that's what I'm most afraid of when I leave the house to go to the market. But when the attack hits, suddenly I feel as if there must be something really wrong with me, something that's going to kill me."

You, too, may fear panic attacks and also, "something really wrong," something more than panic, something deadly. The additional fears are difficult to recognize at times because they are frightening and because the process happens so rapidly, *almost automatically*. But the possibility of "under-the-surface" catastrophic thoughts is worth pursuing.

One way to conduct the pursuit is to use *sequential questioning:* Try completing this sentence, "So I'm going to have a panic attack and..." And then what? "And then I'll humiliate myself?" "And then I'll lose control?" "And maybe this time, it really does mean I'm going to die?"

With each catastrophic answer or vision you generate, ask the further question "and then what?" Continue till you reach the absolute worst, the deepest level of your fears, because that's the fear you need to tackle ultimately.

Notice the word, "vision." Sometimes, as for Caroline, the catastrophic image has never been put into words; it is, in fact, only a visual image. In fact, it's been reported that eighty percent of those with anxiety disorders identify images connected with their anxiety. So when you're asking the question, "And then what?" don't neglect to consider visual images as your answer.

If you can't identify any specific catastrophic thoughts, you might try asking yourself this question: "If I *did* have a catastrophic thought about a panic attack, what would it be?" What do you picture happening if you *couldn't* leave a situation, if your panic *didn't* stop? If your panic symptoms *did* have a basis in organic disease, what disease would it be? Heart attack? Brain tumor? Psychosis? What's your *worst fear?*

Consider, also, whether you might possibly be misidentifying a physical sensation, triggering panic instead of a more appropriate response. Susan, who entered treatment for panic disorder after four years of intermittent attacks, noticed that when she was at work, which involved fairly intense concentration hunched over a computer, she often developed feelings of uneasiness in the late morning, which could then initiate panic symptoms. As she explored the situation more carefully, she realized that what she was experiencing was actually fatigue, not anxiety — but the sensations readily led to anxiety because of her worries about panic attacks.

Susan decided to begin taking a mid-morning break, eating a snack, and taking a brief walk. She took the break even if she didn't feel particularly tired, in the thought that it might prevent later fatigue. And, indeed, taking the breaks diminished her spells of "uneasiness" quite markedly. On the rare occasions that she did develop discomfort, she simply reminded herself that she was merely fatigued and was able to rapidly "breathe away" her symptoms.

The "Special Help" Summary on page 103 offers a handy review of the main categories of triggers for panic. Since the "triggers" for panic attacks — unlike the triggers for a fear of water or of storms or of spiders — are usually internal (bodily sensations, mental images, thoughts, feelings), they're often harder to identify. But your attempts to identify them — so that you can intervene early and tackle them directly — will be well worth your effort.

Looking for early triggers of panic is an ongoing process. You need to consider your first attack, examine your latest attack step-by-step, and look for feelings or thoughts that may have preceded physical sensations. Consider emotions you were feeling — or perhaps trying not to feel. Try to get into the sequence one step earlier.

Next, consider what response might follow the sensations: Ask yourself what you fear at the time of an attack, then ask the question, "and then what?" Continue to ask this question, whether the answers are verbal labels or images, till you arrive at your deepest, most fundamental fear.

Finally, simply using SRB repeatedly, the first instant you experience a sensation or faint whisper of anxiety, will gradually sensitize you to earlier and earlier opportunities for intervention. And early intervention is an important key to success.

Common Triggers for Panic Sensations

A. Physical triggers:
These are usually the easiest to identify and would include such things as overheated rooms and rushing about (which can elevate heart rate), skipping a meal or grinding your teeth (which can lead to headache), a mild bout of the flu (producing nausea), and too much caffeine (leading to "extra" heartbeats.) All these can prompt the sensations leading to the thoughts that fuel anxiety.

B. Very specific cognitive triggers:
These, too, can prompt the physical sensations of anxiety, leading to further anxiety and panic. Examples: You take a new medication and have the sudden, fleeting thought, "I wonder if I'll have a bad reaction?" You think, "What if I have a panic attack in the meeting and make a fool of myself?"

C. "Current" emotional triggers:
You see your child fall and feel instant distress for him. You catch a glimpse of a former friend who hasn't called and feel sudden hurt. Your guts begin to churn and you respond with alarm.

D. "Deeper" Emotional Triggers:
These triggers are often feelings related to a long-ago event, perhaps sparked by something recent: You feel a pain in your side and you feel what you felt as a child when your father was dying of pancreatic cancer, or feel a sudden fear about your own health. Or maybe, in a fight with your husband, he shouts something that is all too close to your father's temper outbursts when you were young.

Remember that SUPPRESSED EMOTION is a frequently-overlooked culprit in triggering panic. Remember, too, that you needn't be wholly aware of a thought or emotion for it to trigger a physical sensation (which prompts catastrophic thoughts and subsequent panic.)

Exercises for Session Seven

I. SRB Practice

Continue to practice SRB twice daily at home and as needed "in real life" when early signs of anxiety or anxiety-producing physical sensations arise. Remember that practicing at home should involve producing anxiety and then using SRB to eliminate it. Record practices and experiences in your journal.

II. Controlled Breathing Practice

Continue to practice controlled breathing twice daily and also whenever you think of it, whenever you need it, or whenever you perform your neutral "signal." Record in your journal.

III. Logging Panic Episodes

Continue to record any episodes of panic or impending panic. More and more, you'll experience days or even weeks when no panic occurs and on those days, you'll just note overall activities and mood.

You'll also find many more occasions when you encounter circumstances that might have led to panic in the past — whether events and emotions that precede sensation or catastrophic responses that follow — but your heightened ability to "catch" these triggers early, and to intervene with SRB will prevent it from becoming anything greater. That's an event you'll want to record since that's precisely the evidence that you're well on your way to eliminating panic altogether! Hurrah!

IV. Daily Journal Writing

Continue to use your journal for "free recording." You'll note that your notebook is now being used for three purposes: for recording practice sessions and experiences with controlled breathing and SRB; for logging episodes of panic, near-panic and, more and more, averted panic; and for spontaneous recording of thoughts and feelings.

V. Identifying Specific Triggers for Your Panic Attacks

A. Go back through your journal and examine the records of your last six panic attacks. For each attack, note the events that preceded the attack and those that occurred just as the attack was beginning.

B. Based on your review, make a list of the bodily triggers that may be important for your attacks: What physical sensations preceded attacks and first aroused your anxiety?

The sensations you identify may be different for each episode, or you may find that the same sensation leads to catastrophic thinking and increased anxiety in almost all cases. If you have more than one sensation on your list (as most readers will), circle the one that appears most important (occurs most often or provokes the most frightening thoughts).

C. Now list *cognitive* triggers for attacks: What thoughts (and/or visual images) occur just before or near the onset of your attacks? These would virtually always include catastrophic responses to very early physical sensations, and possibly also self-statements about your expectation of panic or fears about that prospect. They might also include self-talk about an upcoming feared situation ("I might fail this exam," or "My mother might be angry with me," or "I might look really stupid.")

D. List *emotional* triggers for attacks. Once again, look for feelings you experience just before the onset of physical sensation, and for events with emotional significance.

E. List other factors in the onset of your attacks — the places they occurred, people present, and activities you were engaged in. Evaluate specifically what it was about those factors that might have generated an attack, and add these notions to the appropriate list.

For example, a *person* present in the situation may lead you to think, "I'm going to look like a fool," a cognitive trigger. A *place* might lead to memories of a painful event, an emotional trigger. A given *activity* might evoke particular physical sensations which then, in combination with thoughts about the sensation, could trigger an attack.

F. In future weeks, try to be especially alert to the triggers you identified so that, when one occurs, you can initiate SRB right away, before the attack has the chance to progress further.

Challenging Catastrophic Beliefs

The uncle of a psychologist friend of mine once told my friend he was "crazy" because the uncle overheard him talking to himself. The psychologist-to-be was nine years old at the time.

The fact is, we all talk to ourselves — though most of us don't do it aloud — and hardly anybody is "crazy." In fact, self-talk is very important in working out our attitudes and beliefs and in guiding us through difficult times. But not all self-talk is healthy.

This session's focus is on challenging the internal thinking — the negative self-talk — that can give rise to panic either directly (you believe that an initial sensation is dangerous, causing a spiraling into panic) or indirectly (you hold a belief that raises your overall anxiety level and thereby increases your susceptibility to panic episodes). Learning to challenge anxiety-producing self-talk and to replace it with more realistic, more helpful self-talk is a crucial skill for overcoming panic in your life — and for ensuring that it doesn't return.

As you're no doubt aware by now, a large percentage of panic sufferers share a core belief that physical symptoms and bodily sensations signal danger. Studies have found, in fact, that panic sufferers associate bodily symptoms with perceived danger more strongly than the average person. What's more, *panic attacks accompanied by catastrophic thoughts are likely to be more severe* than those that aren't.

The notion that physical sensations spell danger was discussed in Session three: Most panic sufferers, perhaps you among them, report a tendency to fear physical illness and symptoms that might be interpreted as potential signs of illness. In Session seven, you evaluated your own tendency to fear adverse consequences of physical symptoms, using sequential questions to arrive at your most fundamental fear in the face of panic symptoms. And in Session two, as you learned about personal histories that often predispose people to panic, you examined some of the events in your own life that may have led to these powerful fears.

You know from Session six that the core belief, "physical sensation is dangerous," can lead directly to panic. Since that belief is commonly held among panic sufferers, this session begins by teaching you to challenge that notion. The basic method will then be extended to other beliefs and attitudes that can raise your anxiety and thus indirectly influence the occurrence of panic attacks.

First, let's review briefly what happens during a typical panic attack, following the diagram presented first in Session six. A physical sensation will be used as the *Stage One* event, since that's the most common precipitant of an attack. And the sequence will be followed all the way to a full-blown attack, although by now that probably happens to you only rarely, if at all.

In a classic panic attack, you experience a physical sensation — an "extra" heartbeat or a feeling of breathlessness or an odd sensation in your head or any of a number of other physical events. That's Stage One. You're immediately propelled into catastrophic, "what-if" thinking: "Oh, no, I'm going to pass out!" or "What if I have a heart attack!" The heightened anxiety generated by this *Stage Two* thinking produces *more* physical symptoms, which then *further* increase the catastrophic belief that something is wrong. Ultimately, the spiraling of symptoms and catastrophic thoughts culminates in a full-blown attack.

You've learned what to do when the process begins to effectively halt it: As soon as you experience the first hints of any Stage One events (typically the first physical sensations), you immediately use the SRB method to interrupt it. You *Stop* the catastrophic thinking. You *Refocus* on the present. And you *Breathe* in a slow and controlled fashion. And to the extent you accomplish SRB, your anxiety subsides.

When you use SRB, you don't *challenge* the catastrophic thinking that helps drive the cycle. You simply *stop* it. And that effectively interrupts the panic sequence. But at other times, you can, in addition, work on challenging the catastrophic thinking and the beliefs that underlie it. And that can diminish the likelihood of panic cycles developing at all.

After all, if you truly believe that tightness in your chest is a sign that you're about to die of a heart attack, the thought is going to raise your anxiety and cause panic. But if you know your chest tightness is most likely the result of normal physical events, perhaps due to your strenuous work-out in last night's exercise class, there may be no resulting panic to interrupt!

Challenging Self-Talk: Laurie's Experience

Laurie sought treatment for panic attacks her sophomore year in college. Her attacks typically started with her awareness of an increased heart rate. Laurie had lost her father to a heart attack when she was a junior in high school and had always feared that she, too, might have inherited "a weak heart." Whenever she was home from college, her mother questioned her closely and worriedly about her health, only amplifying Laurie's own secret fears.

One day in a gym class, Laurie pushed herself harder than usual and became alarmed when her heart began to race and to "flutter." She began to feel faint and ill and was convinced she must be having a heart attack. She was taken to a local emergency room and found to be healthy. But the experience was so terrifying that Laurie began to monitor her heart even more closely than before — and to respond with intense anxiety whenever she noticed any unusual sensation. Laurie eventually sought treatment when her attacks became so frequent they were interfering with her class attendance.

Laurie responded extremely well to the initial steps in her treatment: learning basic facts about panic disorder and panic attacks; mastering SRB and using it successfully to interrupt symptoms; and coming to understand how her history had contributed to her fears. But she still harbored immense fears about her health and her heart, believing she'd one day suffer a heart attack and die without warning. And when she experienced any sensations at all in her chest or arms, or any feelings of impending panic, she still felt she was about to die. Tackling her fears about her heart directly was Laurie's next task.

Step One: Identifying Self-Talk. To begin, Laurie was asked to sit down, relax and make a list of the thoughts she had whenever she experienced any sensations in her chest or felt any anxiety or had thoughts about her heart. She was asked to put the thoughts in the form of statements that she implicitly made to herself, as though she were "thinking out loud."

A portion of Laurie's list of self-statements looked like this:

-There must be something wrong with my heart; otherwise, why would it flutter like this?

-I probably inherited a weak heart from my dad; I'm probably going to die from a heart attack. (This thought was accompanied by grief as well as fear.)

-It's dangerous to overlook these symptoms; I need to monitor my heart so that if something happens, I can get help.

Step Two: Evaluating and Challenging Self-Statements. Laurie's next step was to take each statement in turn and to evaluate it as realistically as she could, considering the evidence supporting the statement and the evidence discrediting it. After evaluating the statement fully, she was to write as many challenges to the original statement as she could, based on that evaluation. Challenging self-talk effectively isn't simply a matter of saying, "It isn't true." It demands a careful exploration of the statement from as many perspectives as possible.

Laurie considered her first self-statement: "There must be something wrong with my heart; otherwise why would it flutter like this?". She asked herself what *evidence* indicated that she did have a bad heart and what evidence indicated she didn't. She looked at her own *history* of previous episodes of heart palpitations and what they'd ultimately turned out to mean. She also looked for *alternative possibilities* to explain her symptoms in the instances when they'd occurred.

Laurie ended up generating the following challenges:

-These flutters have been happening for six months now and I haven't died yet. If they did mean something were seriously wrong, surely it would have happened by now.

-The flutters do diminish when I use SRB. That wouldn't make sense if the flutters came from heart disease. SRB doesn't affect heart disease, but it does affect symptoms of anxiety. And that suggests that the flutters probably come from anxiety.

-Lots of other people have sensations like this and they ignore them. They're not all dropping dead.

-I know that lots of people with panic disorder have these kind of symptoms. And since I know I have panic disorder, that's probably a more likely explanation of my symptoms than a bad heart.

-I had more caffeine than usual this morning, and I know that sometimes seems to cause these flutters.

-I've seen a doctor and he said I was fine.

The last challenge generated a rejoinder, an additional self-statement:

-But doctors make mistakes. Even though the doctor said I was fine, he could have missed something; I could still have a bad heart.

When Laurie then evaluated the evidence for that statement, though, she in turn generated further challenges:

-Doctors do make mistakes but I've had a physical exam and blood work and an EKG and even a 24-hour reading with a Holter monitor. The chance of a serious problem being missed after all those tests is really very slim.

-My doctor is very careful; he's never fouled up with me before and I do trust him.

-Doctors worry about malpractice as much as I worry about my heart; I know my doctor would have been as thorough as possible in his examination of me.

Laurie next took up her other self-statements and tried to generate separate challenges to these as well. To her self-statement, "I probably inherited a weak heart from my Dad, and I'm going to die of a heart attack," she responded:

-Dad was fifty-nine when he died and he had high blood pressure and was overweight. I'm twenty-one years old and healthy. If I did inherit "his" heart, I should still have thirty-eight good years left so I can at least delay my worrying for a few decades!

-The probability of a heart attack in someone only twenty-one years old is really very low.

In response to her third self-statement, concerning the dangers of failing to monitor for heart symptoms, she concluded:

-Dad got no warning of his attack, so even if I were going to die like he did, my monitoring isn't likely to help me. And it's hurting me in lots of ways, like making me miss out on activities and making me miserable. So I'm going to try to put it out of my mind and get on with my life!

Step Three: Daily Work to Reinforce More Adaptive Beliefs. After Laurie finished the "challenging" exercise, she reported that she now saw "why those things aren't true and I don't need to think them anymore." But it was important that she not stop there. Laurie was instructed to work with her self-talk each evening to begin to incorporate her challenges into her belief system — so that she could truly come to believe them at an emotional, not just an intellectual level; so that she could believe them even at her most vulnerable times.

Laurie was told that when she had panic episodes (or merely increases in anxiety) during the day, she was to handle them in the usual manner, with SRB. But when evening came, she was to sit down with her notebook and at that time, to evaluate the thoughts and self-statements that had occurred before and during the early stages of anxiety, looking particularly for statements about the meaning of the early symptoms. In most cases, Laurie's self-statements were versions of the thoughts she'd already analyzed, but she nonetheless wrote them down again, evaluated them and again wrote challenges to them.

Note that Laurie didn't address the self-statements and catastrophic thoughts at the time of panic; she was too busy refocusing her attention and using controlled breathing. But later, calmer, she recalled the episode and considered the thoughts more carefully. At that time, she evaluated and challenged them in a manner that would ultimately reduce their power — maybe by the time of the next attack.

Of course, there were days when Laurie didn't experience panic or even the mild anxiety that might prompt her to "check" for heart symptoms. The evenings of those days, Laurie still spent about twenty minutes "working" on her self-statements, but in this case, she simply took out her original or most recent list of self-statements — whichever she felt was most powerful in its influence over her — thought through each statement on the list, reconsidered her challenges, and added others as they occurred to her. In effect, Laurie used the time to remind herself of all the good reasons not to fear the sensations she'd feared in the past, to reinforce her new and more adaptive thinking.

The Final Step: Enjoying the Results. After several weeks, Laurie's challenges became increasingly automatic. Her attitudes gradually changed; she realized she wasn't at risk. The attacks diminished greatly — almost ceased in fact — and she sensed a greater resilience to physical sensations that previously would have greatly alarmed her. On the rare occasions when anxiety arose, she still used SRB, but in parallel, found herself automatically recalling some thought that decreased her anxiety.

In fact, Laurie's comfort level reached the point that sometimes a sensation that would have increased her anxiety in the past instead prompted a thought that prevented it. For example, on one occasion she noticed an increase in heart rate while rushing to get to class on time, but she realized almost instantaneously, "Oh, right, my heart rate is up because I'm rushing — I'm exerting myself and I'm also a little nervous about being late."

Something else happened to Laurie, too. As she pondered the day's situations that had triggered increased anxiety, she realized that situations which reminded her of her father often sparked physical sensations — which in the past had then prompted almost instant fears about her own heart. It became clear to her that she'd never worked through her sense of grief at losing him. In fact, she'd actively tried to avoid thinking of him. Ironically, and tragically for Laurie, in an effort to escape pain, she was robbing herself of the very experiences that ultimately would soften it. This new understanding led her to begin some grief work that probably contributed further to the elimination of her attacks, but more important, gave her back her many happy memories of her father.

Tackling Other Anxiety-Related Beliefs. Laurie also became aware through her journal work that she held other beliefs that interfered in her life and lowered her threshold for anxiety. For example, she felt it was her duty to anticipate and tend to others' feelings, preventing any dissatisfaction or discomfort they might potentially experience. If she were with a group of friends and a conflict threatened to erupt, for example, she became nervous and rushed to smooth things over. And in the past, at least, her anxiety about this situation could raise her heart rate — and provoke a panic attack.

Laurie found she could tackle this set of beliefs, too, with her new "challenging" methods. At night when she sat down, journal in hand, to evaluate her day and to consider any anxiety that had arisen, she found that these self-statements had sometimes been significant. As before, she listed the self-statements she'd made in each situation, evaluated them realistically and wrote challenges to them — precisely the same method she'd used to evaluate and challenge self-statements about her heart.

Over time, she was able to ease herself away from taking responsibility for everyone else's feelings — and her own feelings responded in a very positive way! In the months that followed, she began to feel calmer and happier than she had since her father was alive.

How to Challenge Your Own Anxiety-Producing Self-Talk

Let's take another look at the steps Laurie followed, putting them in the form of instructions you can use in your efforts to challenge negative and catastrophic self-statements.

1. Identify and record self-statements. During the day, whenever anxiety arises, reduce it with SRB. Then, once you're comfortable, either soon after the episode or that evening, ask yourself, "When I became anxious, what was I saying to myself? What thoughts was I having?" List the thoughts in your notebook, putting them in the form of self-statements, such as, "I'm going to pass out."

It's helpful to organize your notebook page before you begin: Divide your paper into two vertical halves by drawing a line down the center of the page, top to bottom. Write the self-statements along the left-hand side of the page, leaving ample space between separate statements. (The room on the right-hand half will be used for recording challenges to the statements.)

To be sure you have as complete a list as possible at this stage, consider whether you've included all your beliefs about the meaning of your physical symptoms — the worst possible outcomes you imagine — including physical disaster ("I'm dying of a stroke"); social disaster ("People are going to laugh at me"); and emotional disaster to yourself or others ("My children will be left motherless" or "I'm going crazy"). Just as in Session seven, try using sequential questioning ("and then what?") to follow every thought to its deepest level.

As you list your self-statements, list, in addition, any visual images that may accompany your anxiety (more about those later).

2. Evaluate and challenge self-statements. Take each self-statement and evaluate it as thoroughly and realistically as you can.

Ask yourself:

-What's the evidence that _____ (some serious medical problem) is the cause of my symptoms?

-Has _____ (the disaster you fear) ever happened to me before?

-If ____ were the cause of my symptoms, would I still be having no further symptoms after ____ (the length of time you've had your symptoms)?

-If ____ were the cause, why would the attacks keep occurring — and usually in particular, predictable situations?

-If my symptoms were really caused by a medical problem, why would they go away when I ran out of the supermarket?

-What else could have caused my symptoms? Anxiety? Fatigue? Exertion? Too much caffeine? Anger?

-What evidence do I have for other possible causes of my symptoms? (Try to look for evidence of other explanations just as actively as you look for evidence of disaster!)

-In the past, when I've had these symptoms, what has been the ultimate outcome?

-What does that suggest about the source(s) of my symptoms?

-Who do I know who's had _____ (the serious medical problem that you fear or suspect)?

-What did he/she experience at the time of the problem?

-How is my situation similar and different?

-What's the actual probability that ____ is causing my symptoms? (For example, if you fear that your headache means you have a brain tumor, you should know that fewer than one headache in a thousand proves to be the result of a brain tumor.)

-What's the actual probability of _____ happening to me? (For example, a sudden heart attack in a healthy young woman who's been given a clean bill of health from her doctor is very unusual. Passing out during panic is extremely rare. There's no association between panic disorder and psychosis — the condition most people picture when they worry about "going crazy.")

-Do I have other symptoms of _____?

-What has my physician told me about these symptoms — and what basis do I have to trust or mistrust him or her?

-If the worst were true and I did have _____, is it treatable?

-Would controlled breathing and refocusing of attention reduce symptoms of a stroke or a heart attack (or whatever you fear is happening)? If not, what might I conclude from the fact that my symptoms disappear when I use SRB?

-In the past, have I ever brought these symptoms on by worrying?

-What would _____ believe or say about these symptoms? (Use as a reference point someone whom you see as being a sensible person and whose "voice" can be a helpful guide to you.)

-If _____ (the feared disaster) *really did occur, what's the very worst that would happen?* (Take this to the very extreme.) *How likely is that? What aspect of "the worst" is most troubling? What would I do if it occurred?*

-When _____ occurred (an objectively dangerous or terrifying situation), *how did I handle it?*

Also ask yourself these related questions to help you further evaluate the self-statements and generate challenges:

-How/when/where did I develop this belief and what gave it such force? Could this be why the belief is so hard to reject, even when the evidence argues that it's not realistic?

-Does this particular self-statement reflect any more general beliefs about myself and about the world in general (e.g., "The worst always happens to me." "You can't trust anyone anymore.")? What's the evidence for those beliefs? How realistic are they?

-How can I prevent or cope with this situation? What coping strategies have I used in the past and how did they work?

Composing Challenges. As you evaluate your self-statements, try to compose challenges for each one, based on the evaluation. Usually this evaluation will generate several challenges to each self-statement. Record each of these challenges on the right-hand side of your paper, opposite the statement that prompted it.

3. Use the Method on a Daily Basis. The first time you generate challenges to your self-talk related to a particular situation, the process will be lengthy and perhaps difficult; it's not easy to look at a situation in a fresh way after years of almost automatic response. The process will be considerably briefer the next time you encounter a similar situation, but it's still important to formally evaluate your self-talk, generate challenges anew, and put them in writing; the very act of writing them down will help to reinforce the new ideas.

If no episodes of anxiety occurred on a given day, you'll have no new self-statements to list, evaluate or challenge. On that evening, take the time, instead, to review your earlier work on your self-statements. Reconsider the challenges, repeat them to yourself, and add any additional challenges you may generate.

Also consider what role you played in avoiding anxiety — and pat yourself on the back! Finally, make a mental note of any useful "lessons" you might take from the anxiety-free day, for example, "When I _____, I don't become anxious and then I don't have chest pains," or, "When I feel breathless but I remember it's only because I was exercising, it doesn't get any worse."

Challenging Self-Talk: Mary's Experiences

Let's consider one more example of the method of challenging self-talk. Mary developed panic attacks in her mid-thirties and sought treatment when they began to interfere with her work performance. One of Mary's work duties was that of taking the minutes in various meetings, and she lived in terror that she'd have a panic attack during one of them. She learned to use refocusing and controlled breathing to avert attacks and became more comfortable in most settings, but she continued to feel quite anxious at work.

When Mary reached the point in treatment when she began to tackle her self-talk, she readily identified a variety of statements which are summarized in the three following remarks:

-I'm going to have a panic attack at work; that would be horribly humiliating.

-My co-workers will think I'm crazy.

-I could never go back to work after I had an attack there; I'd be too ashamed.

With assistance from her therapist, Mary evaluated her self-statements, applying somewhat more realistic standards. First, she asked herself how likely she was to have an attack at work and realized that since she began treatment, she hadn't had a single attack. She acknowledged that it *could* happen, but she also admitted that the probability was very low unless, for some reason, she suddenly forgot all her newfound skills!

Next, she admitted that if she did have a panic attack, her co-workers probably wouldn't even know it was happening. At most, they might notice that she'd become pale, sweaty, and perhaps preoccupied. Mary noted that if she ever noticed someone looking pale or preoccupied, she wouldn't think "crazy"; she'd probably think "not feeling well." Her co-workers would no doubt do the same. And even if they knew it was a panic attack, they'd probably feel sympathetic.

In the process of evaluating her self-statements, Mary decided to tell one trusted co-worker about her panic disorder. She also planned what to do if she did have a panic attack at work: She'd say she was feeling a little faint and would excuse herself. She found that simply having a plan in mind about how to handle "the worst," should it actually occur, relieved some of her anxiety about it. Finally, Mary decided she wouldn't truly be forced by her embarrassment to quit her job if she had an attack. She wouldn't enjoy an attack at work — it would embarrass her — but she'd expect more sympathy than horror from others (if anyone even noticed!). And the incident would pass in a short time — about the same amount of time it took for something else of interest to occur in the office.

Mary wrote her challenges and plans in her notebook and reviewed them each day. She told her friend at work about her attacks, and she began to remind herself, just before each meeting, what to say if an attack developed. Thus far, it hasn't happened.

Mary's example raises a crucial point about the value of examining and challenging your self-talk. Before doing the self-talk exercises, Mary was aware of her belief: "If I have an attack at work it would be horrible." But because she found the whole topic too upsetting to even consider, she never really pressed herself to examine *how* it would be horrible, just *what* she imagined happening. It was only through examining her thoughts — all of them — that she could see the distortions and exaggerations in them. The problem with unexamined thoughts is that they have no chance to be modified by logic or experience. Like monsters in a child's closet at night, they seem to grow bigger and more terrifying when our eyes are closed. It's only by facing them head-on that you can shrink them down to size — and, ultimately, defeat them.

Other Common Self-Statements:
"I Can't Handle This!"

One belief common among panic sufferers when they're in a fear-producing situation is the catastrophic self-statement, "I can't handle this!" If this is familiar to you, spend a few minutes right now — while you're not anxious — considering the statement in light of your last panic attack and generating challenges to it. When you next encounter an anxiety episode in which this statement occurs, you should still go through the formal method of challenging it; this exercise will simply give you a head start. You might ask yourself some specific questions to get started:

-*Do I have any methods to use when anxiety does strike?* (If not, you need to reread Sessions five through seven!)

-*When I've had panic attacks in the past, at their very worst, before I even knew what they were, did I pass out? Throw up? Have a heart attack?*

-*Are there times I've prevented anxiety from turning into a full- blown panic attack? How did I do it? Was it a fluke, a lucky one- time event? Or is it something I might be able to repeat?*

-*How do I usually feel two hours after an attack? Based on past experience, can I expect to go on reasonably well after an attack ends?*

-*Are there any places or people I can turn to for help if I need it?*

-*Have I ever coped with anything difficult in my life before?* (List some of the occasions and obstacles you've coped with in the past.)

-*What are some of the arenas in my life in which I've demonstrated good coping? (Child rearing? Friendship? Job? School? Homemaking?)*

-*Have I overcome any problems in my life? Had any successes?*

Compose challenges based on the answers to those questions. In addition, add some general positive coping statements of the form, "I can handle this!" (See page 123 for some examples.) Write yourself a pep talk — and read it every now and then!

"I Just Know It's Going To Be Terrible!"

Many times, people with panic attacks overcome their attacks quite rapidly, but find that the anxiety they feel at the prospect of entering a situation — anticipatory anxiety — remains quite high. This usually reflects self-statements of the sort, "I'm going to have a terrible time in this situation."

Even before you've eliminated your attacks completely, you can do a lot to change the self-talk that increases anticipatory anxiety. In fact, working to eliminate that talk will decrease the likelihood that you'll have an attack in the first place, by allowing you to enter the situation in a more positive, less anxious frame of mind.

Think back to the last time you experienced anticipatory anxiety. Reconstruct your self-statements, record them in your journal, then evaluate the statements and generate realistic challenges to them. Below are some of the challenges you might include. Be sure to "personalize" them to fit your own particular situation.

-I know I'm better off once I'm actually in the situation; I always feel frightened beforehand, but once I get there, I almost always feel better.

-The last five times I was in this situation, I didn't have a panic attack. So I'm not likely to have one this time either.

-If I do have a panic attack, I know what to do. But I know what to do before that point, too, so it's unlikely my anxiety will have a chance to get all the way to full-blown panic.

-I'm worrying that if I have an attack, someone may notice. I know from experience that's unlikely. When I told _____ I was having a panic attack, she was amazed! And if someone does notice, so what?

-I know this is anxiety. It's miserable but not dangerous.

-When I faced a real emergency, I didn't have a panic attack; I can certainly handle this.

-The worst that can happen in this situation is that I'll feel terribly afraid. If I do, I'll survive it.

The next session will teach you a method for eliminating panic attacks that's been found successful for a very high percentage of panic sufferers. You'll also learn about some further strategies for coping with anticipatory anxiety. You'll surely experience some successes — which will provide you with even more positive statements to add to the list!

Challenging Your Self-Talk at Times of Anxiety

As you begin to work at challenging your negative, catastrophic self-talk, it's most essential that you spend time every day evaluating those thoughts, and replacing them with more adaptive statements. That takes time and attention, so you need to do it outside the anxiety-producing situation. But you can, in addition, begin to apply the fruits of that work at the very times the catastrophic thoughts arise. Here's how:

After you've successfully halted panic with SRB for several weeks and feel quite confident with it, begin to make one modification in your SRB procedure. When you experience anxiety, stop your catastrophic thinking (as before), control your breathing (as before), *then begin to challenge your catastrophic thoughts on the spot.* You may find that this has happened already, almost automatically, as it did for Laurie. But if not, begin to do so deliberately. This will further strengthen your ability to keep your anxiety at a "normal" and manageable level.

Challenging Other Unhelpful Beliefs

Remember Laurie? After she worked on the self-statements that *directly* elicited her panic — her core beliefs about the dangerous meaning of heart palpitations — she identified and tackled beliefs and self-statements in other arenas that raised her anxieties and thus contributed more *indirectly* to the likelihood of panic attacks.

It's useful, in fact, to keep in mind just how general this method is for tackling all sorts of self-talk — the self-talk that directly evokes panic; the self-talk that raises your anxiety and contributes to the potential for panic; and even the self- talk that simply makes you feel lousy about yourself. The last can be helpful to you as a means of improving your quality of life, of course. But it can also help you in your mastery of anxiety — because feeling lousy about yourself can increase your sense of vulnerability and make you more susceptible to the onset of anxiety in any situation.

Let's say you were in a social or work situation and said something rather silly. We all do sometimes. But now you're fretting endlessly over it, replaying the situation in your head, telling yourself that everyone must be laughing at you, and feeling about as crummy as a person can feel. And you know that over the next few days, you'll be sleeping poorly, snapping at your family, and feeling reluctant to leave your house and face other people.

Pull out your notebook and write down all your self-statements. Then consider the evidence and write challenges to them. Your notebook page at the end of the process might look something like this:

That was such a dumb thing to say; everyone must think I'm a complete idiot.	*Yes, it was a silly thing to say, but most people in the group know me pretty well; they know I'm not an idiot. After all, I_____ (jot down some of your accomplishments).*
I always say the stupidest things imaginable. No one is ever going to want to talk to me again.	*I don't always say stupid things; I say plenty of other things too. And everyone says dumb things once in a while.*

*Most people don't judge
others based on one
remark; they judge the
whole person.*

*Most people have plenty
of other things on their
minds; they're not going
to pay that much attention
to one chance remark or
remember that long.*

*If someone else in the
group said that, I might
laugh, but then I'd forget
about it. It's reasonable to
assume others will react
to my statement the
same way.*

*How can I face these
people again after making
such a fool of myself?*

*I'm sure I'm paying more
attention to it than
anyone else.*

*If I'm really agonizing
over this, I can mention it
to a friend and ask her
how bad it sounded.*

One thing to notice about this example — something that's often true of self-talk — is that there frequently is *some* basis for the self-statements on the left-hand side of the page. After all, if the statements were one hundred percent false, completely without grounds, totally crazy, chances are you wouldn't be making them in the first place. In this particular case, yes, you did goof up and you'd rather not have done that.

The problem is not that the left-hand statements are totally crazy or completely false (though they may be). The problem is that the statements on the left-hand side are tremendously *exaggerated*, vastly overstated and stated as absolutes — "always," "complete idiot," "stupidest thing imaginable." And by repeating the left-hand statements so often, without ever questioning them, you've given them incredible power — at incredible cost to yourself. You've come to focus all your attention on them, to accept them automatically and absolutely, and to completely overlook the right-hand statements, which are more true and certainly more helpful to you.

This method helps you to make a place again for the statements on the right, to elevate the challenges at least to a position of equal weight with the destructive beliefs. In fact, if challenging your self-talk helps you even to begin to *question* your self-statements as they pop into your head, to *consider* that they might be erroneous or overstated — to remember, even, that another side *exists* — the process will be of great help to you.

More Ideas for Challenging Your Self-Talk

Other self-statements that commonly increase anxiety include these: "I can never make a mistake," "Something awful is going to happen if I don't _____," "Other people always do things right but I always goof them up," "He's going to think I'm a mess," and "I shouldn't do this for myself; I should sacrifice for others." And of course there are countless others — about as many as there are panic sufferers. (One of the exercises following this session will instruct you to generate your own "favorites.")

Remember, no matter what the *content,* the *process* of challenging self-statements is the same:

-Identify the statement(s) you're making to yourself, explicitly or implicitly, at times of anxiety.

-Evaluate each statement realistically, considering the evidence from a position of neutrality and actively looking for positive, encouraging and calming statements you can make. Write challenges to each statement based on your evaluation.

Since the self-talk most commonly and directly involved in producing a panic attack relates to fears about bodily sensations, the "Special Help" Summary on page 123 provides a list of twelve useful questions you can use in evaluating those self-statements.

You may want to make a copy of it to carry with you, so you have it handy when and where you need it.

-Do this on a daily/nightly basis, while still using SRB at the times anxiety hits.

12 Questions to Challenge Your Catastrophic Self-Statements

(Use these anytime something happens in your body that raises fears of disaster.)

1. What do I *fear* is happening? What's the worst that could happen?
2. What *evidence* do I have for that fear?
3. What does my *doctor* say about the fear, what evidence is that based on, and can I trust my doctor's judgement based on my past experiences with him or her?
4. How often does the disaster I fear happen to someone in *my* circumstances?
   (How often, for example, does a 35-year-old woman in good health with no history of heart disease have a heart attack without warning and die from it?)
5. Who do I know, personally, who've experienced this disaster, and how did their situations *differ* from mine?
6. What *else* could be causing my symptoms?
   (Could it be something physical, like rushing around, or too much caffeine? Worried thoughts about my child's safety on the playground, or a meeting at work? Something emotional, like unhappy memories or trying not to get angry at someone?)
7. Does anyone else with *panic* experience these same symptoms, and what might that mean for my situation?
8. What ultimately *did* happen the last five times I had these symptoms, and what does *that* tell me?
9. Is it possible my symptoms *might* be anxiety-related? If so, how might they have been generated?
   (Remember, for example, that muscle tension can cause aching in your chest wall, overbreathing can cause dizziness, adrenaline can cause a rapid pulse, and noradrenaline can cause difficulty remembering and thinking clearly.)
10. If I slow down my breathing, do my symptoms *decline?* What does *that* suggest about the cause of the symptoms?
11. Where did my fear of this disaster come from in the *first* place?
    (Remember, if the source of your fear was some awful event in your life, that gives your fear extra *power,* but it doesn't make the disaster any more *likely* to happen to you.)
    Power ≠ Probability
12. What would my best friend say about my fears right now, and can I say that to *myself?*

Add any other questions you can think of to fit your particular situation and to help you consider more realistic and adaptive views of your situation. In time, you'll come to believe them.

Here's one more step you might add to the basic method:

-Review the challenges frequently. Give them a chance to become as powerful, as well-learned and as automatic as the self-statements that have caused so much trouble!

You might, for example, select the challenges you find most compelling and condense them to very brief statements. Write the statements on a three-by-five card. Then post the card on your mirror so you read it every morning. Carry a copy in your pocket to review during the day — at times when you feel the most need to be reminded of the challenges and any other times you happen to think of it. This extra review can only speed along the process of change. After all, you've been repeating the original, *unhelpful* statements to yourself for years; it's only fair to give your helpful challenges equal time!

Finally, you may find it useful to come up with some global encouraging, positive-coping kinds of statements to periodically review — some "generic" challenges to the chronic feelings of doubt you may have about your ability to handle anxiety. If you followed the recommendations on pages 117-119, you've already generated some specific challenges to the statement, "I can't handle this," that arises at times when you become anxious. But in addition, make up a more general list like the one below, carry it with you and review it frequently, to help make these realizations more prominent in your life:

-*I'm really brave to be venturing out in the world and tackling my anxiety this way.*

-*I really have a lot of backbone to stick with it.*

-*I've learned a lot of ways to cope with anxiety.*

-*I'm seeing some real changes in myself.*

-*I'm getting more self-reliant every day.*

-*I can handle a lot of new situations.*

-*I thought ____ would be tough, but it went just fine.*

-*I'm starting to feel different. Most times I feel OK and sometimes I feel downright daring!*

-*I'm starting to really understand that my anxiety doesn't hurt me and won't hurt me, even though it's unpleasant.*

-*Things are going to get better yet as I keep up the program.*

-*I like feeling braver!*

Working with Images

Sometimes the mental events that bring on or heighten your anxiety aren't really *thoughts* that translate readily into *verbal* self-statements. Rather, what you experience — like Caroline, in Session seven — is a sudden *visual* image that terrifies you, an image that reveals and captures your most basic fear.

Janet sought treatment after a near-fainting episode that soon evolved into several daily episodes of light-headedness. Like Laurie, she responded well to SRB. The controlled breathing, in particular, halted the hyperventilation that was behind the episodes of light-headedness. But she continued to feel mildly uneasy much of the time. It was time for her to begin to address underlying fears and self-statements.

At first, as Janet examined the triggers of her symptoms, she was only aware of anxiety about passing out from the light-headedness. But as she examined the sequence of fears more closely, she realized that whenever she became light-headed, she had a sudden image of herself lying on the ground and people walking right past her, even stepping over her, neither noticing her nor stopping to help. Pressing deeper yet, she realized that she had a profound fear of *dying alone* — a fear that seemed "silly" to her but one that, she reported tearfully, was in fact very real.

Janet wasn't able to reconstruct how she came to develop this fear. (Reconstructing the origins of an image can be very helpful in relieving the fear, since it allows you to see quite clearly the differences between the current situation and the one that led originally to your fear.) But Janet was still able to address the visual image and the associated fear till it eventually lost much of its power over her and the last vestiges of her light-headedness disappeared.

Janet's situation is by no means unique; numerous panic sufferers report that when they experience anxiety, an image of some disastrous event is connected with it. An image is nothing more, really, than a visual version of a self-statement. And certainly one way to work with an image is to translate it into words. In Janet's case, for example, the image could be translated into the statement, "I'm going to die alone." But because the image is most powerful in its visual form, it probably responds best to a "visual challenge."

Janet elected to challenge her image by coming up with a *counter-image* — one involving a significant, new ending to the old, upsetting image. She imagined herself fainting and being stretched out on the ground, a faithful replay of the early part of her usual image. But then she imagined someone coming over to her, speaking gently, loosening her clothing, herself "coming to," and the person helping her up, fully alive and no longer alone.

After a couple of weeks, Janet decided to modify the image again, this time into an even healthier and more active and empowering version. She imagined herself *starting* to feel faint, then pictured herself using SRB, imagined the feelings passing and pictured herself moving on, feeling powerful and calm.

Janet chose to practice her new image nightly, as she lay in bed. She relaxed, pictured herself fainting, then created her counter-image in her mind, making it as clear and detailed as she could. She took care to imagine as vividly as possible not only the visual features of the new image, but the new *feelings* she experienced as well — a deep sense of mastery and calm. Sometimes she varied the small details, but the central features were always the same. In time the old image lost power and eventually came to her less and less frequently.

Janet used the imagery techniques in addition to challenging her self-talk in the more usual manner. In fact, most of her self-talk was verbal and needed to be addressed in a verbal format, but the "image management" gave her one more weapon in her frontal assault on panic.

Review

To summarize, at the time you notice physical sensations or early signs of anxiety, use SRB, just as you've learned and have been doing for some time now. Later, when you're calm, identify the self-statements you made at the time of your anxiety, evaluate them and develop challenges to them based on your more realistic thinking. Write them all down in your notebook. And review your "new thinking" as frequently as possible to strengthen that new and more adaptive voice in your head.

Once you're confident of your abilities to halt a burgeoning attack on command, try to use your new thinking at the time you feel anxiety: "I know this is just some anxiety about the exam tomorrow. I'm not ill, I'm just a little nervous. I'm going to deep-breathe it away." Early on, though, simply use SRB when anxiety hits, and work on your self-talk some time later that day.

Choose a time when you can devote enough time and thought to it to truly receive maximal benefit from the strategy. Because challenging your catastrophic beliefs on a regular basis can be an important technique for ridding yourself of panic *for good.*

The following session will introduce a method for overcoming panic known as "exposure." Although the formal target of exposure is not catastrophic thinking, but rather, panic attacks and avoidance, studies have shown that exposure therapy by itself does lead to a reduction in catastrophic thoughts. So even if you're still struggling a great deal with these, move ahead and take heart!

Exercises for Session Eight
I. Journal Writing
Continue using your journal to record panic episodes and any other pertinent information.

II. Controlled Breathing and SRB
Continue your practice.

III. Challenging Your Catastrophic Self-Talk
A. Each day, identify the self-statements that occurred in conjunction with any anxiety episodes and record them in your notebook, either soon after the episode or that evening.

B. Evaluate the statements by asking the kinds of questions suggested on pages 114-115. Compose challenges to each self-statement based on the evaluation. Write them down in your journal next to the self-statements they address.

C. On days when no anxiety episodes occur, review your earlier work and note factors that may have contributed to your anxiety-free day.

IV. Assessing the Impact of Negative Beliefs
A. Consider the down-grading, pessimistic, negative statements you find yourself making to yourself across situations and list three to five "favorites" — statements you make quite frequently or habitually. Examples might include such statements as:

Nobody cares how I'm feeling.

I can't do anything right.

Don't be so _____ *(silly, stupid, demanding, etc.).People just can't be trusted; they always let me down.*

Awful things happen if I don't watch myself at every step.

B. Read through the list slowly, allowing each statement to really sink in. How did you feel as you read the list and after you'd finished? Sad? Anxious? Incompetent? Guilty?

V. Altering Chronic Negative Beliefs

A. Pick one statement from the list you just completed which you feel is the most destructive and which you'd like to change.

B. Evaluate and challenge the statement as you've learned to do, considering evidence from current and past experience and seeking more realistic and positive statements. Ask yourself where the statement came from in the first place — whose "voice" it is — and consider whether it's a voice, or a message, you want to perpetuate.

C. In the next week, try to "catch" yourself anytime you repeat this particular statement or belief to yourself. Challenge it at those times; and each evening, review your challenges and try to add to them.

VI. Generating Positive Alternatives

A. Some evening when you feel able to devote about thirty minutes to complete a one-time assignment, sit down, relax and bring to mind a successful time or experience in your life. It might be from the week just past or from some time ago. You might choose a time, for example, when you completed a task despite anxieties and then felt especially proud, or a time in your life when, for whatever reason, you felt bold and happy and strong.

After you've recalled the time, spend a few minutes making the memory as vivid as you can, to enjoy it, to really absorb the feelings.

B. Now take out your notebook and generate a list of all the positive, reassuring, confident self-statements you can think of — about yourself and your capabilities, about overcoming your fears.

C. Anytime you're feeling vulnerable or frightened or inadequate, review the list. Take time to remember and recreate the positive feelings you experienced during the exercise. Try to "adopt" the statements as your more constant companions, to strengthen that positive voice inside yourself.

And when you have successes, good days, good feelings, add to the list!

Taking Back Your Life

If you're reading this book because you have panic attacks, your life has almost certainly been restricted in some way by your panic. You may have begun to avoid a whole range of situations. Or you may force yourself to face anxiety-producing circumstances, but make all sorts of adjustments to reduce the chance of attacks.

You may have changed the stores you frequent, from large, impersonal establishments to smaller, less-crowded shops. Perhaps you shop only at less crowded times, or only when your spouse or one of your children can accompany you. You may have shopped for pleasure in the past, whereas now you do so only out of absolute necessity. Or perhaps you've given up shopping altogether.

Your driving may have been affected. Maybe you drive only during daylight hours, only on secondary roads, only in town or only in the outside lane (the better to pull off the road if need be). Perhaps at times, you leave your house only to be forced by your anxiety to turn back, halfway to your destination.

You may find that although you greatly value your independence, you're suddenly reluctant to go places by yourself or even to stay alone in your own home. In an unfamiliar city, the first thing you may do is locate all the emergency rooms in town "just in case."

Whatever the restrictions — whether fairly mild or quite extensive — you probably resent them greatly. And you should, for your freedom has been taken away: your freedom to go where you wish, when you wish, with whom you wish; your freedom to make choices in your life without always having to consider your panic.

This chapter is about taking back your life.

*   *   *

First, let's review briefly how avoidance develops in the first place. Consider a child who was bitten by a large dog in an unexpected, frightening attack. From that point on, the very sight of a dog — even one behind a fence — is likely to raise feelings of anxiety.

In a similar fashion, entering a situation where you've had a panic attack previously is likely to raise feelings of anxiety in you because all sorts of cues in the situation "remind" you of the previous episode; you now connect formerly benign cues — the sights and sounds and smells of the place — with anxiety. And unfortunately, the anxiety you now feel in the situation, because the situation has been linked with attacks in the past, can *increase* the very sensations you're trying so hard to avoid.

You may simply give up on entering the situation again because of your heightened fear. Or you might try to reenter, and when you do so, feel more anxiety because of the previous experience, and conclude that you were right to fear the situation in the first place! All too often, the end result of these sorts of experiences is that the avoidance worsens over time and gradually spreads to more and more situations.

One Step at a Time: The Graduated Exposure Method

Exposure is a systematic method for resuming the activities you've been avoiding by gradually and repeatedly reentering the situations until you feel comfortable with them. In brief, the method involves identifying the situations that elicit anxiety; breaking each one down into a series of manageable steps; then working your way through the steps, one by one, till you achieve comfort in the situation.

The first part of this session will guide you through the process of preparing an exposure hierarchy, which is just a fancy name for a list of activities and situations you fear, broken down into segments or manageable tasks and placed in order from easiest to hardest. The second part of the session will teach you how to use the list (the hierarchy) in a systematic way to gradually reduce your anxiety in those situations and activities.

How Graduated Exposure Works. To best illustrate this process, imagine for a moment that you're terrified of water. If you were to develop an exposure hierarchy to gradually overcome that fear, the first task, or item in your hierarchy, might involve sitting on the beach for five minutes about twenty feet from the water. After completing this task several times in succession — as many times as necessary for you to feel comfortable — you'd move to the next one, perhaps sitting just one foot from the water. The next item might involve dipping your toe into the water; next, wading up to your knees; then, to your waist; and finally, wading in all the way to your neck. At some point, after you could comfortably enter neck-deep water, you might move to splashing water on your face and, ultimately, to putting your head underwater.

The point is, you don't try to overcome a fear of water by leaping off a pier. It's best to approach the situation in a *gradual* fashion — in *small steps* ranging from easiest to most difficult. Each time you tackle a new task, you experience some anxiety at the prospect. (The first time you sat even twenty feet from the water, you were probably nervous.) But with every experience, your anxiety declines.

So what might an exposure hierarchy for a person with panic disorder look like? Let's look at one example.

Ned's Exposure Hierarchy

Ned's panic disorder started when his marriage was in trouble and his mother was dying. Late one afternoon, as he was driving to the hospital to visit her, he suddenly felt as though he were going to pass out. He pulled over to the side of the road and, after a few minutes, was able to proceed, but he felt weak and shaky the rest of the afternoon.

From that point onward, Ned began having more and more difficulty driving. His attacks in the car increased in scope and frequency. He reacted by making more and more modifications in his driving until, eventually, he felt able to drive only at specific times of the day along specific routes. Although he often drove without experiencing an attack, he was always anxious, fearful that one might occur at any time. He ultimately found driving under any conditions almost impossible.

Fortunately, Ned mentioned his difficulties to his doctor who referred Ned for treatment before his panic attacks spread beyond the confines of his car. Resuming normal driving was his primary goal.

Developing his hierarchy. Ned's first task in treatment was to master the controlled breathing and SRB techniques you learned in Sessions five and six. Then he began to tackle some of his catastrophic thoughts (e.g., "I'll pass out and crash the car.") Once he'd accomplished these, he and his therapist set out to develop an *exposure hierarchy.*

Ned realized that his level of discomfort in driving varied depending on a variety of features of the situation. For him, these included:

-whether or not he was alone. (Ned was less anxious when someone else was with him in the car, even though he himself was driving.)

-whether it was day or night. (He was more anxious at night when it was more difficult to see what was ahead.)

-whether traffic was light or heavy. (He was more comfortable in light traffic where he could drive more slowly and keep a greater distance between his car and others'.)

-whether or not he could pull off the road easily. (Ned preferred two-lane roads or, on a four-lane highway, the outermost lane next to the shoulder.)

-whether or not the road was familiar to him. (Familiar routes were more comfortable.)

After he'd considered the different features that influenced his anxiety level while driving, Ned simply varied them to come up with his exposure hierarchy — his own list of driving-related tasks, ordered from easiest to hardest. The first eight items looked something like this:

1. Driving out in the country, in daylight, with a companion (easiest).

2. Driving out in the country, in daylight, alone.

3. Driving in town on a familiar route, not at rush hour, with a companion.

4. Driving in town on a familiar route, not at rush hour, alone.

5. Driving in town on a familiar route, at night, with a companion.

6. Driving in town on a familiar route, at night, alone.

7. Driving in town on a four-lane highway, not at rush hour, during daylight, with a companion, and staying in the outside lane.

8. Driving in town on a four-lane highway, not at rush hour during daylight, alone, and staying in the outside lane (most difficult of the first eight items).

In final form, Ned's items actually described specific, concrete tasks. Item #1, for example, was the following: "Take a drive on Midtown Road at 2:00 in the afternoon with my buddy Jerry." The more general descriptions (1-8) are provided here since they highlight the way in which Ned varied the different features to achieve gradually increasing difficulty levels.

Using his hierarchy. How did Ned then *use* his hierarchy to overcome his anxiety about driving? He set a start date for himself and when that date arrived, he completed item #1, a drive on Milltown Road at 2:00 in the afternoon with his buddy Jerry. He was quite anxious before and during the early part of his drive, but decreased his anxiety somewhat using SRB. And he stayed with the item — driving along on Milltown Road — till his anxiety had declined and he felt fairly comfortable, then ended the exposure session for that day. After he returned home, he recorded the experience in his journal, rating his anxiety level during the session. The next day, Ned repeated the same task, and he continued to do so every day till he could accomplish it with little or no anxiety. He then moved to item #2 and followed the same procedure. Ned continued with his exposure practice sessions till he'd completed all the items in his hierarchy — in other words, till he found himself able to drive in all circumstances without undue anxiety, just as he had before the onset of his panic attacks.

Before you leave Ned's hierarchy and move to your own, there's one thing you should note: Ned's hierarchy began at the point that was appropriate for *him*, but his initial item is one that would be much too difficult for many panic sufferers. For example, if you hadn't driven for years because of a panic disorder, you might have selected, as *your* first task, simply sitting behind the wheel of your car as it's parked in the driveway. You might then have moved to starting the car and just sitting in it with the motor running. Next, you might have driven around the block with a companion, and so on.

In other words, the first item in your hierarchy should be a task that's slightly anxiety-provoking, but not so frightening that you feel you can't accomplish it; you don't want to set yourself up for a failure. And it never hurts to start with an item that's too easy; you'll simply move to the next item that much more rapidly.

Developing Your Own Exposure Hierarchy

Identifying Situations. A good hierarchy forms the "backbone" of your exposure program, so this session will go through instructions for developing yours in some detail. The first step is to make a list of all the situations and circumstances you avoid or find uncomfortable. Ned's hierarchy focused on only one situation — driving — but that's unusual; more often, those with panic struggle with anxiety in a whole host of situations. These might include particular places (the supermarket, elevators); specific circumstances (being rushed, alone, or forced into a large social gathering); or specific activities (exercising or standing in a steamy shower).

First, simply make a list "off the top of your head." Then check the list against your log of panic episodes (Session four exercises) to be sure you haven't overlooked any circumstances that make you anxious. Also check the log for episodes of anticipatory anxiety, to identify situations you dread a great deal, and add those to the list.

If there are no situations you consistently avoid or dread, you don't need to complete the exercises in this session. But be sure to read the chapter carefully, since the information you learn will be important for the next session, where you'll learn a different sort of exposure technique, one that's important for anyone experiencing panic attacks.

Developing Items. You now have a list of situations you avoid or fear. Now, *for each situation,* list several items, or tasks, to represent it. Your goal is to create a group of items that vary in difficulty level from easiest to hardest. You do this by:

1) selecting an initial item — a task you can accomplish, but that raises your anxiety somewhat;

2) considering what features influence your anxiety level in the situation; and

3) varying those features to generate additional tasks, each one slightly more anxiety-producing than the one just before it.

Mary Ann, an attractive, thirty-four-year-old homemaker, had difficulties with grocery shopping, accompanying her husband to his various business functions and attending her children's school activities. She decided to develop an exposure hierarchy for grocery shopping first. Her first (easiest) item was that of going into a fairly empty grocery store with her husband to walk through the aisles without buying anything, staying until she felt comfortable. Then, she gradually "added" anxiety in several ways to create additional items:

a) She increased the number and difficulty of tasks to complete while in the store. (First, she selected groceries but sent her husband through the check-out; next, she went through the check-out with him with just a small number of items; finally, she went through the check-out on her own.)

b) She changed the times that she went to the stores.

c) She began to go to the store by herself.

d) Eventually, she went to *different* grocery stores.

Mary Ann ended up with a total of twenty-three items in her entire grocery shopping hierarchy.

You may be wondering just how many items to include in your hierarchy. It depends; some situations require several, while others may require only a couple. *Start with a task you feel you can accomplish* and create just as many additional items as you need to fully represent the levels of anxiety you feel in all possible "versions" of the situation.

At this point, try to develop a set of items that involve only *small increases in difficulty level from one item to the next*. This will help to prevent "glitches" in your progress which could slow you down and shake your confidence.

Finally, build into each item *sufficient time for anxiety to be felt and to diminish before you leave the situation*. An ideal way to achieve this goal is to include anxiety reduction as a part of the item, for example, "I'll walk into the store, stand near the magazine aisle and leaf through a magazine till I realize my anxiety has diminished." Or you might designate a specific amount of time sufficient for anxiety to subside (e.g., fifteen minutes), based on previous experience. Usually, longer exposures are more effective than shorter ones.

Don't fret too much at this stage about creating the perfect hierarchy. You'll probably make changes and find ways to improve on it as you go along.

If, like Ned, you have only one feared situation to tackle, your hierarchy is now complete and ready to put to use. If your circumstances are more typical, though, you'll have identified several different situations and created a list of items for each of them. In this case, you have one final decision to make before you can begin using your hierarchy: You need to decide whether you'll tackle your different feared situations one at a time or combined into one single hierarchy.

Assembling Your Hierarchies. Remember Carol, from chapter one? Carol, you'll recall, feared eating out, going to the movies, entering stores, and sitting through church services. After she had created a separate list of tasks for each of these situations, she combined them all into one "mega-hierarchy," simply by putting them all together into one list and placing the combined set of items in order from easiest to hardest, based on the degree of anxiety she expected to experience with each one.

Here's a portion of Carol's completed hierarchy:

6. Go to a movie with my husband and sit on the aisle.

7. Go to church with my family on an "ordinary Sunday" (not Easter or Mother's Day) and sit toward the back.

8. Go shopping with my sister on a weekday evening.

9. Go to the mall by myself at midday during the week.

10. Go to church with my family on an ordinary Sunday and sit near the front, not on the aisle.

11. Go to a restaurant with my husband on a weekday evening and sit near the exit.

12. Go to a restaurant for lunch with a close friend and sit near the exit.

You might think this list seems "mixed up" since it includes items from several different feared situations, but there is a type of order to it, an order *based on the difficulty level, for Carol, of each of the items.* And that's precisely the kind of order every hierarchy requires.

Carol might have chosen a different strategy: Instead of combining all her separate hierarchies (lists) into one, she might have chosen to tackle all her "restaurant" items first, followed by all her "church" items, then all the "shopping" items and so on till she'd completed all the items on all the lists in succession. She could have started, in this case, with whichever group of items she chose — possibly, the group that were the least difficult for her overall, or perhaps those that caused the most disruption in her life.

The choice of how to arrange your hierarchy is up to you. There are no rigid rules. Remember, *this is your program.* You're the one in charge.

And now, on to the exciting part: using your hierarchy to overcome your anxieties.

Using Your Exposure Hierarchy to Eliminate Anxiety

Now, how do you use your hierarchy?

1. You *choose the first item* on the list as your starting point — for example, going into a small grocery store with your husband to purchase three items at 8:00 in the morning.

2. You *select the day you'll begin* the program. You commit to that day and when the day comes, you stick to the plan.

You're likely to feel some anxiety when the time arrives, but by following the program, your anxiety will diminish reliably, often quite rapidly. And since that's your goal — the whole point of undertaking the program, in fact — you muster your courage and do it.

3. When the day arrives, you *complete the assigned task* described by the item. You head out with your husband at 8:00 in the morning, enter the store, select and purchase three items, and leave.

4. While in the store, it's important that you stay there till your anxiety and the urge to escape have diminished and you've completed the assignment.

If you stay in the situation and allow your anxiety or panic to subside (it *will* subside), *over successive experiences, your anxiety in that situation will disappear, simply because of your repeated exposures.* This process, called *habituation,* is extremely predictable and has been demonstrated repeatedly and powerfully in research studies and in clinical situations. You'll demonstrate it yourself as you proceed through your own hierarchy. *Guaranteed.*

You might think about habituation as simply the process of getting used to a situation by encountering it over and over again — a situation that's distressing but not dangerous. A commonplace analogy might be that of a first-time father who picks up his newborn daughter for the first time and feels genuinely terrified that he'll drop her or that she'll "break." After he's picked her up several times though, his anxieties have disappeared and he feels comfortable with the experience. He's *habituated* to the situation.

5. While in the situation, you may do what you can to remain as comfortable as possible. That means, first and foremost, you use SRB to diminish any anxiety you feel. **S**top "what-iffing," **R**efocus on the present, and control your **B**reathing.

If you need to use SRB several times during a single exposure, that's fine. If you need a hug from your companion to help you through the exercise, or a reminder of the value of what you're doing (e.g., saying to yourself, "I can do it!"), that's fine too. Do what you need to, but *stay in the situation.*

Despite any strategies you may use to diminish your anxiety, you will feel *some*, of course, and that's actually a good thing. Why? Because you *need* to experience some level of anxiety in a feared situation for the process of habituation, described above, to occur. But the SRB can give you the courage to enter the situation in the first place, and can help you to stick it out during the roughest times, and eventually, that remaining anxiety *will* disappear, simply from your repeated exposures.

As it does so, your use of anxiety-reduction strategies will gradually disappear as well, simply because you no longer need them!

It *is* important that you fully *experience* the situation during the exposure, that you pay attention to the situation itself rather than trying to distract yourself from it — for example, by pretending that you're really lying on a beach in the Caribbean. This allows you to break the connection between the worrisome aspects of the situation and your anxiety. Fortunately, the SRB method, with its emphasis on refocusing on the present, builds this in automatically.

6. Once you've completed the item and you've left the situation, you *record your peak anxiety level during the exercise.* Recording is important. The records you keep will help to guide you through the program, indicating when you're ready to move to the next item in the hierarchy. And your records will offer important proof to you that the program is working.

A handy format for recording your progress is illustrated below. (And a copy is provided for you in Appendix VI). Along the left-hand side is a scale to indicate how much anxiety you felt in the situation at its worst. Along the bottom are the days of practice. The records you see in this example are Ned's exposures to the first item in his hierarchy: an afternoon drive out in the country with a friend.

	Mon	Tue	Wed	Thu	Fri	Sat	Sun	Mon
10								
9								
8	x							
7	x		x					
6	x	x	x					
5	x	x	x					
4	x	x	x					
3	x	x	x	x	x	x		
2	x	x	x	x	x	x	x	x
1	x	x	x	x	x	x	x	x

Ned completed his first practice on a Monday. After he got home, he rated his highest anxiety level during the drive at 8 by writing 8 x's above Monday. Each day thereafter, he completed his practice, then rated his anxiety in the same fashion.

You'll notice a couple of things about Ned's record. First, and most important, *his anxiety did drop,* from 8 to 2 over eight days of practice. This overall decrease in anxiety over successive practices is very predictable.

You'll also notice that the decrease in anxiety didn't occur in a completely regular fashion. The overall trend is downward, but it happens somewhat unevenly; some days simply go more smoothly than others. This, too, is predictable.

What isn't predictable is the number of exposures required for anxiety to drop in an individual situation. This number will vary for different people, and for different items. Ned, for example, continued his "drive out in the country with a friend" item for twelve days before he felt totally comfortable. But his next item, which involved driving out in the country alone, required only four days before he felt anxiety-free and prepared to move to the next item.

7. You *repeat the exercise daily* (or as close to daily as possible).

8. You *stay with the item till you feel no significant anxiety with it.* Then you proceed to the next item on the list and follow the same steps until that item, too, is comfortable for you.

Choosing when to move on to the next item is up to you. Many people stay with an item till they've experienced four or five practices in which they felt no significant anxiety. Others feel prepared to move ahead once they've conducted two successive exposures to an item and felt minimal anxiety.

A good rule of thumb is to stay with one item until your level of comfort approaches the level you feel in day-to-day life. You may not feel one hundred percent anxiety-free, but you're sufficiently at ease to enter the situation without holding back. For some people, this means a rating of 2, while others want to achieve a rating of 1 or 0 before they move forward.

9. You then move to the next item in your hierarchy and follow steps 1 through 8 as before. And you *continue the process till you've reached an end-point that satisfies you.*

Once you've achieved comfort with standard versions of your feared situations, it's important to challenge any superstitions you hold about your ability to enter and remain in a situation. For example, suppose you feel you can go to the supermarket successfully only if you carry your lucky rabbit's foot with you. Next time you go to the market, leave it home. Or perhaps you feel comfortable being alone in your home only if you have the TV on full-blast. Add a few exposure practices in which you gradually lower the volume and eventually turn the TV off altogether. Practice entering situations without using SRB, simply to reassure and remind yourself that your anxiety truly *has* decreased simply as a result of the repeated exposures to the situation. Use exposure techniques to develop a feeling of comfort in the setting *without* the need for lucky talismans, rituals or special conditions. It's the only way to reduce your vulnerability to anxiety and regain true freedom from your fears.

To help you remember them easily, the steps to follow in conducting exposure can be reduced to four:

1. Enter the selected situation and perform the task as the item instructs you to do.

2. While in the situation, you may use SRB and other strategies to help you remain more comfortable, but stay "in contact" with the situation and *don't leave till your anxiety has diminished.*

3. Afterwards, record your anxiety level.

4. Repeat daily.

Encouragement About Your Exposure Program
At this point, you may be looking over your hierarchy (whether it represents one situation or many) wondering just how long it will take you to master the entire list. Once you start conducting exposures, you'll likely be surprised at how rapidly you move through the items.

You might spend only one or two practice sessions on an item and realize that, having mastered previous items, your comfort level has "spread" to the current one; your anxiety is already quite minimal on the very first exposure. You may even skip an item or two. The hierarchy is only a guide. You might follow it exactly as it's written, but you won't be unusual if you choose to modify it as you go along.

It's also helpful to remember that if you do nothing more than *enter* your selected situations as planned, and *stay* despite the anxiety you feel initially, you'll experience the predicted drop in anxiety over time, and eventually be able to enter the situations without undue anxiety. A strategy like SRB is likely to ease and speed the process for you (and may give you the extra reassurance you need to enter a situation in the first place), but in a sense, exposure works automatically: *As long as you repeatedly enter the situations on your list, exposing yourself to the sensations and cues that occur in those situations, including, inevitably, the sensations of anxiety that occur, your anxiety will "extinguish" or disappear.*

In addition to the "automatic" element, there's an important cognitive component to exposure. When you conduct your exposure practices, you *observe* yourself entering the various situations and you experience yourself, over successive practices, as a calm, competent person rather than a helpless, frightened victim. Each experience diminishes your "old" view of yourself and increases your confidence in your new, calmer self. And, as you know, once your *expectation* and *fear* of panic attacks decreases, you're far less likely to experience them, since the fear of panic erupting is one of the triggers that can lead you into a full-fledged attack.

In fact, exposure therapy is a well-established method clearly proven to reduce and eliminate panic attacks, agoraphobia and the catastrophic thinking associated with both. (Different variations of exposure therapy, in fact, are used to treat some of the other anxiety disorders.) All panic sufferers, but *particularly those with more severe levels of avoidance*, should devote the time needed to thoroughly eliminate the avoidance *and the discomfort* that prevents them from living the lives they want to live.

You've now learned the elements necessary to begin your own exposure program to take back your life. The exercises that follow this session will instruct you to do just that. First, though, some final "how-to's"—how to use imagery in exposure, how to overcome anticipatory anxiety, and how to use the method of exposure to its fullest advantage.

Using Imagery for Tricky Situations and Better Results

Sometimes certain situations cause anxiety and you'd like to tackle them with exposure, but there doesn't seem to be any way to do so following the usual procedures. Perhaps the situations happen so seldom, it's difficult to plan a sequence of exposures frequent enough to be effective. Or maybe they simply don't lend themselves to the gradual variation in difficulty needed for the exposure method.

That was the problem David encountered. David was required to attend weekly planning meetings on his job at a large engineering firm. He hadn't *avoided* the meetings — he couldn't, and still keep his job! But he was chronically anxious and fearful of having a panic attack during a meeting.

David had used exposure methods successfully to decrease his anxiety in various social settings, but he didn't see how he could use similar methods in these weekly meetings. For one thing, he couldn't create "easier" items by modifying different dimensions of the situation: He couldn't ask half the people not to attend the meeting, or take a companion along with him, or attend the meetings only as an observer. And the meetings were held *weekly*; he didn't see how he could manage *daily* exposures.

Fortunately, there's a solution to this dilemma: When you can't create (or alter) a situation "in real life," *create it in imagination.* In fact, *systematic desensitization,* a method that pairs the deliberate imagining of a feared situation with relaxation, was for many years a primary method for helping people conquer their fears. Later it was discovered that people could overcome their fears more rapidly using exposure to the actual situation (called in vivo exposure), but exposure in imagination remains an effective technique and is particularly useful in circumstances where "real-life" exposure is impractical or impossible.

David's Strategy

David created a *hierarchy* of meeting-related items just as he would have for any exposure program, but instead of planning to enter them in reality, he planned to enter them in imagination. He altered the difficulty level of successive items by adding or modifying various features of his (imagined) scenarios.

David's first item involved imagining himself in the very easiest situation he could think of — a meeting of only a few co-workers that did not include his boss. Successive items involved picturing himself in increasingly larger and larger meetings, imagining people focusing on him, imagining co-workers arguing with him, and imagining himself beginning to panic in the midst of a meeting.

David conducted daily exposures following the same procedure each time: He used controlled breathing to relax himself, then he imagined himself in a meeting according to the details of his item, using all his senses to create as vivid a scene as possible.

It was important that David include features in the scene that involved *his own responses* as well as external elements. As he imagined himself in a meeting, for example, he included details about the conference room, the people present, the speakers, and the discussion; and *he also imagined himself experiencing certain sensations, having certain thoughts and behaving in certain ways* that were typical of his anxiety responses (noticing his heart start to pound, feeling his face heat up, thinking he was about to have an attack, seeing the horrified reactions of his co-workers, and looking around the room fidgeting).

Once he felt somewhat anxious, David stopped his catastrophic thinking, used controlled breathing to reduce his anxiety and *imagined himself coping with his anxiety* — responding calmly to a question, smiling in a relaxed fashion at others, leaning back in his chair feeling confident — however he'd *like* to be able to respond in the particular situation.

David conducted exposures daily, and he stayed with a practice session till the scene ended and his anxiety had diminished. Once he'd experienced three exposures of a particular item with little or no anxiety, he moved up the hierarchy to the next item.

In other words, David followed the same basic exposure guidelines you've learned, with minor modifications: His exposures were to imagined, rather than to "real-life" items. Instead of anxiety arising spontaneously in response to a real situation, he imagined himself becoming anxious — really letting himself feel it, in fact, before starting his panic-control strategies. And for panic control, he used a variant of SRB: He stopped catastrophizing; refocused on the present through the strategy of picturing his coping responses; and used controlled breathing to reduce his physical reactions.

Incidentally, this imaginal technique can be used for any situation *in conjunction* with your real life exposures, as a means to speed your progress and increase your comfort with feared situations even more: Periodically, choose a quiet time and simply conduct an imaginal practice session or two *in addition* to your planned exposures to the actual situation.

"Inventing" Situations for Extra Power Practice

David eventually worked his way through all his imaginal items, but he still felt the need to reduce his anxiety in "live" meetings even more. The strategy he and his therapist eventually developed for this was to invent items in which he tried to replicate different elements of his feared situation.

For one item, he used a tape recorder and pretended he was giving a brief presentation, something that occasionally happened in "live" meetings. When he became anxious, he simply used SRB as he would have in a real meeting. Because certain people at the weekly meetings intimidated David a bit, another item in his program involved deliberately going to the office of one of these co-workers to ask a question or make a comment. He continued this practice daily with different "target" individuals until *that* task, too, was much more comfortable for him.

Eventually, David felt he'd done all he could to expose himself to *imagined versions* of his ultimate feared situation and to the *real-life elements* of it — and by that time, he'd experienced a significant drop in anxiety in the real-life situation itself.

Overcoming Anticipatory Anxiety

You've been told that exposing yourself gradually and repeatedly to anxiety-producing situations will cause the anxiety you feel in the situations to drop reliably over time. But as you learned in the last session, the anxiety you feel before you enter the situation — the *anticipatory anxiety* — often takes much longer to disappear. You may be entering a given situation repeatedly without experiencing anxiety *once you're in the situation,* but the prospect of entering it still fills you with dread.

Remember that this is quite normal. It simply takes time to develop faith in yourself and in the program you're following — faith that you can enter a situation without difficulty; faith that the disappearance of anxiety is real and lasting; even faith that, should anxiety arise on occasion, you can handle it.

When you find anxiety arising at the prospect of entering an upcoming situation, remember to use the methods you learned in Session eight to cope with it: Identify any catastrophic self-statements about the situation; explore the realism and accuracy of those statements; and try to generate challenges to them, similar to the ones suggested on pages 116-119. And you can now add two more challenges to the list:

"Yes, the situation is difficult, but every time I enter it serves as one more 'exposure,' which helps me get over my anxiety that much quicker!"

"I've managed this situation X times now, and I'm still going strong!"

The most important thing is not to let yourself fall into a pattern of avoidance again. Ultimately, the *single best cure* for anticipatory anxiety is to *continue entering the situation* until even the anxiety at the *prospect* of doing so disappears.

Joan's Experience

Joan developed panic in her late thirties when, all in the same month, her teenage daughter began to rebel against the house rules; her father developed a chronic illness; and Joan learned, completely out of the blue, that she'd been adopted as an infant. She got her panic under control quite rapidly using a combination of behavioral methods to eliminate symptoms (controlled breathing, SRB and exposure) and psychotherapy to address some of her feelings of grief and dismay. At a follow-up meeting about a year after her last panic attack, she described her experiences with anxiety this way:

"First, I had to actually force myself to go into a restaurant, and I was miserable the whole time. Soon, I got to the point where I wasn't nervous once I got inside, but I didn't exactly enjoy myself; I was just there. Eventually, I actually started to have fun in restaurants once I got through the door. That's when I defined myself as being over my panic disorder. But then, about six months later, I realized that, for the very first time, I'd go into a restaurant and *it wouldn't even cross my mind* that I might experience panic. That's when I knew my panic was *truly* behind me."

Joan's experience reflects a characteristic pattern of recovery from panic: at first, the experience of marked anxiety in a situation; next, the absence of anxiety but not much enjoyment either; next, the enjoyment of a situation, but still some uneasiness in approaching it; and, finally, *not having the notion of panic even cross your mind.*

You will probably be delighted when you reach even the second stage, but, as Joan can attest, it gets even better. The more experiences you "log" entering a situation without anxiety, the more the anxiety will recede into your past, until finally you experience true and unmitigated enjoyment — you've gotten your "old self" back.

If you've experienced a much longer course of panic than Joan, entering a situation without even thinking of panic may take longer for you to achieve. But simply being able to enjoy yourself while in the settings will be a tremendous gift, a gift you've given yourself.

Troubleshooting

If you encounter difficulties of any sort implementing your exposure program, Appendix III, a "trouble-shooting" appendix for exposure, can help. It offers strategies for solving all sorts of dilemmas, from how to tackle an unexpectedly difficult item to how to reverse disappointing results. And whether or not you're having difficulty with exposure, the information discussed in the appendix will be of help to you in maximizing your own results using the method.

A Few Final Points on Using Exposure Successfully

Many panic sufferers find that by the time they reach this session, they've virtually eliminated avoidance already; with newfound skills and confidence, they've simply returned informally to previously-avoided situations on their own. Or, when they began formal exposures, the process went so well that they sailed through the items and soon found — often to their own amazement — that they could enter almost every situation without problems.

Even if you tend to dismiss exposure because you no longer have significant trouble in specific circumstances, it's still useful to "hit" all the situations you *previously* avoided, simply to get a few anxiety-free experiences of that situation "under your belt." These experiences boost your confidence even more and help you build a reserve of experiences to draw on when you occasionally feel more vulnerable. And if you do hit vulnerable times, your successes with exposure will help to prevent any tendency to resume avoidance.

Similarly, if you get anxious in a situation but don't outright avoid, use exposure formally *just as though the situation were one you avoided routinely*. It will help extinguish your anxiety in the situation so that the question of avoidance doesn't even arise.

The best strategy with exposure, as with any other anxiety-reduction method, is to *overlearn*, to go farther than necessary, to push the envelope" as the saying goes. If you used to have trouble with ordinary shopping trips, don't stop after you achieve the ability to resume normal, day-to-day shopping. Take your exposure practices a few steps further; shop in bigger malls, unfamiliar locations, busier "super-sale" times. You'll feel a much greater and more enduring level of comfort — a result well worth the extra effort.

The next session will teach you a different sort of exposure — one that follows the same basic principles of this one. Before you continue reading, though, don't neglect the exercises that follow. They'll help you to solidify your understanding of exposure principles and use the procedures to take back your life.

Exercises for Session Nine
I. Controlled Breathing and SRB

Continue your practice. You may have noticed that when you practice SRB at home, coming up with some imagined scene or memory or thought to create anxiety and then using SRB to eliminate it, you're not only solidifying your skill in the panic-control technique, you're also conducting a "mini-exposure." You're repeatedly exposing yourself to cues of anxiety and then *experiencing a reduction in anxiety in the presence of those cues*. This added element has probably contributed to significant reductions in anxiety by now. So keep it up!

II. Daily Recording

Continue to write in your journal daily, recording your practice experiences, logging any episodes of panic, near-panic or averted panic, and noting other observations regarding your anxiety.

III. Ongoing Challenges to Your Self-Talk

Continue nightly to evaluate and challenge your self-talk — challenging self-talk related to any instances of anxiety during the day and, if none occurred, reviewing earlier challenges to common catastrophic beliefs.

Also try to use the method for tackling any other negative, self-destructive beliefs as described in Session eight and recommended in the exercises that followed the session.

IV. Developing Your Exposure Hierarchies

A. Make a list of the situations (including activities) that you avoid or modify because of your anxiety. For suggestions, see page 134.

B. For each situation, develop a list of items, ordered from easiest to hardest, according to the guidelines on pages 134-135. Use a separate sheet of paper for each list (hierarchy).

C. Decide whether you'll conduct exposures for one situation, beginning to end, then move to the next situation; or whether you'll combine items for all your situations into one large "mega-hierarchy" as described on pages 136-137.

If you choose to use the "separate hierarchies" approach, arrange the separate hierarchies in the order in which you want to tackle them (simply put the different pages in that order).

If you choose to follow the "combined hierarchy" approach, combine all the items from all the hierarchies in order from easiest to hardest. This process will involve rewriting one long list that will contain the items from all the separate pages.

V. Conducting Exposures Using Your First Hierarchy

A. Select a start date to begin exposure, and from that date forward, every day, conduct one exposure practice.

B. Conduct your practices following the detailed procedures described on pages 137-140.

a. Enter the situation as described by the item.

b. Use SRB and other strategies to remain as comfortable as you need to, in order to remain in the situation.

c. Stay in the situation till your anxiety diminishes.

d. End the practice and record your anxiety level.

C. When you judge that you're truly finished with one item (see page 140), move up to the next.

D. Continue planning and conducting at least one exposure every day, or as close to every day as possible.

It's best to stay with this session's exercises exclusively for two or three weeks before moving on, as exposure is truly the core technique for overcoming panic attacks and agoraphobia.

Session Ten

Internal Affairs

By this point in your program to overcome panic, you've mastered an impressive list of tasks and techniques and have very likely seen a marked reduction in panic episodes as a result:

-You've learned how to use controlled breathing to decrease the physical sensations that arise with anxiety and to keep the body at a comfortable level of arousal.

-You've learned how to use SRB — the Stop-Refocus-Breathe method — to interrupt the panic cycle whenever you need to — not to eliminate normal bodily sensation, but to prevent it from prompting the catastrophic thinking that, through spiraling, can culminate in panic.

-You've been working over the past several weeks to understand how your panic arose in the first place and, in Session eight, to revise the kind of thinking that can keep panic alive — in particular, the notion that physical sensations are danger signs, signals that something's wrong with your body.

-And you began, through the exercises presented in the latest session, to gradually and repeatedly enter situations that previously caused you discomfort and avoidance, experiencing a successive drop in anxiety as you did so.

The focus of the exposure exercises of Session nine was on external situations — places and activities. But the impact of the exercises occurred on two fronts: You became more comfortable with the external situations, *and you became more comfortable with the physical sensations that arose in the situations* (sensations such as an increased heart rate). In exposing yourself *explicitly* to the situations, you exposed yourself *implicitly* to the associated physical sensations — and as you know from your own experiences in Session nine, successive exposures lead to a reduction in anxiety.

"Internal" Exposure

This session extends the exposure method to internal sensations. In this session, you'll learn how to develop hierarchies of items reflecting the physical sensations that cause you needless anxiety. And the exposure method you've learned for *external* cues for anxiety can function in the same fashion for *internal cues: Expose yourself repeatedly to a specific situation or a specific sensation and your anxiety to that situation or sensation will drop over time.*

Research has shown that the method of direct exposure to internal sensations, formalized originally by psychologist David Barlow and his colleagues, is very effective in helping people to overcome panic attacks. But wait a minute. If exposing yourself to *external* situations as you did in the previous session exposes you *implicitly* to *internal* sensations, thereby increasing your comfort with them, haven't you already achieved this? And is the internal method any better than the external for doing so? A lot of other people have wondered the same thing.

Which is Better? External Exposure, "Internal" Exposure, or Both?

Until 2001, whether the external exposure methods described in the previous session or internal exposure strategies (also called interoceptive conditioning) worked better for eliminating panic attacks and avoidance was a matter of conjecture. Well-controlled studies of cognitive behavioral therapy using external exposure as part of their treatment for panic yielded about the same success rates as those using interoceptive conditioning. Therapists' recommendations were therefore based on personal preference or, perhaps, intuition about which method might work best for a given client.

In 2001, however, the first controlled study was published which directly compared the effectiveness of external versus internal exposure methods for eliminating panic and avoidance. The study also looked at the benefits of using both methods together, evaluating outcomes at the end of treatment and after one year's time. The study found, essentially, that the two methods worked equally well. And to many people's surprise, they found no real advantage to using both methods together over either one alone.

If you feel you've already achieved the results you want in overcoming avoidance and panic attacks and increasing your comfort level across a range of situations, you may choose to simply scan this chapter for your own information, holding it in reserve should you ever wish to use the techniques it describes. If you still have farther to go to achieve your goals, however, you have two options: You may choose to continue working solely with the methods you learned in the prior session, practicing till you achieve, then maintain your goals; or you may elect to learn the methods outlined in this chapter, practicing till you do reach your goals.

Do remember, in either case, the purpose of the method is *not* to rid you of *normal* physical sensation or the variations in sensation that occur in your body from day to day. Like many of the other techniques you've encountered, the aim is to rid you of the fear and *discomfort* with normal sensation — to increase your tolerance to normal sensation and in doing so, to help eliminate the anxiety and catastrophic thinking that can then lead to *excess* physical symptoms and initiate the spiral into panic.

In fact, to truly eliminate panic from your life permanently, it's absolutely necessary to become comfortable with physical sensation, to realize that physical sensation (a) isn't dangerous in and of itself, (b) doesn't signal tragic outcomes, and (c) needn't worsen anxiety and anxiety symptoms.

The Method of Exposure Revisited

Let's review the essentials of the method of exposure presented in Session nine, since the method of this session is simply a variation on it. In Session nine, you selected a situation that caused you anxiety — sitting in a movie theater, for example — and developed a set of items to represent the situation, ranking them from easiest to most difficult. You then "exposed" yourself to the initial item, using SRB to manage any anxiety that arose. Once you'd completed the task specified by the item and experienced a drop in anxiety, you left the situation, recording your level of anxiety during the exposure. Over successive exposures to the same situation, you observed a consistent reduction in anxiety level, and after several exposures that elicited little or no anxiety, you moved on to the next item.

This session's work follows the same basic sequence. First, you'll select a physical sensation that increases your anxiety level, and you'll develop items to represent it, ordering them from easiest to hardest. However, the items will involve not going into a feared *situation,* but rather, producing and experiencing a feared *sensation.*

Starting with the first item, you'll expose yourself to the sensation just as you might expose yourself to sitting in a movie theater, and you'll use SRB to manage any anxiety that arises. After your anxiety has subsided, you'll end the practice ("leave the situation," as it were), recording your overall level of anxiety during the exposure. And you'll repeat the practice till you've experienced the designated sensation on several successive occasions with only minimal anxiety.

Exposure Method for Internal Sensations
Let's go over the steps one at a time, looking at each in detail.

The first step: Generating a list of feared sensations
Make a list of all the physical sensations that you find alarming. Include those that clearly produce anxiety in you (e.g., "Feelings in my chest make me worry about heart attacks") and any others that seem to be triggers for panic or early signs of impending attacks (e.g., "Tingling in my hands doesn't worry me, but it always happens when a panic attack is coming on").

Include, too, any sensations that constitute features of your panic attacks (e.g., "I always feel a sense of unreality in the middle of a full-blown attack"). You may not have experienced an attack in some weeks, but you'll recall quite clearly the sensations that were a part of them!

In other words, include in your hierarchy any physical sensations that may play a role in your panic cycle. Then order these sensations according to how much anxiety they typically produce in you.

The second step: Developing a hierarchy of items for each sensation

Now take each sensation in turn and create five items to represent it. This involves two elements: first, how to produce the basic sensation and, second, how to vary level of difficulty to create a hierarchy of items.

Producing the sensation. What methods can you use to produce the sensation you need? Imagine that an increased heart rate is one sensation on your list, as it's likely to be for virtually every panic sufferer. One way to produce increased heart rate is simply to jog in place for a designated amount of time — two minutes, perhaps. If feeling overheated is a trigger for panic, putting on a winter coat over a sweater and sitting in the warmest room in your house should produce the sensation fairly readily. If you need to create feelings of dizziness, sitting in a rotating office chair and spinning the chair around several times, or standing and twirling the way children sometimes do for pleasure should produce the desired sensation. (Do the standing-and-twirling near a couch or bed so that if you should lose your balance, you have a soft place to land!) If feeling "off balance" is a problem for you, standing with your feet close together and closing your eyes may duplicate the off-balance feeling, and so on.

Table A lists a variety of sensations and various methods for producing them. Chances are, you can come up with other methods for the different sensations and for any sensations that don't appear on the list. (Before you begin, please read the "Additional Notes," near the end of this session.)

Varying item difficulty level. Now that you know how to produce a specific sensation, how do you create a hierarchy of items for that sensation? In Session nine, you produced a completely individualized set of items, or hierarchy, by varying the different dimensions of the experience that were related meaningfully to your own anxiety. In this session, the process is a bit simpler. The same basic format can be used for creating a hierarchy for each different sensation, at least as a starting point.

For your *first* item in the hierarchy, use *imagery* to produce the sensation. Sit down, close your eyes, relax and imagine the sensation in question. Make it as real as possible. Then, once you're aware of mounting anxiety associated with the sensation, use SRB to reduce it.

For your *second* item, use the appropriate *physical strategy* to create the desired sensation and conduct your practice in the

Table A
Possible Methods for Production of
Physical Sensations*

*Increased heart rate***	Jog in place for 2 or 3 minutes, longer if necessary to elevate your heart rate.
	Step rapidly up and down on a stair tread or foot stool for 2 or 3 minutes.
	Do 25 vigorous jumping jacks.
Shortness of breath	Same as above.
Dizziness, light-headedness, wooziness, "disorientation"	Shake your head from from side to side for 30 seconds.
	Place your head between your legs for 30 seconds, then lift it quickly to an upright position.
	Spin in a rotating chair for one minute or till sensations of dizziness are produced.
	Twirl quickly while standing, placing yourself near a bed or couch so that you can sit down once sensations are achieved.
	Hyperventilate: While seated, breathe as rapidly and deeply as possible, 25-30 breaths per minute, taking large, gasping breaths and vigorously forcing the air out. Continue up to three minutes. *This method should not be used by pregnant women or those with known medical problems.*
Choking and smothering	Press along the sides of your throat while breathing normally for one minute or till sensations are achieved.

	Fold up a cloth handkerchief, place it on your tongue as far back as necessary to produce desired sensation, and close your mouth. Breathe for one minute.
Difficulty breathing, feelings of suffocation	Pinch your nostrils closed with one hand and breathe through a straw for one minute or till desired sensations result.
Shakiness and trembling	Tense every part of your body and try to maintain the tension for one minute before releasing.
Chest pain	Tighten your muscles, curl your shoulders forward as much as possible and try to breathe as deeply as possible for up to a minute.
Pains in the head	Hyperventilate for one minute or till the sensation is produced (see above instructions and cautions for hyperventilation).
Overheated sensation	While dressed in regular clothing add a sweater and winter coat, then sit in the warmest room in your house till the sensation is produced.
Feelings of unreality	This method requires the help of a companion. Ask a companion to talk to you nonstop and stare at his or her mouth for one or two minutes, till feelings of unreality develop.

*Pregnant women and those with known medical problems should always check with a physician before using any of the sensation-producing exercises.

**Which method best produces the anticipated sensation for you is quite individual. Pick your "best guess" and if, on the first attempt, you find it unsuccessful, try again with a different method. Be an inventive as you can in thinking up methods for producing the desired sensation. If you actually can't produce a sensation despite trying all the methods you can think of, you can use imagery instead, simply imagining the desired sensation as vividly as possible.

presence of a companion. If you want to produce elevated heart rate, for example, you might use the method of jogging in place for two minutes. Once again, if you become anxious, use SRB to reduce your anxiety.

For a *third* item, use the same physical method for producing sensation, but conduct your practice *alone.*

And for a *fourth,* conduct your practice alone and use the same method to produce the sensation, but this time, aim for as *intense* a sensation as you can produce — really let yourself feel it — then use SRB.

As a *fifth* and final item in a given hierarchy, produce the sensation as you've learned to do, and then time yourself till you've experienced the sensation *for a full thirty seconds* before using SRB to calm yourself. Then, once your anxiety has diminished, you may end the exposure session.

One note about the "prescribed" hierarchy: If you feel quite confident about tolerating a particular sensation without undue anxiety, as you well might after having experienced successful exposures during Session nine, feel free to drop items from a given hierarchy and start wherever you think appropriate, or to "collapse" two or three items into one.

Similarly, of course, if there's a gap between two items that feels too great to you, generate additional items between the two so that finer gradations of anxiety result. You could, for example, vary your method of producing sensation so that less intense sensation results initially (e.g., doing three jumping jacks might elevate your heart rate very slightly, while doing twenty-three would result in much greater elevation — a more intense sensation). Just be sure that the very last item in your hierarchy involves thirty seconds of exposure to the sensation before moving on.

The third step: Conducting exposures and recording results

This step needs little explanation; by now you're an expert in conducting exposures. As in Session nine, you need to select a time each day to conduct your exposure and commit yourself to it — no weaseling out. When the time arrives, begin with the first item in your first hierarchy and conduct the exposure: Do whatever the item specifies, using imagery or physical means to create a sensation, then use SRB to diminish anxiety.

You should use SRB immediately when anxiety arises except for the final item in your hierarchy, which specifies a thirty-second exposure to the sensation before moving to SRB. And once you've begun SRB, continue to use it for a full two minutes to ensure that you feel quite comfortable, then declare the exposure finished.

Now record your anxiety level during the exposure the same way you recorded it in Session nine. What you'll record is not the intensity of physical sensation itself, but the *anxiety* you experienced with it at its maximum. Below is a copy of the simple format used for recording, identical to the one shown in session nine. Remember, a copy is found in Appendix VI which you can duplicate if you wish.

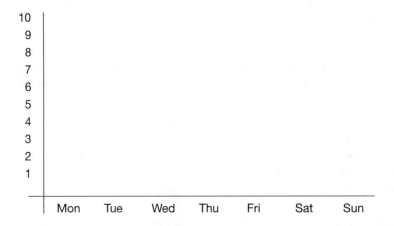

Conduct four exposures per day. At this point, one difference in procedure from Session nine arises. In Session nine, exposures were frequently lengthy, involving sitting through movies, shopping for the week's groceries, or going for a long walk. In this session, an exposure takes just a few minutes to conduct, typically less than five. So after you conduct one exposure and record your anxiety level, take a few minutes to become completely calm — perhaps by using controlled breathing — then do a second exposure of the item.

After you've finished the second exposure, take another brief "recovery time" to become fully relaxed and again repeat the exposure. Finally, complete one more cycle of recovery time, then exposure.

In other words, each day you'll conduct four exposures, taking a short "recovery time" to become fully calm before each new repetition.

The fourth step: Moving to the next item

After you've completed four exposures of a single item with minimal anxiety, move to the next item. (The four exposures could occur on the same day, since you're completing four exposures per day. But usually they would occur over more than one day.)

One more addition to the method occurs at this point: Once you complete the last item in your hierarchy for a given sensation, do two things:

1. Move to the first item of the next hierarchy (the hierarchy for a different sensation) *and*

2. For two successive days, *repeat* just one exposure of the last item of the previous hierarchy, simply to maintain your full level of comfort with it.

Summary of Steps of an Exposure Method for Internal Sensation

In summary, to conduct exposure to internal sensations and eliminate your anxiety to them:

-List feared sensations and order them from least to most frightening.

-For each sensation, generate a hierarchy composed of about five items ranging from easiest (using imagery) to most difficult (producing intense sensation for thirty seconds before using SRB).

-Starting with the first item of the first hierarchy, conduct four exposure practices each day, recording anxiety after each practice and taking needed "recovery time" before the next.

-After four successful experiences with one item (i.e., minimal anxiety during the practice), move to the next item.

-Once you complete all the items for a given sensation, move to the first item for the next, but "review" the previous item (i.e., conduct one exposure of it) on two successive days, as well as conducting exposures to the new item.

Terry's Sequence of Practice

Let's look at an example that illustrates how someone might proceed through a hierarchy. Terry, a twenty-seven-year-old high school chemistry teacher, was working on the anxiety he felt whenever he experienced increased heart rate. He'd had to give up exercising as a result of his difficulties and was determined to overcome them.

Let's assume Terry has already worked his way through three or four "easier" sensations (five items each) and has completed the first four items of his heart rate hierarchy (imagery; using ten jumping jacks to elevate heart rate in the presence of a companion; using ten jumping jacks without the companion; and using twenty jumping jacks, aiming for more intense sensation before using SRB). Now he's ready to tackle his fifth item — using twenty jumping jacks to elevate heart rate, continuing his exertion at the level necessary to maintain the elevated heart rate for thirty seconds (which for Terry meant doing another jumping jack every several seconds), and only then using SRB to diminish any anxiety he still might feel.

On the first day that Terry tackled item five, he conducted his first practice and, after the practice, rated his anxiety level at 7. He took a couple of minutes to allow the anxiety to diminish more fully, using controlled breathing and reading an article in the newspaper before proceeding.

He then conducted a second practice in the same manner, but this time, his rated anxiety was only 4. He again took some recovery time and on his third practice, rated his anxiety at 4 again. After a recovery period, he conducted his final practice of the day and this time, recorded an anxiety level of 2.

On the following day, he went through the same sequence, but this time, his anxiety ratings were 3, 2, 1 and 2.

On Terry's third day of exposure to item five, all four practices yielded anxiety ratings of 0, 1 or 2, so he decided he was ready to move on to his next hierarchy. (Terry also went out with his wife for a celebration that night; a month earlier, he wouldn't have believed he'd ever again experience a rapid heart rate and feel so completely comfortable!)

On day four, Terry repeated one practice of the fifth heart-rate item (his "review"), then moved to his next sensation — light-headedness — conducting three practices of item one, producing light-headedness through imagery.

On day five, Terry again "reviewed" his heart rate exposure once and again conducted exposures for light-headedness. From that point on, he focused each day exclusively on light-headedness till he'd completed those five items as well.

Incidentally, such a rapid, regular decrease in anxiety is not typical; there are usually a few more "ups and downs" when people reach the more difficult sensations in their hierarchies. Terry was chosen for this example since he illustrates the progressive steps of the method so clearly.

Additional Notes
That's the method in full, but a few additional notes are in order.

First, a note about medical safety. You may have concerns about the safety and wisdom of provoking the different physical sensations. If so, remember that all these sensations occur naturally in your body and are perfectly benign experiences — you've simply learned to interpret them as risky.

This program assumes that you've had a physical exam recently and been declared healthy. If you have any specific concerns about what a given sensation means or about producing it deliberately, contact your physician. And of course, if you're pregnant or have an existing medical condition, talk with your doctor about the exercises before you begin any of them.

If you've had a heart attack in the past, you're likely to have particular concerns. Again, go over them with your physician and find out the advisability of each of the exercises given your specific circumstances. Also, get a clear statement from your physician, if you haven't already, of what signs and symptoms ought to trigger action from you (e.g., a phone call or a trip to the emergency room) and *which ones need not.*

Second, even if you now feel comfortable with various physical sensations that used to alarm you, it's best to "overlearn," to push the limits of your comfort to ensure continued comfort over time and in different situations, inoculating you against future outbreaks of panic.

Third, you may feel, for whatever reason, that you'd prefer to do "internal" exposures somewhat more informally than the methods outlined here. That's fine, so long as you make certain to *build into your schedule every day* some activities that involve increasingly intense bodily sensation. And be sure they include the specific sensations you've identified as especially anxiety-producing for you. Examples might include running up stairs, sports activities, watching scary movies, standing up quickly, heavy lifting, cranking up the heat in your car full-blast, taking hot showers — any activities you can think of that cause elevated heart rate, lightheadedness, feelings of warmth and the like.

Finally, a confidence-building note: Remember that you're tackling the explicit production of uncomfortable sensation at a point in your treatment program when you've already overcome much of your discomfort. For many of you, this session is simply a cementing of gains already made.

Exercises for Session Ten

I. Well-established Habits

Continue practicing controlled breathing and SRB. Continue recording panic episodes — if you have any to record — and other observations in your journal. And continue exposure practices "out in the world" at least twice weekly.

II. Ongoing Challenges to Your Self-Talk

Continue the nightly work on your self-talk, especially related to any instances of anxiety you experienced during the day and, if none occurred, reviewing challenges related to common catastrophic beliefs about physical sensation and panic.

III. Internal Exposures

A. Assuming that you've chosen to use the exposure method outlined in this session, develop a list of feared sensations and a hierarchy for each, following the guidelines on pages 153-159.

B. Each day, conduct four exposures. Pages 158-159 describe the procedure for selecting the appropriate item(s) for each day's practice session.

The Question of Medications

Should you take medications in your efforts to overcome panic attacks? It's an important question, one on which not even the experts agree. It's also a highly individual one.

There are medications available that, for most panic sufferers, can control their symptoms quite effectively. There are very good reasons why many people with panic choose to take them, and they often find them immensely helpful.

On the other hand, it's important to realize that medications can't do the job alone: If you were to rely solely on medications to overcome your panic symptoms and did nothing else, when you eventually stopped taking them, your symptoms would very likely return. And as you know, it is possible for most individuals to overcome their panic symptoms without medications, using strategies of the sort you're learning in this book.

So the question remains — should you take medications or not? Unfortunately, that question can sometimes evolve into a debate about whether medications are "good" or "bad" for you, or whether those with panic "should" or "should not" take them. Those questions are not only unanswerable, they're not terribly helpful. The more useful question is this: Given your unique situation (your symptom picture and personal circumstances, your family and medical history, your success with other panic control measures and *your own preferences)*, what is the best choice for *you?* Medications or no medications?

Of course, no book by itself can give you individualized medical advice. What it can do, though, is offer the information you need to help you consider the question of medication sensibly and without prejudice. This session describes the major classes of medication useful in treating panic, outlines their benefits and drawbacks and suggests guidelines for using medications wisely, should you decide to do so.

Why Medication for Panic May Be Needed

You may be wondering why you or anyone else with a panic disorder would choose to take medication in the first place. There are several possible reasons.

First, your *anxiety level* may be so intense and constant that without medication, you don't feel able to even attempt the methods in this book. As you know, behavioral techniques for overcoming panic involve experiencing a certain amount of discomfort in the process. In the case of many strategies, in fact, it's that very *exposure* to anxiety that leads to its decline. If your anxiety is so severe already that you don't feel able to tolerate one more ounce, you may decide you need medication to allow you even to go forward with a treatment program.

Or perhaps you're simply too depressed right now to undertake a treatment program without the extra boost medications can provide. Studies have suggested that roughly one third of people with panic disorder suffer a major depression before the onset of their panic. An additional third develop major depression in reaction to their panic disorder. Some of the medications prescribed for panic also treat depression effectively, so if *depressed mood* is a significant problem complicating your struggles with panic, medication can be especially helpful.

You may have *another anxiety disorder* that you're battling along with your panic. Some of the newest medications for panic are also being found effective against other anxiety disorders. So if you are troubled by another anxiety condition in addition to panic, your doctor may encourage you to try one of these and treat both problems simultaneously.

Perhaps you've been practicing various panic-reduction strategies for some time, but you still haven't experienced as much improvement as you'd like. In this case, you may decide to try medication in hopes of *improving your overall success* at controlling your symptoms.

Or, finally, you may simply be looking for *more rapid relief from your symptoms.* The non-medication strategies can take longer to yield complete results, so you might choose to take medications alongside your other efforts, simply for greater comfort during the early phases.

In short, the nature and intensity of your symptoms, your experience with other methods of treatment and your own preferences can all propel you in the direction of trying medications for panic.

Medications for Panic

The most frequently prescribed medications for panic fall into two major classes, the antidepressants and the high-potency benzodiazepines. Carefully-controlled studies have found several medications from each of these classes to be effective in controlling panic symptoms.

Antidepressants

Antidepressants have been well-studied for the treatment of panic disorder, and several have been shown to reduce the frequency and intensity of panic attacks and even to eliminate them altogether. They can help you deal with avoidance as well, since the reduction in panic can make it easier for you to brave the world again. Antidepressants normally have positive effects on mood, of course, and also on overall anxiety level. And, as mentioned earlier, several of the newer antidepressants help to treat symptoms of other anxiety disorders you may have (including social phobia, obsessive-compulsive disorder, PTSD and possibly generalized anxiety disorder). Finally, the antidepressants are nonaddictive and, taken as directed, are very safe medicines.

People are often confused when they're prescribed an antidepressant for their panic attacks, especially when they aren't depressed. Although these medications are classified as antidepressants (since they were originally used for that purpose), they are just as effective against panic whether you're depressed or not. In other words, they could just as easily be called "antipanics."

_. ._.ul classes of antidepressants have now been well-studied for the treatment of panic. The first, oldest, and still effective are the tricyclic antidepressants (or TCAs) and the MAO inhibitors (or MAOIs).

Recent evidence suggests that antidepressants that act on the serotonin system of the brain (most of them, "serotonin-specific reuptake inhibitors," or SSRIs) and certain other antidepressants are also effective against panic, and are rapidly becoming "first choice" medications for the treatment of panic disorder. Their effectiveness against panic symptoms matches that of the older medicines, and they are somewhat less likely to cause problematic side effects. Some examples of these medications (listed by trade name) include Zoloft, Paxil, Prozac, Luvox and Celexa. Effexor, Remeron and possibly Serzone are other antidepressants with SSRI activity which also work against panic, and which are often referred to as "atypical agents," given that they possess other forms of action in addition to their impact on serotonin.

It should be emphasized, though, that the tricyclics and MAOIs remain perfectly good medications and suit many people very well given their specific circumstances. Unless there's a specific reason to make a change, if you are already taking them comfortably and with good results (and you don't have another anxiety disorder potentially treatable with an SSRI), you would probably be advised by your doctor to continue them, particularly as they're often less costly medicines and available in generic forms.

Antidepressants: The Drawbacks

The Relapse Issue. So if the antidepressants work so well to control panic, why are other methods even needed? Why not simply take the medication and be done with it? The primary reason is quite simple: If you take a medication to control your symptoms *and do nothing else,* when you stop the medication, you're likely to have a *relapse* — your original symptoms are likely to return. Different studies report different rates of relapse, but all agree that, to quote one clinician-researcher in the area, "Relapse is the rule." Some studies have found that relapse rates are lower if the medications are taken for eighteen months or longer before stopping. But relapse is still a problem for many.

That's not to suggest that medications have no useful place in the treatment of panic. But you need to be aware of the relapse issue when you make your decision about medication. In other words, medication is not a *complete* nor a *permanent* solution to panic.

Delayed Results. There are other issues in the use of antidepressants you should understand as well, to ensure that your experience with these medications is a successful one. First, it may take several weeks to receive full benefit from the antidepressants. It generally takes two to four weeks on the right dosage to experience initial antipanic effects of the medication; and further improvement is likely to occur over several more weeks, perhaps even a few months, before you achieve the *maximal* benefit. It's important to know this so you don't conclude that the medicine isn't helping and go off it before you've given it a fair chance.

Trial and Error Period. You should also know that the process of medicating for panic involves a certain amount of adjustment. Typically, your doctor will start you at one dosage level and then, depending on your response, will increase the dose gradually till both of you are satisfied with your results. In addition, since having panic disorder typically means your nervous system is on "high alert," your doctor will very likely start you on a lower dosage than the typical starting dose for depression, and your final dosage may, likewise, prove to be somewhat lower.

On occasion, finding the best medication for you may even involve switching to a different medication altogether; sometimes different medications work best in different individuals for reasons that aren't completely predictable. It's important to realize that a trial-and-error period is normal, so you'll tolerate the whole process a little more easily.

Side effects. All medications have side effects. Unfortunately, neither you nor your doctor can predict whether you'll experience any, or what they might be. One person may have no side effect problems at all, whereas someone else on the very same medication and dosage may experience side effects they find quite unpleasant.

The tricyclics most commonly cause dry mouth, constipation, weight gain and some minor effects on blood pressure called orthostasis. (If you get up too quickly after sitting or lying down, you may feel faint or dizzy for a moment; the best way to minimize this, if it happens, is simply to rise more slowly and, if you're lying down, to sit up slowly and pause for a moment before standing.)

Potential side effects of the SSRIs include sleep disturbance, gastrointestinal complaints such as nausea and diarrhea, dry mouth, increased sweating, and sexual problems such as delayed ejaculation in men and lowered arousal and orgasm in women. If you're experiencing sexual problems, don't be shy about mentioning the issue to your doctor, since it's not at all uncommon and the two of you can discuss together whether a change in medication is in order. Before you rush to change medications, though, remember that most side effects diminish or disappear over time, so at the outset, try to be patient until it's clear whether that may be the case for you.

One of the most troublesome side effects which can occur with virtually any of the antidepressants — older or newer — is a "jittery" feeling which, unfortunately, can feel a lot like the anxiety you were hoping the medication would alleviate. It can often be minimized by starting on very low doses of the medications and increasing them very slowly and gradually. Unfortunately, this side effect, like the others, can be especially acute early on, before you've experienced any improvement in symptoms (which, remember, can take as long as three weeks). As a result, many people end up discontinuing the medicines before they discover the true benefit they might have experienced, had they given the medication slightly longer to take effect.

Anxious expectations. Finally, some panic sufferers experience a slight increase in anxiety early in their use of an antidepressant which they label as a side effect, but which is really due mostly to their own *anxiety about taking medication in the first place.*

That can happen in two different ways: First, you may simply be so anxious at the prospect of being on medication that your anxiety alone causes more symptoms — which you then blame on the medicine.

Or, your anxiety about the medication can make you so hypervigilant that you react strongly to any minor change in sensation that is a result of the medication (a slightly increased heart rate, for example). That initial reaction can lead you into a spiraling of catastrophic thinking and greatly *amplified* symptoms — which, once again, you may blame solely on the medication.

If you experience increased anxiety after starting a medication, don't instantly assume the medication was responsible. Remember that you probably have an exquisite sensitivity to sensation, and new sensations are likely to occur when you start taking a medication for the first time or when you adjust your dosage. Spend some time exploring what's the most likely basis for your increased jitters before you decide what to do.

The final tally. In short, antidepressant medications are safe, nonaddictive drugs and several of them are known to help panic symptoms a great deal. They also improve mood and may help with other anxiety problems. But it can take some patience and faith to get through the first couple of weeks, and you may need to tolerate some initial discomfort before you experience their full benefits. Most important of all, you need to remember the absolute necessity for additional measures to overcome panic, both with the antidepressants and with the second major class of medication for panic, the *benzodiazepines.*

The Benzodiazepines

High-potency benzodiazepines — most people think of these as anti-anxiety drugs, or "tranquilizers" — are also frequently prescribed for panic. Within this class, alprazolam (Xanax) and clonazepam (Klonopin) are probably the most common, and both have been found quite effective in controlling panic symptoms. There is also evidence that other benzodiazepines such as diazepam (Valium) and lorazepam (Ativan) are effective against panic disorder for some people, but because alprozolam and clonazepam are so much more commonly prescribed, this discussion will focus on those two medications.

These medications carry a couple of advantages over the antidepressants. First, they generally work more rapidly; instead of waiting two or three weeks before you experience relief on the medications, you're likely to feel some immediate improvement. And the benzodiazepines have very few side effects, with drowsiness and slightly impaired coordination the most common complaints.

Benzodiazepines: The Drawbacks

Relapse. So if the high potency benzodiazepines (HPBs) also work well against panic symptoms, and on top of that, they take effect rapidly and cause few side effects, the question again arises, so what's the problem? Once again, why not just take a pill for your panic?

The answer, in part, is one you know already: If you simply take medicine for your symptoms and you do nothing else, when you eventually go off the medications, your original symptoms will almost certainly return; you'll *relapse.* If you want to overcome your panic fully and permanently, and without relying on medications for the rest of your life, you must do more.

Dependency and withdrawal. The benzodiazepines, particularly alprazolam, have another, more serious drawback associated with their use: They produce a physical dependency if taken for a long enough time period. That means they have the potential for abuse. You can experience withdrawal symptoms when you stop taking them, and if you stop the drug abruptly, severe withdrawal reactions could occur (symptoms which could include agitation, sleeplessness, muscle pains, dizziness, diarrhea, increased heart rate and confusion). These withdrawal symptoms occur somewhat less with lower doses and can be minimized by tapering off the medications very slowly, decreasing dosages by minimal amounts and over a long period of time.

It should be noted that many doctors worry less about dependency issues with clonazepam than with alprazolam, an impression that appears to be supported by studies of the two medications. This is probably because clonazepam has a longer half-life than alprazolam. That means that the medicine is used up by your body more slowly, so you need to take it less often and you're less likely to "feel" it when your body runs out of its supply. Still, withdrawal symptoms do occur for some people, whatever the medication and tapering schedule.

Finally with alprazolam, at least, *relapse* is complicated by a phenomenon known as *rebound* — the return of the original symptoms once medication is withdrawn, *but at an even greater level than before.* A recent study did confirm that rebound is not generally a problem with clonazepam, however.

In other words, though, depending on the medication chosen, as well as the dosage and tapering schedule, discontinuing an HPB can result in up to three separate processes to contend with at once — a return of the *original* panic symptoms *(relapse),* the potential prospect of even more *intense* symptoms *(rebound)* and the additional discomfort of *withdrawal.* You'll want to be aware of these issues, and discuss them with your doctor before starting an HPB so that you'll be able to make a well-informed choice.

One final point should be mentioned with respect to the use of benzodiazepines for panic disorder: Recent studies have shown that, if you do use a benzodiazepine in combination with cognitive-behavior therapy, it's important to use it on a *regular* schedule, prescribed by your doctor. Taking it "prn" or "as needed" (that is, only when you become anxious) actually reduces the positive benefits of cognitive-behavior therapy quite dramatically, perhaps because you come to rely on the medication to reduce your anxiety instead of using the new strategies you've learned.

Additionally, it's extremely important that after you *stop* using the benzodiazepine, you *keep practicing* cognitive-behavioral strategies until you are confident that your panic difficulties have been eliminated altogether. Otherwise, you're at high risk to see a return of your panic, again, because your body has not "learned" to overcome symptoms in the absence of the medication. (This is actually good advice no matter what medication you may have been taking, but is especially crucial with the benzodiazepines.)

Combination Options
Thus, medications can help relieve the symptoms of panic, but none of the effective medications is perfect. Antidepressants don't produce benefits immediately and may even involve some increased discomfort at the outset of treatment. On the other hand, they don't present problems with physical dependence and withdrawal. The high potency benzodiazepines are more rapid-acting and usually generate fewer troublesome side effects, but they do have some potential for abuse.

In light of these relative advantages and disadvantages, many doctors who prescribe medication for panic choose to start someone on an antidepressant *along with* a benzodiazepine. While the antidepressant is just starting to take effect, the benzodiazepine helps to ease any initial discomfort. Then, once the antidepressant is working well (usually within a few weeks), the benzodiazepine is discontinued or tapered down to very small doses. What little research there is on this approach suggests that it may be less effective than most people believe. However, some people do report that the method works well for them.

Finally, if your symptoms aren't responding to your primary medication, your doctor may try "augmenting" it by adding a small amount of a different medication. You can see why it's important to work with a physician who's up-to-date and familiar with all the options.

Most important to remember as you consider the use of medications for your panic is a principle that can't be overemphasized: If you use medication, *combine* it with a program to teach you panic-control strategies, and to address features that medication can't address — features such as anxiety-producing self-talk, low tolerance for normal physical sensation, and any life circumstances or emotional factors that may contribute to your panic.

Indeed, in many clinical settings, therapy using medication- and non-medication-based strategies in combination is a common approach to panic disorder.

What kind of results can someone expect from this sort of approach? Unfortunately, the answer to that question is less than crystal-clear. There *are* a number of studies showing that, at the end of treatment, those treated with medication in combination with cognitive-behavior therapy show greater improvement than those treated with only one or the other. They generally indicate, however, that cognitive-behavior treatment is necessary to prevent relapse after treatment ends. For example, one very well-controlled study compared medication (in this case, Luvox), cognitive-behavior therapy (a treatment similar to the sort you've learned in this book), and a combination of the two. This study found that while the cognitive-behavior treatment was necessary to *maintain* gains, adding medication to the cognitive-behavior therapy increased the *speed* of improvement, and added slightly to the comfort level of those going through the treatment while they continued the medication.

Another study found that while those taking *only* medication for their panic disorder were highly likely to relapse after stopping the medication, for those who combined medication with cognitive-behavior therapy, 85% were still panic-free for an average of more than five years' time after treatment had ended. On the flip side, though, an analysis of three large studies by a highly-regarded researcher in the field has suggested that the addition of medication, despite initial benefits, may actually *interfere* with the long-term benefits of cognitive-behavior therapy. This may very likely be due to the fact that the medication interferes with *habituation*, described in Session nine. (Remember, habituation is, in essence, the process of "getting used to" a feared situation after repeated exposures, until it no longer frightens you.) It may also reflect, in part, the fact that the panic sufferer attributes the absence of panic to the medication, rather than to the internal changes that have come about as a result of the therapy.

So how do you make sense of all this and make the best decision for yourself? Perhaps the best advice at this point is to choose the approach that best fits your instincts and preferences, the advice of your treater, and the results of any treatment experiences you may have had in the past. If you decide to add medication to your treatment regimen, once you feel ready to discontinue the medication, do so gradually, as outlined on page 174 and reviewed on page 190, continuing to use the cognitive-behavioral techniques you've learned in this book till you feel truly confident of your panic-free state. Above all, don't neglect the emotional work you've begun, nor the relapse-prevention strategies described in the next session, which will maximize your resilience to future difficulties.

What Should You Do?

So the question arises anew: Should you use medications or not? You now have much of the information you need to make a decision:

-You understand the complications of panic that might lead you to choose medications — perhaps depression or another anxiety disorder, perhaps unmanageable levels of discomfort, perhaps frustration with the time lag or with your results using the other methods alone.

-You recognize the positive effects a medication can have: Medications can offer an easing of your misery and effective panic control while you work at mastering more complete, permanent strategies for overcoming panic.

-You recognize the potential drawbacks of medication, and the importance of working closely with your doctor to manage these appropriately.

-You recognize that some people are immensely helped by medications, while others overcome their panic successfully without medications; and that either choice is perfectly acceptable, and depends on individual circumstances.

-You realize that no decision is cast in stone: If you try behavioral methods *without* medication and aren't as successful as you'd like, you can decide at a later date to add medications to your program. If you try medications in conjunction with the other strategies and find they don't agree with you, you can discontinue the medications and continue with your other strategies for controlling symptoms.

-You understand the *absolute necessity* to use non-medication methods in conjunction with the medication, and to *continue practicing* those non-medication methods (that is, cognitive-behavior methods like those in this book), after you discontinue the medications

-Most important of all, you remember that it's your life, and your choice — yours and only yours to make.

Guidelines for Using Medications Well

If you and your physician do determine that you'll try medications, what can you do to maximize their contribution to your total treatment plan? There are really only two important guidelines.

1. First, you're well-aware that *it's crucial to combine the use of medications with other, non-medication approaches* to controlling panic. Many people need or want to stay on their medications quite long-term or even indefinitely. Perhaps more typical are those people who prefer to use medications while they develop and consolidate other panic-reduction strategies, then to discontinue the medications once their panic is under good control.

Used in this manner, you might think about the use of medications as comparable to the use of a cast for a broken leg. A cast is worn for support — to "manage symptoms" as it were — while internal healing occurs. Once the internal healing is complete, the cast is no longer needed and is removed; the patient's own resources take over the job of supporting the once-broken leg. Similarly in panic, medications can provide needed support, then when "internal healing" has progressed enough and they're no longer needed, they can be "removed."

2. The second critical guideline in the use of medications is *to work closely with your physician* throughout the process:

-*Inform your doctor* of any medically-related conditions that could influence your use of medications both at the outset and as they arise throughout treatment. This includes other medical conditions, the possibility of pregnancy, and any other medications you're taking.

-*Follow your doctor's instructions* concerning how to take your medications, what to expect from them, appropriate dosages, changes to watch for and, especially, safety guidelines. Some of the SSRIs, for example, can affect the absorption of other medications, which may alter the amount of the medication you need or even cause an accumulation of the medication in your system.

Taking an MAO inhibitor requires *absolutely* that you follow certain dietary restrictions and observe very stringent prohibitions regarding other medications (prescription or over-the-counter medicines) along with it. Failure to observe these restrictions could be extremely dangerous.

-*Don't ever go off a medication abruptly.* This guideline, too, merits special emphasis. In the case of the benzodiazepines, abrupt discontinuation could result in serious physical reactions. If and when you wish to discontinue your medications, meet with your doctor to discuss the decision and to develop a plan for doing so gradually. Review your strategies for managing panic and be sure you're practicing them fully so that your withdrawal doesn't result in a resurgence of difficulties. You'll probably feel a bit "different" temporarily, but now can manage these differences in sensation without allowing panic to rise in response to them.

In short, *stay in communication* with your doctor about any concerns, questions or problems. Remember, this is a partnership. Your doctor's aim is the same as your own: to allow you to live the life you want, unlimited by the restrictions of panic attacks.

Exercises for Session Eleven
There are no new exercises for this session. The most important strategy to practice, to ensure that you become and remain panic-free, is that of exposure: Continue to expose yourself to outside situations, twice weekly if possible, and internal sensations if you've chosen to do so. Also evaluate and challenge your self-talk whenever anxiety arises, as well as any other times you feel it's needed.

Where Have You Been?
Where Are You Going?

As you near the end of your formal program to master your panic and take back your life, it's useful to review how far you've traveled in the past twelve weeks — to see all you've achieved.

The following list of items, numbered by session, is a summary outline of the program you've just completed.

1. You've learned that your panic disorder is a *distinct syndrome* with many features that you share with other panic sufferers. What you have is real and recognized, and you've stopped feeling totally alone with it.

2. You've come to understand the *potential roots* of your difficulties, whether they be in your biology or inborn temperament, or perhaps in early experiences — experiences that taught you to fear the world as a dangerous, unpredictable place; to fear physical sensation as a warning sign of disaster; perhaps to fear that there was no one you could rely on in the world, least of all, yourself.

If childhood experiences have resulted in a fearful adulthood, perhaps you're beginning to recognize the difference between your life then and now, and to let some of the old fears go. And ideally, you've stopped blaming yourself for developing panic disorder, realizing that it's understandable in light of your experiences — or perhaps recognizing, as you scan your family tree, that you came by your panic disorder quite naturally!

3. You've considered your own *personality features* that may relate to your panic, resulting in greater acceptance (many features are a result of your disorder or are heightened by it), greater awareness (which allows you more choice and control in your life), and perhaps a new-found determination to moderate the tendencies that may increase your panic problems.

4. You've examined the *timing* of your panic outbreaks both globally (when in the course of your *life* you've experienced attacks) and specifically (when in the course of your *week* or your *day* panic arises). Understanding your vulnerable times has helped you to recognize and interrupt impending panic earlier in the cycle, and to begin to address the emotional issues that underlie your own panic, whatever they may be (feelings of inadequacy relative to others, sensitivity to loss or separation from loved ones, discomfort with anger, or any of the countless other possibilities unique to you).

5. You've come to understand how closely breathing style can be related to anxiety outbreaks, and you've learned *controlled breathing* both as a technique used daily to maintain lower susceptibility to attacks and as one step in a formal method to interrupt attacks as they arise.

6. You've mastered *SRB* — the stop-refocus-breathe method for halting anxiety symptoms before they spiral into full-blown panic. You not only use it in situations as it's needed, but practice it on a daily basis at home. Thus, you're as prepared as you can be to use it effectively when you need it most. Ultimately, through repeated exposures to your feared situations (and sensations), it's expected that your panic attacks will have stopped altogether. Perhaps you're already there. But it still gives you extra confidence to have this tactic available to you, should you ever need it.

7. You've become skilled at recognizing *early cues* of anxiety that can spiral into panic, allowing you to intervene early to interrupt or even prevent the panic cycle altogether. You've come to realize that even physical sensations not clearly identifiable as anxiety *per se* can provoke the cycle and you've learned to respond to these, too, with your methods for halting panic in its tracks.

You've examined the way in which unrecognized, mounting stress, other emotions, mild uneasiness, and seemingly innocuous events of special significance to you can sometimes trigger panic.

Previously inexplicable, out-of-the-blue attacks now make sense — and offer you a chance for early intervention.

8. You've learned how to "tune in" to underlying beliefs and self-talk that can lower your threshold for panic, heighten your anxiety, and play a crucial role in the panic cycle. You've learned to evaluate and *challenge catastrophic self-talk,* replacing it with more realistic and adaptive statements. In particular, you're recognizing the central role played by your beliefs that physical sensations spell disaster and imminent danger. You're learning to challenge those beliefs and, over time, to break their destructive power over you.

9. You've developed your own program to *re-enter situations* you'd begun to avoid, exposing yourself repeatedly to those situations (places, activities) and witnessing, over time, the drop in anxiety that occurs as a result.

10. You've developed the capacity to *tolerate physical sensation* without experiencing the rise in anxiety that previously resulted from it. You may have developed this capacity by direct, *explicit* exposure to sensation, or by the exposure to sensation that happens *automatically* as you re-enter previously-avoided situations. (After all, you can't enter a feared situation and feel subjectively anxious without experiencing the physical symptoms linked to your anxiety.) Either way, you're learning that you needn't fear these sensations: They aren't dangerous in themselves; they aren't signs of impending physical disaster; and they needn't signal an onrush of anxiety.

11. You've learned about the use of *medication* for panic — how it can help you if you need it and, if you decide to use it, how to do so in a manner that yields the best outcome.

Now that we've reviewed where you've been, let's take a look at where you are now.

Savor Your Successes
By this point in the program, it's likely that you're seeing substantial results from all your hard work. This is a good time to stop and take note of them. You can probably identify measurable improvements on several fronts:
    -reduced frequency of your panic attacks;
    -reduced intensity of any attacks that occur;
    -your improved ability to "catch" and interrupt an attack that may be arising;

-the places you're going and activities you're enjoying that you had been avoiding before;

-the degree of physical sensation you can tolerate that, before, would have alarmed you (e.g., perhaps you can now tolerate the increased heart rate, shortness of breath, and sensations of warmth that occur with moderate exercise);

-the degree to which you're able to identify your anxiety-producing self-talk, evaluate the underlying beliefs realistically, and challenge them energetically;

-the degree to which you're realizing at an emotional level that physical sensations won't hurt you and aren't signs of danger to be feared; and

-your overall level of anxiety as you go about your day-to-day tasks.

You'll also note accomplishments that are unique to you, changes that arose out of the emotional work you did during the program. Perhaps you spoke up to your mother for the first time or told your husband some changes were needed around the house or stopped waiting hand and foot on your teen-age son. Perhaps you visited a family member in the hospital and let yourself cry about it for the first time or talked with a therapist about some early traumatic events. Maybe you traveled out of town for a conference or stayed alone in the house for the first time in years or started dating again, even though it terrified you. Don't overlook these equally important accomplishments — important in their ultimate impact on panic and on your overall emotional health and well-being.

Be sure to note the important steps you've taken, even if you don't feel completely finished with your work. If you now *identify* a particular theme as highly emotional after a lifetime of not letting yourself even think about it, that's an important change. If, in day-to-day interactions, you now *recognize* a vulnerable issue as it arises, whereas before you were totally unaware of it, you're making progress. And if you now handle an issue differently, even though you still may feel intensely upset *inside*, you're almost there.

Accepting and Letting Go

As you consider your progress, you may discover changes in your deepest beliefs and attitudes about yourself and the world. The exact "look" of these changes will be unique to you (and it may be that, for you, the changes are still yet to come), but they usually have to do with increasing levels of *acceptance* and of *letting go.*

The acceptance might be an acceptance of yourself and your own history; of sensation; of emotion; or perhaps of life's fundamental uncertainties. You may be letting go of your hypervigilance; of old griefs and hurts that never healed; or perhaps of all your efforts to guarantee an absolutely risk-free life. In the process, you may have experienced a deepening of faith — faith in yourself and your coping, in the probability of good outcomes in life, perhaps in your spiritual faith.

It's important to note that these core changes are not the kind of changes you learn through instruction and practice, in the same way you learned SRB or exposure techniques, for example. But through your *experiences* using the different techniques, such changes evolve. You do exposures and discover that you can experience different sensations and disasters *don't* happen. You *don't* die. Oftentimes, you don't even have a panic attack. Or perhaps you have one and you learn that people respect and care for you anyway. You learn that symptoms come and symptoms go, just as life's events come and go.

Maybe you even learn things *from* your panic — how to tune into important issues in your life, for example, or what those issues are; how to be more open to the feelings life brings. All these changes are important ones, worthy of your attention.

Make Note of Your Progress

How you choose to evaluate your progress is completely up to you. Some people like to recall a difficult time six months ago and simply think about the differences they notice in themselves now. Some choose to skim early journal entries and compare them with more recent ones. Others like to make formal charts or graphs of panic attacks or compile written lists of the places they've gone and activities they've undertaken in the past month. However you choose to record your progress, whether in your mind or on paper, the point is to notice progress and to praise yourself for all the positive changes.

Celebrate!

Now that you've noted all your accomplishments, it's time to celebrate them, in whatever way suits you best. Call up a friend and share the news of your success. Write in your journal, savoring the feeling it gives you to recognize your accomplishments. Write yourself a letter of congratulations, a letter to save and reread on occasion. Reward yourself with a present, something you might buy that will remind you, each time you use it or wear it or see it, of how far you've come. Or celebrate your achievements by doing something you weren't even able to do before you took back your life — go to a movie, dine in a fine restaurant, take a car trip, go on a shopping spree.

Find some way to celebrate, any way that suits you, but don't neglect the celebration. You deserve it.

Overcoming Problems and Increasing Your Success

You've come a long way in mastering your panic, but what if you haven't achieved the level of success you desire? Perhaps you've followed the program conscientiously, but you're still having significant difficulties with panic or related symptoms. Or maybe you see gains, but you want to progress even further. This section explores some key steps you can take to overcome problems and improve your results. Even if you're happy with your progress in the program, be sure to review this section; the guidelines suggested are equally important for *maintaining* your hard-won gains:

1. Keep practicing. This is perhaps the most important point of all — for *initial* success, for *further* improvement and for *ongoing* maintenance. Essentially, *you continue to make the program a part of your daily life.* Every day, you:

-practice controlled breathing and SRB at home;

-continue to practice exposures to internal sensation;

-remain active in the places, situations and activities that you used to avoid because of your discomfort;

-use the SRB method whenever you sense the slightest hint of rising anxiety or notice a physical sensation that can lead to anxiety;

-evaluate your self-talk whenever you feel uneasy and challenge any anxiety-producing statements you identify; and

-record your practice sessions, your day's experiences, and any panic episodes in your journal or on a calendar. (This means, of course, that you'll also identify panic-*free* days.)

Maintaining all the elements of your program can be difficult. But the payoff is worth it: powerful panic control. If you're having difficulty maintaining regular practice of all your new skills, the following strategies can help:

a. Enlist the help of a friend, perhaps forming a partnership to work jointly on your respective goals. ("You report to me each day how you did with your diet; I'll report how I stuck with my panic-management strategies.")

b. Choose a manageable goal for each day, for example, practicing controlled breathing and completing one session of exposure to internal sensations. Set your goal first thing in the morning and try to accomplish it early in the day, before you get preoccupied with other tasks.

c. Record your daily practices on your calendar (your breathing practice, exposures and anything else related to anxiety management).

d. Commit yourself to doing something (e.g., an exposure-related outing) *with* someone. It's much more difficult to break a commitment made to someone else than one you've made only to yourself.

e. Develop a reward program to reinforce the behaviors you want to maintain. As rewards, use stars on a calendar, fifteen minutes of an enjoyable activity, or even self-praise in some deliberate way. In your reward program, you should reward yourself for the behavior itself (e.g., the exposure, the practice) and not whether you judge the *outcome* to have been successful (e.g., whether you felt anxious or panicky during the activity).

f. Tell the people in your life just how they can help you. People you care about don't have to *understand* everything about panic disorder to appreciate your hard work and offer you support. In fact, you might tell them directly, "You may not understand exactly what this process is like for me, but you can help me by _____."

g. Remind yourself explicitly that progress in managing your anxiety will happen unevenly, at different rates for different people, and that it reflects the influence of external events you have little control over, not just the effects of your practice of anxiety-management techniques. That's one of the reasons it's important to praise your *behavior* (which you do have control over), not the outcome of that behavior on one particular occasion. But remember, too, that *overall,* the more you practice your panic-control strategies, the more your anxiety will diminish. So take heart and keep it up.

2. Push the envelope. Whenever and wherever possible, stretch the limits of your practices. Extend your exposures past the bare minimum, from normal, everyday situations to those that arise rarely or not at all. Coping with the *exceptional* situations will make the day-to-day ones that much easier to handle comfortably.

Practice controlled breathing under a variety of conditions, not just sitting in an easy chair in comfortable clothing with the phone off the hook. While that's a good place to *start,* once you've mastered controlled breathing in that situation, remember to conduct your second practice session of the day in different physical positions, in different settings, while performing different activities, until you feel confident that you can achieve the desired results *whatever* the circumstances.

When you practice the SRB method at home — generating anxiety imaginally then eliminating it by stopping your catastrophic thinking, refocusing your attention and "breathing it away" — don't stick to one single scene to create anxiety. Use a whole variety of scenes to expand your ability to relax in as many different situations as possible.

3. Analyze any problems that arise. If you've hit stumbling blocks in your progress, first try to determine where they seem to occur. If you're having difficulty with a particular technique — challenging your catastrophic self-talk, for example — be sure to review the pertinent sessions in the book and any relevant troubleshooting appendices.

If, despite following the program carefully, your results simply aren't satisfactory — you're still having lots of panic attacks or troublesome physical sensations or you're still avoiding or you're feeling a little bit anxious all the time — Appendix IV can be of help. It outlines different dilemmas that arise most frequently and discusses remedies for them. As before, even if you're satisfied with your progress, you can benefit from reading this appendix since it reviews general principles and offers ideas to enhance success.

You might also examine your journal for clues to the source of your difficulties. Perhaps the same life stresses keep arising again and again, or maybe you haven't resolved one particular emotional issue — grief over a loss or ongoing marital conflict or anger at a family member. If so, you might consider seeing a therapist for help. You needn't necessarily resolve an emotional issue before overcoming panic, but trying to understand and acknowledge your feelings often helps relieve the underlying tensions that can keep panic alive.

If low-level but constant anxiety is a problem — and perhaps is lowering your threshold for panic — be sure to read the special section that follows session twelve. It offers strategies for general stress reduction and can have a marked, positive effect on your overall level of tension and anxiety.

Finally, consider the possibility that you might be depressed. Remember, as many as a third of people with panic experience a major depression *before* they develop a panic disorder and another third develop depression *after* the onset of panic. Ongoing depression can make overcoming panic a lot tougher. Typical indicators of depression include sleep problems, a change in appetite or weight, poor concentration, difficulty making decisions, loss of energy and motivation, withdrawal from friends, irritability, feelings of worthlessness, crying spells, and thoughts of suicide.

If you suspect that you're depressed, consult a mental health professional who can evaluate your situation and discuss treatment options with you. Treatment of your depression can occur jointly with your work on panic (as you know, some medications treat both simultaneously), and resolving the depression can oftentimes boost your success at controlling panic.

4. Be fair to yourself. If you're not totally satisfied with your success at panic control, the proposed strategies can help. But you also need to consider whether you're being fair to yourself, if your vision of success is realistic. Once you begin improving — especially when you've been working so hard at it — it's easy to feel that you ought moving faster. But think about where you were six months ago. Think about how many months or years you've struggled with panic. It's understandable that you're impatient, but you do need to *give yourself some time.*

Also, remember that the reductions in your panic symptoms aren't simply a reflection of your new skill at controlling anxiety; they're also subject to the ups and downs of life. If you achieved some initial success in overcoming panic but lately, some symptoms have returned, you need to *consider what else is going on in your life.* It may be that you really have made genuine gains, but external stresses are counter-balancing or masking them.

Remember, too, that *success often occurs unevenly,* in spurts followed by plateaus followed by new spurts. It's possible that you're simply at a plateau just now, one that will pass eventually as you continue to use the methods you've learned in the program.

Don't inadvertently underestimate real success because of unfair standards. Toni came to a clinic for treatment after having been housebound for years by her panic and agoraphobia. She'd overcome the most severe avoidance on her own, with great courage, and then came in for additional help. Her therapist felt Toni had been doing well in treatment, but Toni herself was often dissatisfied with her progress.

One day, as she and her therapist discussed their differing perceptions, Toni realized that whenever she tried to enter a feared situation and *managed* it, but felt anxious *inside,* she considered this a failure. Her therapist considered it a shining success; after all, it takes the most courage to do the things you fear most. After that conversation, Toni began to give herself credit whenever she *undertook and completed* a difficult task, whether or not she experienced anxiety during the task. She began to feel better about herself and eventually, her anxiety diminished as well.

If you become discouraged every now and then, go back and repeat an exercise that *used* to be difficult but now is easy. Remind yourself of your successes. Post a list. Give yourself credit for the small steps. They're important. And they will, in time, add up to big ones.

Looking Ahead

Even as you complete the final steps toward overcoming your panic problems, consolidating your achievements and celebrating your successes, you're probably wondering what the outlook is for someone who's conquered panic symptoms. You might be wondering, "Is panic disorder something I can truly get over? Or is it something I'll have all my life?"

Is panic a chronic condition? The question can't be answered with a simple yes or no. There *are* significant percentages of people who, with cognitive-behavioral treatment (with and without medications), overcome their panic symptoms and, at follow-ups extending as long as two years or more, report no further difficulties. In fact, one study of 100 people in Italy followed people for *seven years* and found that over two-thirds of those treated with cognitive-behavioral therapy were still panic-free. Of course, as you can see from numbers like these, some people *aren't* successful in their efforts.

The problem is, no research study, no therapist, *no one*, in fact, can tell you what you *really* want to know: "Will *I* be successful in mastering *my* panic?" This book can't answer that question either. However, revisiting the concept of susceptibility to panic can help you to evaluate your current situation, and your future, in a useful way.

Susceptibility to Panic

The notion of susceptibility has threaded its way through this book, explicitly and implicitly. It provides a useful framework from which to look back and understand your panic disorder from its very inception, through the course of its development and on to its present status. It may even offer information about the future and what it holds for you.

As you've learned, a number of factors may have contributed to your unique vulnerability to developing panic disorder at some point in your life. First, you very likely inherited a *predisposition* to the disorder. In addition, unfortunate events in your early life may have contributed — possibly an early loss or traumatic separation, or perhaps growing up in a household marked by chaos, unpredictability, or even abuse. These experiences may have resulted in the feeling that you needed to be constantly vigilant — on chronic alert, as it were. Your brain might well have become more likely to interpret a situation as an emergency, and your body to respond accordingly, with a panic attack. (It may even be, for a few of you, that growing up with a parent you experienced as very critical and controlling left you feeling unsafe and chronically on guard.)

In a similar vein, it's likely that *cognitively*, you oftentimes interpreted events (especially physical sensations) as emergencies or as signs of impending disaster, possibly due to an early history in which disaster really did strike "out of the blue," or, for others of you, perhaps the result of a style you learned from an over-anxious parent.

Physically, you probably shared with other anxiety sufferers a tendency to engage in "anxious" (rapid, shallow) breathing. This increased your physical arousal level, bringing you closer to your panic threshold. It also, through changes in your blood chemistry, made you more responsive physically to small increases in anxiety, likewise bringing you even closer to your panic threshold.

And you may have developed a style of *avoidance of feelings*, believing this was safer or more acceptable within your family (or perhaps because feelings during your childhood were often painful). Ironically, as you learned in Session seven, those out-of-awareness feelings may have emerged, instead, as increased anxiety. And your style of avoidance may have extended to situations of conflict, to new situations, and to situations in which panic had previously occurred, giving you little opportunity to overcome your fears or to experience yourself as an independent and capable person.

In short, your history and habits in the emotional, the physical and the cognitive realms may all have created increased susceptibility to panic before you ever developed your first panic attack

As a result of your work over the past several weeks, though, it's likely that physically, you've developed a more relaxed breathing style and therefore are farther below your panic threshold. Cognitively, you've learned to evaluate situations more realistically, and are less likely to automatically assume disaster. And having achieved a greater understanding of your early history and its impact on you, you may be less vulnerable to its effects. You've recognized that your life situation has changed, and that the need for ultra-vigilance has ended. Situations of separation and loss are still difficult, it's true, but you now recognize the feelings for what they are, which diminishes the likelihood of panic arising in response. And perhaps you've become more willing to face situations, feelings, even conflicts, "head-on," rather than trying to avoid them.

If panic should begin to emerge at some point down the road, you'll recognize it early on for what it is, respond rapidly and effectively (now that you know how!) and very likely prevent it from developing into a full-blown recurrence. So while you cannot alter your inheritance, you may truly be, in all other regards, less susceptible to panic.

The concept of susceptibility, then, offers you a framework to understand both your original development of attacks and your increased resilience to future attacks. Are there ways to heighten or even ensure that resilience? You bet there are.

Preventing Relapse

You already know that one important way to keep panic out of your life is to keep practicing your panic-control strategies with vigor and regularity. There are four additional guidelines that will help you to prevent a return of symptoms:

Respond to signs of trouble early. Be alert for times when you might be vulnerable to a return of anxiety. Anticipate potential problems and take steps to prevent them before they arise; don't wait till you have a panic attack to take action. Are you facing a job change? An ailing parent? Financial reverses? A teenager with problems? Marital tensions? Recognize that extra stresses can "lower your threshold," and take *preventive* measures accordingly.

Take care of yourself. Build in some extra time for your own needs, a time of quiet meditation for renewal and relaxation or a playtime for fun and emotional release. Seek out extra emotional support from family, friends, a support group or a spiritual advisor. Find ways to express your feelings — to someone close to you, in your journal, perhaps to those directly involved in a stressful situation when appropriate. Consider if life changes to reduce stress are needed and if so, take steps to initiate the process; the special section coming up can be of help. Think about your values and priorities and consider ways to live according to their guidance. Spend more time laughing.

Address the potential return of symptoms head-on. Reread this book and beef up your practices if needed. Schedule an appointment with your therapist for an extra "booster" session or two. In fact, many people see a therapist for a course of treatment for panic; then once things are "on track," they elect to continue with some form of "maintenance" therapy, perhaps meeting with the therapist every several weeks to review and consolidate treatment gains, tune in to any problems on the horizon, and prevent "slippage" in continuing to follow the program. This practice can be an important part of your plan to prevent relapse, a bit like a periodic weigh-in for someone striving to maintain a previous weight loss.

Analyze any return of panic. If panic does threaten to return despite your best efforts to resist it, *remember to ask yourself what that might mean.* What emotional turbulence could be bubbling under the surface? Strengthen your panic-control efforts, yes. But look at possible underlying factors, too. For just as pain is a signal that something is amiss physically, alerting you to create conditions for physical healing (bandage the finger, treat the infection), so panic can be a signal that something is amiss emotionally, alerting you to the need to create the conditions for *emotional* healing. Don't ignore your body's signals.

The "Special Help" Summary on page 190 offers a list of good strategies for preventing relapse. Review it, post it in a visible spot, and practice the suggestions faithfully, to keep panic from re-entering your life.

Discontinuing Medications

What about discontinuing medications? When to do so is a decision for you to make in cooperation with your physician.

Let's assume that you've completed the program and have tackled all the different elements of your panic — the symptoms themselves, the avoidance, the anxiety-producing self-talk and even the emotional issues you identified. You've reached your goals of overall comfort level, resumption of normal activities, and ability to tolerate physical sensations more comfortably. You still experience normal anxiety, of course, but you're aware that it's normal and harmless and are confident that you can manage it appropriately. Let's assume, further, that if you've been taking an antidepressant medication, you've been taking it for at least eighteen months (or at least that you've considered the enhanced maintenance this might offer).

You and your physician now conclude that you're ready to discontinue the medications. How should this process proceed? Ideally, you'll work with your physician to gradually taper off the medication *as you continue to implement the panic-control strategies* you've learned. You and your doctor, and your therapist, if you have one, will monitor your progress and troubleshoot as needed. You'll expect a certain temporary increase in anxiety due to the change, but you know you can manage it, just as you manage anxiety from any other source.

Relapse Prevention Strategies for Panic & Anxiety

1. *Continue* the new habits that helped you "lick" your anxiety and panic in the first place: Continue daily controlled breathing or relaxation practice; continue your usual activities despite occasional discomfort; continue to use healthy self-talk; and continue to make the choices that promote good health.

2. Try to *anticipate* possible rough spells ahead of time and plan for them: Allow yourself extra time. Practice the specific skills you'll likely need to handle an upcoming challenge. Review your journal and the chapters in the book that addressed your own situation most directly.

3. If you notice some symptoms of panic, *don't over-react:* Everyone struggles more at vulnerable times with their own particular reactions to stress; yours simply take the "shape" of heightened anxiety. If your anxiety does recur full-force, remember that this time, you have the knowledge and the skills to overcome it much more rapidly, and with far less anguish.

4. *Ask yourself* what your additional anxiety might be signaling: What's going on, perhaps out of awareness, that you may need to examine further? Consider the timing and possible triggers of your increased difficulties. Ask yourself, "What's the important 'message' in my anxiety?" If you determine there *is* one, *listen to it.*

5. Also *remember* that a certain amount of *physical sensation is normal.* Try shrugging your shoulders and reminding yourself that sensations needn't propel you into a panic attack; it's only your catastrophic thoughts in *reaction* to sensation that can do that.

6. Keep *"inoculating" yourself* against future anxiety: Deliberately produce the physical sensations that used to cause you panic over and over again. Let them become so commonplace that they truly lose their power over you.

7. Periodically *examine your life* for balance: Are you attending to your needs for physical relaxation and pleasure? For intellectual stimulation? For spiritual renewal? If not, think about remedies for the "gaps."

8. Take the resources that have been freed up, now that you're less occupied by your battles against panic, and use them toward improving your life in more enriching ways: *Have some fun!* You deserve it.

If the changes don't go smoothly despite your efforts, and you conclude that you still need medications, you resume them and plan for discontinuation later, perhaps after you've achieved some specified target goal (e.g., "after I've experienced twelve successive weeks with no panic symptoms").

Enhancing Your Success

Now you've finished the program, you've achieved the successes you sought, and you're vigorously involved in relapse prevention. The end? Perhaps.

Then again, you may find that the whole experience of coming to understand and master your panic has opened up new possibilities and generated new goals for you, goals beyond merely eliminating panic. Perhaps your work has led you to some specific plan — to return to school, to seek a new job, to mend a broken relationship. Or, with panic behind you, maybe you simply have a new-found urge and new-found confidence to set your sights higher — to strive for a more fulfilling life, a greater sense of emotional health and well-being. But how do you do that?

You might first consider your mental vision of the life you'd like to lead — how might it look different from your current life? What might it take to reshape it in that direction? Consider parts of your life that you once valued but that have fallen by the wayside. Explore ways to recapture them. Did you love bicycling but give it up when anxiety struck? Tune up your old bike. Join a biking club. Start to race.

Consider the sorts of changes that would offer you more time for yourself and your needs, more peace in your life. Hire someone to mow the lawn for you; cut back on your hours at work; say "no" to the extra requests for your time. Or perhaps trade some neutral activity for a more meaningful one: Step down from a boring committee and volunteer instead for an inspiring program that matters. Learn a meditation technique to enhance relaxation or spirituality.

Entertain ways to broaden the scope of your life, to add positives. Learn a new skill. Take a class. Explore a long-standing interest in greater depth. Join an exercise class for the chance to build friendships along with fitness. Consider all the ways you might bring more joy into your life, more passion, more thrills. Then take the first steps.

Above all, don't be afraid to dream, to imagine the possibilities, to envision the life you want and to go for it. The path you choose is wholly up to you. As for where it can lead... the sky's the limit.

Exercises for Session Twelve
I. Assessing Your Progress

A. Turn to the review list on pages 176-178. Read through the list again and this time, as you do so, rate your progress in each area using the scale below.

Rating Scale

1. I feel I've mastered this area quite thoroughly and have little or no more work to do here beyond very simple maintenance.

2. I feel I've made good progress in this area. To maintain will require my ongoing attention, efforts and practice in the area, but I don't feel it will be too difficult for me.

3. I feel I have a good understanding of this area and have made some changes, but I'm still working at it, hoping to see greater improvement in my day-to-day life.

4. I'm continuing to struggle in this area. I see some very small evidence of improvements, but I need to work extremely hard and pay very close attention to hold my own with them.

5. I'm having lots of trouble in this area. I haven't really been able to progress on my own, and I think I may need some outside help with it.

Mark your ratings according to how you feel you're doing now relative both to where you began and where you'd like to be. You can simply pencil your ratings in the margin of the book or write them into your journal along with any additional notes.

You'll notice that a rating of 1 is possible, and was included to provide an anchor point, but a rating of 2 is a wonderful achievement.

B. Your ratings offer you a profile of your current status in the different skill areas of the program. If there are areas giving you difficulty, jot down in your notebook any theories you have about them, based on your reading.

Write down at least three plans for remedying any problems and/or for continuing your progress in the areas of panic control.

II. Recognizing Successes

A. Record in your journal the three accomplishments with regard to panic control in which you take the most pride. These might involve efforts you made, new behaviors you've established (like practicing controlled breathing every day), or positive results you've experienced.

B. Now identify one success from the past few weeks relating to any arena at all, not necessarily related directly to panic.

Perhaps you dealt in a positive way with an interpersonal situation. Maybe you addressed an aspect of your life that had been troubling you. Maybe you tried some new activity for the first time ever. Or maybe you listened to your inner voice and acted on your own feelings rather than going along with someone else just to keep the peace as you might have in the past. Write about the success in your journal.

III. Self-Exploration and Nurturance

A. Pull out your journal and make a list of all the responsibilities in your life. You can write first "off the top of your head," then try mentally going through your day so that you overlook nothing. Scan your completed list and ask yourself if you see "responsibility overload" problems. If so, ask the next question: What it would take, panic issues aside, for me to feel less rushed, more serene in my life?

Now make a list of all the satisfactions and pleasures in your life. Some of these will be rather abstract (my close relationship with my friend Amy) while others will be very concrete (my undisturbed hour at the library). Scan this list and ask if it seems too brief. What would you like to have on your list that *isn't* there?

Jot down any ideas this gives you about ways to modify your life in satisfying ways. Consider some of the ideas in the chapter for making changes in your life. Read the special section to follow, especially part II that covers stress-management techniques. Browse through the self-help section of your bookstore for more ideas to help you with the endeavor.

B. Make up a three-part chart that lists all the ways you can think of to take a break if you have only five minutes available, if you have half an hour, or if you have the entire day to spend. Include items like daydreaming, washing your face, stretching from head to toe, singing a song, working a crossword puzzle, drinking a cup of tea, looking at photo albums, listening to music, calling a friend, reading a chapter of a beloved book with your feet up, taking a hot bath, going for a run in the park, writing a letter, watching TV. Think of ideas as you're doing laundry or driving to work. Be as creative as possible. Brainstorm with friends. One person's pleasure is another's misery, so be sure to make this your list and nobody else's.

Next time you need a break, try to remember your list and find a way to take one, even if it's only a five-minute "mini-break."

IV. Celebrating

Be sure you make time in the coming weeks to celebrate your work and achievements, your life, yourself. *You deserve it.*

Everyday Anxieties

Some of you may not have panic disorder per se but you're still likely to struggle with anxiety from time to time — or even every day. Going to the dentist may trigger it for you, or on-the-job pressures. Or maybe it's always a bit higher than you'd like.

The good news is that all the strategies and skills you've just learned are readily transferable to what might be termed *"everyday anxieties."* The controlled breathing (described in Session five) will reduce the physical symptoms that accompany anxiety of any type. The cognitive techniques (Session eight) can help you moderate any self-talk that contributes to your anxiety. And if you routinely experience anxiety in a specific situation, the exposure techniques of Session nine can offer you valuable help.

In addition, the framework suggested throughout the book — the emphasis on careful evaluation of the sources and triggers of your anxiety, on the ways deeper emotional issues can contribute to your fears, and on the importance of facing your feelings head-on —all will be important in mastering your "everyday anxiety" as well.

This special section considers how to manage your anxiety in two realms. First, we'll examine what can be done to control the anxiety that appears only in *particular situations,* whether predictable in advance, or those that arise without warning. Second, we'll look at ways to reduce day-to-day, *chronic* anxiety and stress.

If you've already read the preceding chapters and have systematically practiced the different techniques, you're well on your way.

Part I: Overcoming Anxiety in Specific Situations

To begin, let's assume that you feel anxious in situations where you have to talk in front of people, whether giving formal speeches or participating in less formal gatherings like monthly PTA meetings.

That was Susan's problem. Susan worked as a computer programmer for a large retail and mail-order company, loved her job and felt quite competent at it. That was a big plus for Susan, who was a bit shy and sometimes lacked confidence. If asked, she'd have admitted to some anxiety about speaking up in groups, but neither her job nor her personal life required much of it, so it didn't really present problems for her.

Then Susan was promoted unexpectedly to head of her department. The good news was that her salary took an impressive leap. The bad news, from her perspective, was that the new position involved a considerable amount of public speaking. She'd be expected to lead weekly meetings in her own department, conduct training sessions, meet periodically with the heads of other departments to provide them with updates and, worst of all, to present information formally to various company executives on a regular basis. Susan was terrified, afraid she'd actually be unable to perform her new job responsibilities and lose her promotion in disgrace. She made an appointment that very day with a psychologist who specialized in the treatment of anxiety problems.

Susan and her therapist tackled Susan's anxieties from several angles. First, Susan addressed her self-talk — mostly self-statements such as, "I am completely inept compared with everyone else in the room — and everyone will realize it the minute I open my mouth." She learned to evaluate these statements more realistically and to develop appropriate challenges to them ("I wouldn't have been promoted if my boss didn't think I could handle the job, so either he's an idiot — which he's not — or I *can* handle the job," and "Yes, the department heads know *their* departments well, but they don't know what's happening in *mine* — that's why I'm meeting with them in the first place," and "Executives are people just like me. They aren't looking for perfection, just information. And if I come to the meetings well-prepared, I can provide it.").

In addition to working on the self-talk that brought on and intensified her anxiety, Susan learned controlled breathing and SRB (Session six) to use anytime she felt anxious. She also practiced the methods daily to increase their effectiveness and to strengthen her overall resistance to anxiety.

Finally, with the help of her therapist, Susan developed a modified exposure program to conduct on her own between sessions. As part of this program, she performed at least one exposure task every day. First, she practiced at home alone, presenting information in the manner expected at work meetings. She simply made certain no one was around to hear her (which would have increased her fears tremendously), then stood at the kitchen table, speaking aloud as if she were in an actual work meeting. If she became anxious, she used SRB to relax herself physically and to refocus her attention on the task at hand.

Once Susan was less anxious with this task, she practiced her presentations into a tape-recorder, then with her husband as her "audience." Finally, for a few nights before each scheduled meeting, she stayed at work after hours to practice speaking in the setting where she'd actually make her formal presentation. In other words, Susan practiced repeatedly in situations that were increasingly close to the "real-life" situation she feared.

As you'd predict from the discussion in Session nine, Susan's repeated exposure sessions helped to gradually decrease her anxiety in public-speaking situations. In addition, since the exposures involved practicing the very skills she felt she lacked, the practice sessions improved those skills and boosted her confidence — and that helped reduce her anxiety even further.

Susan also took some time to consider in advance any features of the meeting rooms that might affect her level of comfort. She realized she'd be less anxious if she had a small podium to lean on and if the chairs were arranged in a semicircle rather than in straight rows. She asked to have the room set up accordingly.

In short, Susan's strategy was to *practice, practice, practice* in situations that gradually became more and more like the situations that actually caused her anxiety. She accompanied this practice with the *use of SRB* to calm herself physically and with ongoing attention to challenging and *modifying her negative self-talk*. And she did as much as she could to *prepare in advance;* and to *structure different aspects of the situation* to increase her level of comfort.

As one additional practice strategy, Susan used an *imagery* strategy similar to the one used by David, in Session nine. While she was driving to work, she tried to envision herself at a work meeting, presenting reports to the group and feeling anxious. She imagined "glitches" that might occur (questions she wasn't prepared to answer, inattentive listeners, or losing her train of thought), felt herself becoming even more anxious, then *imagined herself becoming relaxed* and responding in a composed fashion. This strategy provided yet another exposure opportunity for Susan, helped her to plan out how she'd handle any challenges that might arise in meetings, and allowed her to once again practice her new skills, contributing further to her new, more confident sense of herself.

Susan's first presentation was scheduled only a week after her first meeting with the therapist. She did what she could to prepare, but she also contacted her doctor and asked for a one-time prescription of medication she could take, if necessary, at the time of her talk. Her doctor was happy to prescribe for Susan (in her case, propanolol, a medication shown very effective for treating performance anxiety), but after the first meeting, she felt able to go into the meetings without it.

Susan saw the very pattern in the reduction of her anxieties that might be expected. Early on, she was fairly anxious throughout the meetings but could admit that, from an outsider's perspective, she managed to do her job quite well. Soon, she found that although she still felt anxious in advance of the meetings, once they began, she forgot her anxieties and became absorbed in her task. And after only three months, Susan announced that she not only felt fairly comfortable in most meetings, she actually *enjoyed* some of them!

Finding Your Own Strategies for Situational Anxiety

So what can you do to deal with your anxieties in specific situations? You can do just what Susan did.

On the spot, use controlled breathing and SRB to manage your reactions. These techniques offer a quick, effective strategy requiring little time to master, but, as you know already, they'll be far *more* effective if you practice daily. An alternative is to use a more extensive relaxation strategy, as discussed in Appendix II.

Alter your self-talk, catching those automatic, anxiety-boosting statements you're making to yourself and replacing them with more realistic and encouraging ones. This method, too, is one to use both at the time you experience anxiety, and to practice regularly, for added power. It's particularly important to spend some time every day evaluating your self-statements, developing positive, accurate challenges and practicing them as much as possible in *any* situation.

Over time, expose yourself gradually to the feared situation, or versions of it, as frequently as possible. This will simply help you to "get more used to it," a well-proven strategy for diminishing your fears. You'll recall that Session nine explains in detail the principles of exposure and gives numerous examples of the kinds of tasks you might develop for different situations. Remember that *imagery* is one useful way to create versions of the feared situation for exposure practices, particularly early on, before you feel quite ready for the real thing. Susan's approach is a good example of how you might do this if public speaking is your particular fear.

Evaluate carefully any aspects of the situation that contribute to your anxiety and consider whether you can *modify* any of them to ease your discomfort.

Prepare in advance as much as possible. If you have a talk to give, like Susan, be sure you've prepared well and practiced several times before the actual event. Practice in your home, into a tape recorder, with a friend or group of friends, perhaps in the actual location. The practice will help due to the "automatic" anxiety reduction that comes with repeated exposure and due to the improvement of your actual abilities (in this case, your public speaking abilities).

And *continue to modify your self-talk,* deliberately replacing old, automatic negative statements with newer, more realistic and encouraging ones — statements that, among other things, *reflect* your recognition of your new-found skills.

Situational Anxiety: Another Example
So now you've seen how the various principles and techniques of anxiety reduction you've learned in the book can be applied to public-speaking anxiety, an extremely common problem. One more example might help to illustrate how these same principles

and techniques can be used to tackle *any* situation that causes anxiety — including the ones that create trouble for *you*.

Mary is one of those lucky folks who actually experiences very little anxiety from day to day. In fact, she doesn't even mind public speaking! But, like many people, she used to be terrified at the prospect of going to the dentist. Mary had no idea how her fears arose; she only knew that since childhood, she'd found every trip to the dentist to be sheer torture.

Mary managed to limp along for years, going to the dentist as infrequently as possible and when she couldn't avoid it any longer, suffering intensely for several days in advance. But as she approached forty, she began making a number of changes in her lifestyle — eating more nutritiously, exercising regularly, breaking the TV habit. She began to feel so positive, so confident in herself that one day, swept along on a wave of exhilaration about all the wonderful changes she'd made, she decided it was high time to tackle her fear of the dentist.

Mary's first step was to learn controlled breathing and SRB. She found that those skills alone made the visits at least tolerable for her. She might have stopped there, but she was determined to overcome her fears completely — to go beyond mere *tolerance* to actual *comfort*. She decided to embark on a full-fledged fear-reduction program, using the principles and methods of anxiety-management she had learned from — of all places — a self-help book!

Initially, Mary puzzled about what aspects of the dental visits raised her anxiety most. She reviewed her last visit mentally, trying to recall exactly what she'd experienced at every step of the process. She realized that the most nerve-wracking elements for her were the smell of the dentist's office, the sound of the drill, and most of all, simply sitting still in the chair as she imagined fearsome, painful procedures to come. In fact, Mary realized after this exercise that she *produced* much of her anxiety herself with her vivid imagination.

Mary vowed at that point to put her imagination to better use — to use it for *relaxation* instead of anxiety; to *help*, rather than hurt herself. She decided to develop a soothing mental scenario to focus on during future appointments — an image to occupy her mind and help her to relax. Mary chose to imagine herself at a spa being pampered. She pictured herself stretched out on a recliner while armies of attendants tended to her — massaging her feet, manicuring her nails, and offering exotic herbal wraps. She used all her senses to elaborate on the basic scene, imagining not only the smells, sights, sounds, tastes, and physical sensations associated with it, but also her internal feelings of relaxation and peace.

Before her next visit to the dentist, Mary practiced her imagery strategy at home several times to be certain she could generate the scene when she felt intense anxiety. She sat down, relaxed, and pictured herself at the dentist. She imagined herself becoming anxious in the chair. *Then as soon as she felt anxious, she switched to the soothing scene,* using controlled breathing as she did so, and became relaxed again. If her attention strayed, she simply pulled it back to the calming scene and added a new "wrinkle" or two to recapture her interest.

Mary wasn't especially surprised at how readily she could generate anxiety simply by picturing herself at the dentist's. After all, she'd had years of practice! But she was surprised and delighted to discover that she could rapidly reverse the process by focusing intently on her soothing images. Still, how well the strategy would work during an actual visit remained to be seen.

Mary also prepared for the appointment by analyzing and altering her "pre-dental" self-talk, realistically evaluating what was likely to happen, reviewing her coping strategies, and assuring herself that this was a situation she could handle just fine, as long as she didn't scare herself with her vivid predictions of excruciating pain — pain, she reminded herself, that she'd never actually experienced.

Last of all, Mary alerted her dentist to her difficulties and, at his suggestion, decided to bring along a favorite music tape to listen to during the appointment.

Mary was certainly nervous as the date of her next appointment approached. Nevertheless, she used her self-talk determinedly, took a few extra tension-relieving walks with a friend to whom she could "unload" all her fears, and worked in a few more sessions of imagery practice. When the visit finally arrived, it went far better than she'd anticipated. In fact, Mary ended up rating her anxiety level during the visit at a 4 on a scale of 1 to 10 — way down from the 9 or 10 that usually characterized her trips to the dentist.

Even now, Mary's dental appointments are by no means her *favorite* activity, but they're vastly more tolerable than they used to be. She still prepares for each visit in advance by using *reassuring, realistic self-talk* (which each time includes mention of her increasing number of successes at the dentist's), by reviewing *controlled breathing*, and by taking any *objective steps* she can to *minimize negative aspects of the experience* (e.g., bringing along favorite music and planning to lunch with a friend after the appointment). She also practices *positive mental imagery*, which she then uses, along with controlled breathing, at the time of the appointment. She's even generated some new scenes for variety, but her original remains her all-time favorite.

Note that the imagery Mary used was an on-the-spot technique which relieved her anxiety at the time of her appointment. But it was also an exposure technique of sorts: Each time she practiced it at home, remember, she first *imagined herself in the dental chair becoming anxious*, then used her own imagery to achieve calm. She became more skilled at shifting her attention to a calming image when she felt anxious, and she gained the anxiety-reduction that comes with repeated exposure (in her case, exposure in imagination).

If Mary had been more seriously impaired by her anxieties, she might have chosen to add other elements to her preparation. *Real-life exposure*, for example, would expose her gradually to the actual situation and all the cues associated with it — the waiting room, the smells in the office, the sound of the drill, and the sight of dental tools. She might have begun by going to the dentist's office every couple of days to simply sit in the waiting area for half an hour, a strategy that — as you know from Session nine — would result over time in a decrease in anxiety in that setting. Most dentists are quite accustomed to people's fears of the dentist and are happy to assist in any way they can — it's to their advantage, after all, not to have to pry their patients off the ceiling!

Mary also might have chosen to learn one of the strategies discussed in Appendix II to lower her overall level of physical tension, perhaps meditation or a method of relaxation taught in a stress management class. These methods are valuable for their daily benefits to your physical and mental well-being as well as for anxiety reduction in specific situations. They do require effort to master in the beginning, and to practice on a regular basis. But if you choose to make the initial investment, you'll find that your time and effort will be repaid a hundredfold.

Don't Forget "The Big Three"

From the examples of Susan and Mary, and with careful consideration of your own situation, you should be able to use your newfound skills to manage and overcome your anxiety in whatever situation troubles you. Remember to think in terms of "the big three" — the three primary modes of attack included in virtually all effective programs for overcoming situational anxiety:

• address the physical elements of your anxiety through some sort of *controlled breathing technique or other physical relaxation strategy.*

• use some means of *gradual, repeated exposure to the situation,* whether in imagination or real life;

• recognize how your thoughts can raise your anxieties, and be sure to use *more positive self-talk.*

It's true, incidentally, that one strategy alone — whether controlled breathing, repeated exposure or modified self-talk — might be enough to control your anxiety, particularly if you match the strategy to the most troublesome aspect of your anxiety. But the very best approach is to include all three. Use the methods on a daily basis for greater long-term benefit and — since you'll become more skilled at using them — for more on-the-spot power. And remember to "push the limits" — to use the methods to go beyond mere tolerance of anxiety to actual comfort — maybe to the point that your anxiety stops interfering in your life for good!

A Special Case: Blood and Injection Phobias

There is one special case of situational anxiety that needs to be discussed separately, since a good strategy for coping with it is quite different than those you've learned for other fears. If you have an intense fear of blood or of injections, and you're suddenly confronted with either, you may faint (from a sudden drop in blood pressure that occurs). The *fear* of fainting is quite common in panic, but blood and injection phobias are the only circumstances in which fainting is likely to really happen.

If, in the past, you've fainted in response to injections or the sight of blood and you continue to feel fearful in their presence, the most useful coping strategy in future situations is to tense all your muscles by clenching your fists very hard. This will cause a rise in blood pressure and should prevent any problems.

It's also very effective to lie down and elevate your feet (i.e., before you receive an injection); but where that's not practical, clenching your fists should be a valuable strategy.

When Situational Anxiety Is Less Predictable

What if you become anxious in various situations, but the situations that trouble you are *different* from one occasion to the next? You're not anxious all the time, only now and then, but when a situation does make you nervous, you wish you had better ways to cope with it.

There are three general classes of situations that can arise less predictably and give you trouble: First, there are the situations for which you have some advance warning, yet still the situations are somewhat unique (unlike trips to the dentist, or work meetings, or other events that come up repeatedly). Second, there are situations that take you by surprise. And third, there are situations that cause stress once the event has ended. Let's tackle each one in turn.

When you have advance warning. Sometimes, you'll face tough situations that you know in advance are likely to be stressful for you — an unfamiliar situation (e.g., visiting a new community), a task that stretches your capabilities to the limit (e.g., a new job assignment), a situation you had difficulty with at some time in the past (e.g., dealing with an "unfavorite" relative). In these cases, where you can anticipate a potentially stressful situation ahead of time, *advance preparation* is a good tactic for reducing your anxiety.

Susan illustrated this principle in overcoming her public-speaking fears, but it's equally applicable to one-time situations. If you can prepare yourself in advance by gathering information, planning well, and practicing appropriately, you'll go into the situation more confidently, simply from the knowledge that you're prepared. And your preparation is likely to ensure greater success, adding to your confidence and lessening your anxieties even more.

You're probably already intuitively aware of this anxiety-reduction strategy. If your son started college last fall, for example, you may have helped him feel less fearful about it by visiting the campus with him in advance, so he could become more familiar with the area. You probably encouraged him to learn as much as he could about college life before his departure. You may have even suggested to him that he consider in advance the challenges he might face there, so he could plan how he might handle them. And that was good advice — good for your son in his situation, good for you in yours.

Perhaps you're nervous about going into your second grader's school to help with a classroom project for the first time. Again, take any steps you can think of to deal with the different aspects of the experience in advance. Drive to the school and locate the classroom ahead of time. Ask your daughter or her teacher or another parent any questions you may have about the project, or the classroom, or the teacher's expectations. If you have to demonstrate something to the class, practice it once or twice the evening before. Every single thing you can find out, plan for, and practice in advance is one less thing to worry about when you actually face the situation "for real."

Your preparation for a difficult situation can include not only *objective* preparation — increasing your store of information and skills for handling the actual demands of the situation — but also *advance work on your self-talk.* In Session eight, for example, you learned about reducing your anxiety before entering situations where you feared a possible panic attack. You can use those same ideas to prepare in advance for *any* situation you expect to raise your anxiety. And of course, it's always a help to review and practice the *controlled breathing and SRB* that you'll likely want to use once you enter the situation.

When situations take you by surprise. What about the anxiety-producing situations that arise without warning, or for which there really doesn't seem to be any way to prepare? Perhaps you become anxious in a whole variety of situations, but the settings aren't the same — which seems to rule out the strategies Susan and Mary used so well — and you just don't see any way to get ready for *all* the different situations in advance.

In this case, you're in a better position to tackle your difficulties than you might realize. First, *analyze the circumstances* of your increased anxiety across several of the situations to see if there are any common factors responsible for the anxiety. If so, try to *address those* (more about that in the next section).

Try to *evaluate your self-talk* and take steps to adjust it appropriately. At first, this may be something you'll need to do after the fact, not at the precise time you're feeling so anxious. But once you have a better understanding of the kind of self-statements that regularly get you into trouble (most of us have our own "favorites") and you've worked out and practiced some challenges to them, you'll be able to use this strategy more effectively on the spot. You may want to review Session eight for a more detailed discussion of this approach.

Learn controlled breathing, practice it on a regular basis, and *use SRB* at the time anxiety strikes. Finally, study the next section and *adopt some of the general stress-management strategies* you find there. They can help you reduce your overall level of tension and thereby become more resistant to those intermittent increases in anxiety.

When situational anxiety hits "after the fact." What if you feel stressed and anxious because of a situation that's *already occurred* — a conflict with a friend or a rough day at work for example — or because of a difficult *ongoing* situation that sends you home every night nervous and upset? To help you feel calmer in these situations, try this two-step procedure: *First,* take some time away from the scene to *analyze* the situation. You can do this "in your head," by talking with a trusted friend or by writing in your journal. Consider the *objective issues,* your *self-talk,* and your *goals* in the situation, and *plan out* your responses accordingly.

Suppose, for example, that you're feeling overwhelmed because you have far too much to do in your job as a supervisor. To analyze this situation, you might list all the tasks that you face and your concerns about each one (e.g., *This* task has to be completed by Tuesday and I'm short-staffed; I'm dreading *this* one because the person I'll be working with on it is so unpleasant; and I'm tensed up about initiating *this* job because I'm sure my staff are all going to hate me for it). Then you might figure out a schedule for the tasks, including some decisions about how you'll handle each of the particular dilemmas, and some positive self-talk where it's needed.

Once you've completed this "sorting out" process, move to the *second step:* "Get away" mentally and physically from your preoccupation with the situation. Accept that you've done all you can; you have your responses planned, both internal and external. Don't allow yourself to keep ruminating. Use SRB to stop the mental wheel spinning and follow it up with something absorbing or very relaxing, ideally something that doesn't *permit* you to keep fretting — dinner with a friend, a rousing game of indoor soccer with your youngsters, or listening to music while your visual imagery transports you to a serene, far-away place.

If you simply try to escape a stressful situation without first sorting through your feelings, you're likely to continue to feel stressed and anxious. You may find it hard to concentrate on anything or to sleep that night. Those issues on your mind will keep nagging at you, demanding to be "heard." But once you've worked through them mentally, figuring out a plan for them and dealing with your self-talk in a more positive manner, you'll be freer to move forward. You'll still need determination to say to yourself, "No, I'm not going to think about this anymore." But you'll be in a better position to do so, knowing you've done all you can at this point to solve the dilemma.

Part II: Overcoming Day-to-Day Anxiety and Stress

You now have a set of strategies to use against anxiety that arises *situationally*. But what if you *always* feel tense and anxious, no matter what the situation? This section summarizes techniques you can use to reduce the *ongoing* level of stress and anxiety in your life, whether stress is a problem for you only during an occasional rough week or during every week of the year. Where do you start? You start at the beginning, of course, with a step that's often overlooked but is critically important in helping you to zero in directly on the factors most important in your anxiety picture.

Analyzing Your Situation

Once again, the very first, all-important step to take is to thoroughly, thoughtfully analyze your situation to determine the primary sources of the stress in your life. Why is this step so important? It's important because the best way to plot your way out of anxiety and stress is to understand as clearly as possible the circumstances that put you there in the first place —the *thinking* ("I know I'm go going to mess this up and the whole day will be a disaster!"); the *habits* (hunching over your desk all tensed up till you have a whopping headache; saying "yes" to every request that comes your way); the *practical circumstances* (living with a man who drinks too much; having barely enough money to make your bills each month; working two jobs and having no time for friends); and even *the early emotional history* (being raised in a family of overanxious worriers; having experienced a succession of painful losses as a youngster; having been mistreated or neglected) that contribute to your ongoing struggles.

You might begin your analysis by talking through your feelings with a friend or family member or therapist, or by sitting down alone to quietly ponder your situation. Better yet, start by keeping a journal for a couple of weeks, making notes every day of *how you felt* at different points throughout the day, *your major activities* — including interactions you have with significant people in your life, and *any other observations* and thoughts you have about what may be affecting your stress level that day. Don't forget to include potentially relevant *physical factors* — a late night, excessive fatigue, heavy alcohol use, the menstrual cycle, or that bad cold you caught the day after you were feeling so inexplicably lousy and stressed.

Just what accounts for most of your feelings of tension may well be obvious at the end of two weeks or even sooner. But if not, analyzing your journal systematically, noting what sorts of activities or interactions or thinking patterns were occurring when you felt most stressed, should give you some pretty good ideas.

Once you understand the factors that increase your anxiety, you're ready to tackle them with the different methods available to you — and you can tailor the methods you pick to your unique situation for the greatest possible impact.

Looking for Solutions to Specific Life Problems

Many times, anxieties arise in response to a very specific problem, and in those cases, working to solve the problem can offer the most rapid and effective "cure" for the anxiety. After all, if you're anxious because you're standing in the middle of the road and there's a truck bearing down on you, you don't use controlled breathing to reduce your anxiety — you get out of the way just as fast as you can! A job change, a new way of handling a difficult child, efforts to strengthen a deteriorating relationship — all are examples of practical maneuvers that target specific problems in your life and can diminish at least some of the anxiety you've been experiencing.

Even when there's no possible "cure" for a problem you identify, looking for ways to tackle the specific stresses it creates can still be the most efficient and effective approach. Suppose, for example, you're experiencing high levels of stress related to raising a developmentally disabled daughter — worrying about her and her future, feeling sorrow about her circumstances, and trying to cope with all the practical implications of the situation. Though you can't change the basic facts of the situation, there still are ways to reduce the stress and anxiety associated with it. A support group for parents of children with disabilities, for example, can offer you immense relief by providing a place to talk about your feelings and reactions, to share practical information, and to consider how best to cope in this objectively tough situation.

This raises an important point: In a difficult life situation, it's easy to feel as though you have absolutely no options, no choices, no ways whatsoever with which you can alter or influence the situation. It's important to challenge those beliefs as vigorously as you can. *Start by assuming that you do have choices.* You might, for example, be miserable and lonesome in your marriage to a critical, controlling man, but feel as though you have to stay in the marriage because raising your two teenaged sons alone would be virtually impossible for you. Paradoxically, recognizing that you *could* leave, but that you choose not to for some very compelling reasons, can actually ease somewhat the stress of staying. As stressful as pure misery is, feeling absolutely, inescapably trapped in it can be even more stressful.

And recognize that there are always several options in a tough situation, not just an either-or choice (leave altogether or stay in the situation just as it is). Look for "mid-range" options, in particular. Some, for example, might stay in an unfulfilling marriage but look for other sources of satisfaction in friendships or hobbies; others might enter personal counseling; still others might try to strengthen the positive aspects of the otherwise difficult marriage. Broadening the range of options you consider only increases your chance of hitting on some ways to at least make your circumstances more tolerable.

When it looks as though you can't change a bad situation (or when the consequences of doing so would be too disastrous in other ways), *consider different ways to react to it.* If your mother is extremely critical of you, for example, you may very well not be able to change her behavior. In fact, continuing to try — and continuing to be amazed when she *doesn't* change — might well be a lesson in how *not* to reduce stress! But try working on your *internal* responses to her, perhaps modifying your self-talk to recognize that your mother's criticisms reflect her contrariness, not some inadequacy in you.

Perhaps you can alter some aspect of the *environment* in a helpful way, for example, limiting the amount of time you spend with your mother, or trying to see her in situations where she can focus on a preplanned activity. You might well choose to tell her how you feel, but if you do, make sure that your goal is just that —

to tell her how you feel; the goal of trying to change her, remember, can be a painful, frustrating trap for you.

Finally, you might work to reduce the *impact* of a tough situation, with strategies that offer you general support or help to build up your resistance — joining a support group or learning some form of meditation, for example.

Using General Stress-Reduction Strategies

In addition to addressing specific stressful situations, there are several general strategies *useful in lowering stress and anxiety.* Begin by selecting strategies that most closely match the factors that play the biggest role in your stress. You'll be able to reduce your anxiety and stress even further by gradually making several of the strategies a regular part of your life — perhaps all of them! As with panic itself, some methods are of the "quick fix" variety while others offer long-term solutions. (And many, such as the use of relaxation, can provide both a short-term remedy for on-the-spot stress and, with regular practice, can also begin to have a more extensive and consistent impact.)

Since stress and anxiety always have an impact on your body, physical methods of stress management are a good place to begin.

Physical Methods of Stress-reduction

You're already well aware that anxiety expresses itself physically, and that finding ways, like controlled breathing, to calm yourself physically can have a powerful impact on that anxiety. Indeed, learning and practicing some physical means of relaxing your body should be one aspect of your stress-reduction program. (Again, Appendix II may offer you some ideas.)

For chronic feelings of anxiety, relaxation or meditation strategies can be particularly helpful. *Which* strategy you select is probably far less important than actually learning a method, learning it well and making it a part of your everyday routine. You can even invent your own if you wish — simply sitting for five or ten minutes breathing slowly and deeply, relaxing your muscles, and imagining a deeply peaceful scene can do the trick.

In addition to developing the formal relaxation habit, following healthy habits in general will help to increase your resistance to stress and anxiety. Adequate rest, a nutritious diet and regular exercise may seem dull, but they're important. Just as fatigue can increase vulnerability to panic attacks, it can also increase susceptibility to anxiety in general — and increase your feelings of demoralization or irritability, which can further amplify the stress in your life. Cutting out caffeine can reduce anxiety levels for some people. And exercise not only improves your health and stamina, it relieves tension and creates an overall positive feeling to carry you through difficult times with greater ease.

Walking is one form of exercise that can be particularly effective at relieving stress. Besides the fitness it provides, it can offer solitude, a chance to organize your thoughts, and a break from the intrusions of life. Walking with a friend can boost your spirits and provide an opportunity for both fitness and friendship. For some, too, simply being outside is restful.

The important thing, of course, is not what form of exercise you choose, but that rather, that you try your best to incorporate it into your life on a regular basis. For some people, subscribing to one of the health or lifestyle magazines that emphasize walking (such as *Prevention* magazine) helps to inspire enthusiasm and keep determination alive. The tips found in Session twelve may give you further ideas about "staying on track."

There's one more "physical" strategy that's useful in helping maintain a comfortably low level of tension from day to day. Pick a regular point in your day, perhaps midway through, and take a moment to mentally "scan" your body for physical tension. If you identify any, relax it away using whatever method works for you. This quick, simple daily strategy can help to prevent the build-up of tension and fatigue which, by the *end* of the day, can be so much more entrenched and difficult to eliminate.

Finally, if you suspect, or know, that you have problems controlling your alcohol use, you need to take steps to address that problem before you do anything else. Otherwise, your drinking will simply create stress in your life faster that you can undo it, no matter what other strategies you may try. An evaluation with an alcohol counselor is an excellent starting point, or if that's not practical, almost every community has an AA chapter available to help.

Expressing Feelings and Seeking Emotional Support

Now that you have the physical side of your tensions and anxieties under control, what about the emotional side? It's a truism, perhaps, that keeping things "bottled up inside" isn't good for you but, like many truisms — it's true! Finding ways to express your feelings is an important part of keeping stress and anxiety at a manageable level.

That doesn't mean that, if you're furious with someone, it's always a great idea to spill all your feelings to that person on the spot — though sometimes it may be. As with any decision, you need to consider the consequences to you and to the relationship of speaking up or staying silent. But having a safe place *somewhere* to "unload," to talk about what you're feeling, is crucial to everyone.

"Unloading" may mean talking to a trusted friend or relative or speaking with someone in your church, or seeking out a therapist or even writing in your journal. The "who" and "where" are up to you, but find some means of expressing what's on your mind, what's in your heart.

Anger can be a potent stress-producer and is a complex, sizable topic all by itself. If chronic fuming is a problem for you, tackling it can have a marked impact on your level of stress. Fortunately, you can apply the strategies you've already mastered quite successfully to the situations that have you steaming. Try to analyze what it is that's most upsetting to you about a situation. Consider what you want to achieve and use some problem-solving to try to get there. Evaluate the realism and usefulness of your self-talk about the issue. Challenge any self-statements that may be making the problem worse for you, increasing your frustration and rumination. Use physical relaxation or exercise to relieve some of your bodily reactions. And talk out your feelings with a friend.

In fact, whatever the situation, we now know without a doubt that *social support* is crucial to mental and even physical health. If you feel you lack this all-important feature in your life, expanding your social network may be an important goal to consider.

Setting Limits

When was the last time you took a full day off from all your responsibilities and worries? If not a full day, what about half a day? An hour? Even ten minutes??? It's easy to get so wrapped up in the demands of life — jobs, homes, children, partners and friends, churches, social groups — that time off somehow gets squeezed out, put off, totally forgotten. But never taking a break can begin to take a serious toll on you.

That's probably not news to you. If your life has become all too hectic for comfort, you probably recognize quite clearly that you need to "slow down" — but you also may feel it's just not possible.

For many people, reducing the demands they face from day to day is one of the most important elements in reducing stress. It does take determination and courage to make the choices and set the limits necessary to reduce daily demands, but consider the alternatives. Is it worse to have to call the PTA president and decline to help with the next fund-raiser, or to give up three nights of your free (your *not*-so-free) time and have to squeeze all that you had planned for *those* nights into your busy weekend? Is it harder to miss out on the political meeting your best friend urged you to attend, or to go to work the next day exhausted and stressed because you stayed up late doing neglected laundry, missed the only TV show you really enjoy, and forgot to pack your lunch?

To begin making some improvements in this arena — and as an instructive, perhaps startling exercise — try making a list of all the responsibilities in your life, all the activities that occupy your time, daily, weekly, monthly and seasonally. (If you made a similar list for exercise IIIB following Session twelve, use that list as a starting point.) Make the list as specific, detailed, and all-inclusive as you can. Organize the items by category — work, family, home life, outside activities, personal goals — whatever system best fits your specific circumstances. Then prioritize the items within each category both by their importance to you and by "necessity." (If you'd lose your job by omitting a certain activity performed at work, for example, it's probably high on the list.)

Now for the really hard part — the part that's crucial to reducing stress: Start to ask yourself what *could* be eliminated — dropped altogether, delegated to someone else, or deferred to another time in your life. (Do you absolutely *have* to organize your children's baby books right now — or can you wait till Jim and Susan are in high school, and you have more free time?) Brainstorm a little, talk to your partner or a friend, be flexible in your thinking. Review the comments about choices and options on pages 209-210. Don't rule out anything at this stage. Ask yourself, "What would happen if I were unexpectedly hospitalized, and I actually *couldn't* do this task? Would the world come to an end?"

Once you decide how you'd like to cut the list down, what new limits you'd like to set, then comes the challenge of actually doing so. That may mean simply learning to live more comfortably with some undone tasks — a less clean house, for example. More often, it involves saying no to others' requests for your time. It's a challenging task, often difficult, but well worth the reward.

Remember, when you set limits, when you say no to a request — when you make a choice that's a positive one for you — you don't need to explain or apologize for it. Learn and practice the phrase, "I wish I could help out, but I'm afraid I just can't. Sorry." Requests that take you by surprise can be especially hard to handle, so try out this response, too: "I'll need to check my calendar (think about it, talk with my spouse); I'll call you later tonight to let you know." That response will give you a chance to think about what you really want to do — and if your choice is to refuse, to practice that first phrase till you can say it firmly, and with finality.

If setting limits and refusing requests is especially tough for you (which then surely contributes to your stress and anxiety), pick up the book *Your Perfect Right* (R. E. Alberti and M. L. Emmons) and do some work on your assertive skills. Setting limits is a skill that will continue to be important your entire life, important in helping you achieve the kind of life you desire. And like so many stress-management skills, the investment you make in learning to set limits more comfortably now will pay off handsomely right away *and* in the years to come.

Setting limits to reduce the demands in your life again touches on the issue of self-talk. (Doesn't everything!) For example, it's harder to refuse to help out at your child's school, even if you're feeling swamped and anxious and really *want* to refuse, if you're unintentionally sabotaging your efforts with self-statements like, "I can't say no; the teacher will think I don't care about my son's education." The next section will address the self-talk issue further.

Self-Talk — Again!

You're certainly aware of how self-talk can elevate your anxiety in a given situation, but have you identified the self-talk that may be creating increased stress on an *ongoing* basis? As they examine their thinking, chronically stressed people often find that there are some self-statements they make on a habitual basis that increase their sense of pressure. "I have to do it perfectly; I can never make a mistake," is a common one. So is, "I'm the one responsible for handling this, and if I don't get it done right, it'll be a disaster!"

Life should be fair," is another that can keep you fuming and tense. You can probably add some more of your own.

In fact, when you analyzed your life circumstances, looking for the factors important in your day-to-day stress, you may well have identified some decidedly unhelpful self-talk. If you struggle with unpredictable situational anxiety, you may have discovered that even though the situations that bring anxiety are different, there are some common self-statements that you're making across different situations. Or you may have realized that you're always operating under the burden of some particular unhelpful self-statements. If you haven't yet become aware of self-talk as a factor in your ongoing stress, carefully consider whether you may be overlooking some. It's unusual for those who struggle with stress not to struggle with critical, demanding self-statements as well. And modifying them can diminish your stress levels immensely.

Review Session eight to help you better identify the negative self-talk that's creating pressure and tension in your life. For many people, altering self-talk is the most difficult, but, in the long run, the single most useful strategy there is to control stress better. Because once you're no longer a slave to the demands of that critical, demanding inner voice, oftentimes the other pieces of life just fall into place.

Taking Breaks and Having Fun
Finally, one last stress-reduction strategy that's downright fun to consider. What is it? Taking breaks and having fun, of course! Taking a break can be used as an on-the-spot technique to interrupt stress as it mounts, and as a regular approach to keep stress lower in the first place.

Consider how you feel on the days when you go full tilt all day long with no breaks at all. Now try to recall a time, if you can, when you interrupted your workday with periodic short breaks. It's likely that in the second case, you felt better throughout the day, felt less exhausted by the end of it, accomplished more, and built up less anxiety and stress besides. It's pretty clear that you feel better and function better when you take occasional breaks. But it's harder to remember that fact — and to act on it — when you're in the midst of your day, faced with a list of responsibilities that's impossibly long.

Taking a full day off to relax and enjoy yourself is certainly lovely
— and highly recommended. But a break doesn't have to be a full
day, a half-day, or even a full hour to be of value. Learning to give
yourself *short* breaks, the brief respites that refresh and renew you in
just a few minutes' time, can noticeably reduce your overall stress.

Check back over exercise IIIB following Session twelve, which
instructed you to generate a list of possible "break-time" activities and
offered several examples of good five-minute breaks. If you haven't
completed the exercise, do it now. Then post your list in a prominent
place in your home and use the ideas any time you sense stress
beginning to mount, or better yet, before it happens. The "Special
Help" Summary on page 217 contains further strategies to try.

To work even a brief break into your day sometimes takes every
bit of ingenuity you possess, but keep at it. In a sense, the more
difficult it is to make time for a break, the more evidence you have
of just how badly you need one! Suppose, for example, that you've
taken the afternoon off work to take a "shift" caring for your ill
father in his home. Your four-year-old twins are with you because
you felt too guilty to leave them at the sitter's. You've been at it for
two hours already, you're exhausted and cranky, and your sister
isn't due to relieve you for another hour. How could you possibly
take a break in this situation, much as you might need to?

What about a cup of tea in the living room for you, with cookies
in the kitchen for the kids? Or ten minutes with your feet up in an
easy chair while Dad naps and the children watch TV? A brisk
walk around the block with your children might revive you if your
father can be left alone for a time. What about setting up a lawn
chair in the backyard and daydreaming in the sunshine for ten
minutes while the kids make a game of picking up sticks in the
yard? A phone call to a friend to let off steam and bask in her
sympathies? Five minutes of jumping around and being silly with
the kids? Anything that "changes the scene" for even a few
minutes can be a big help.

You can also use breaks to keep stress levels low by building in
a regular break as part of your daily routine. This may mean
adopting a certain time of the day as your "break time" and using
the time for whatever sounds appealing to you that day. Check
your list if you can't think of anything.

Or you might consider adopting a *specific*, unvarying routine as a
regular part of your day — reading the paper for fifteen minutes in

Self-Soothing Strategies for Anxiety Prevention and Reduction

Strategies for self-soothing can help you recover after a distressing interchange or simply renew your spirits at the end of a busy day. They can help you to maintain a steady, serene frame of mind and in that way, increase your resilience in the face of stress.

Use the following list of ideas as a starting point. Consider them all, try out a few and develop your own personal list to draw upon when you most need to bring peace and comfort into your life.

1. Recall a particular event from your past that captured feelings of being cherished and comforted, or of mastery and strength. Simply enjoy the recollection without trying to achieve any particular goal.

2. Go biking or running or attend an exercise class. Work up a spectacular sweat, take a hot shower, then collapse onto your bed and savor the feelings of fatigue and relaxation in your muscles.

3. Devote some time to aimless pottering about — time spent with absolutely no goals in mind.

4. Hug a cherished stuffed animal, or in some other way connect with an object associated with a secure time in your life.

5. Arrange for an hour — or even fifteen minutes — of total solitude. If you wish to, use it to meditate using whatever method you find most calming.

6. Throw a pot, perform a hand craft you enjoy or cook something just for the pleasure of it.

7. Go for a drive and empty your mind of everything but the sights and sounds around you or enjoy whatever thoughts drift through.

8. Leaf through a photo album and reminisce about some of the funny, warm times you've had.

9. Go through some harmless routine you enjoy: Make a cup of tea and drink it while sitting in your favorite chair with your favorite quilt over your legs. Draw calm from the regularity of the routine, as well as from its content.

10. Invent a delightful daydream and savor it thoroughly, beginning to end.

Permission granted to reprint. From *Master Your Panic* ©2004 by Denise F. Beckfield, Ph.D. Impact Publishers, Inc., Atascadero, California.

the morning when no one else is awake, taking a short walk each noon, perhaps watching the 6:00 news every evening — watching it live at 6:00 if that's what fits your routine best, or maybe videotaping it to watch after the kids are in bed. In these cases, the activity itself reduces stress and, in addition, the sheer fact of the routine, over time, can add to the relaxation and comfort it provides. As in the case of children's bedtime rituals, it's not just the warm bath or the pj's and story that are soothing; the routine itself adds to the feeling of security and calm. Treat yourself like a kid for a change. Create a cozy ritual for yourself. Give yourself a break.

Aim for brief breaks, both regularly and when you need them. But try for a longer break on occasion, too. Granted, it's much tougher arranging for a half-day of free time than for five minutes, but it's well worth the effort. Be as creative as you can. If you have young children and need a break, but you can't afford or don't feel comfortable hiring a sitter, consider an exchange with a friend who's also feeling stressed ("You watch my kids one Saturday, I'll watch yours the next.") If you can find a sitter but money is tight, ask yourself if you can cut the budget somewhere else. Call on a relative. Put yourself first for a change.

Most people think of *relaxation* as the opposite of tension but laughter, too, can be a great antidote to stress and anxiety. Watching a hilarious movie is a great way to relieve stress and renew your spirits.

And if you're feeling that the fun has gone out of your life, slipped away somehow when you weren't looking, it may be time to analyze the problem and recapture the fun. Then, too, it can be difficult to have fun when you're weighed down with the burdens of panic and anxiety. By tackling those, you may already have taken the most important step yet in solving the problem!

Moving Ahead

You're now aware of several general methods for reducing your overall level of stress and anxiety: Pay attention to your physical well-being, including regular exercise in your day; scan for physical tension daily and adopt some sort of regular strategy for tension reduction; find ways to express your feelings and obtain emotional support; set limits and make adjustments to reduce the number of demands in your life; keep working on your self-talk as it relates to your stress and anxiety; and find ways, both on a regular basis and "as needed," to take breaks and "get away from it all." Reading this section, you've probably come up with other strategies of your own.

In addition to general strategies, you have strategies to apply if anxiety in particular situations troubles you. And you know that it's important to keep using your strategies every day, and to ask for help if you need it.

It's as simple (!) as that. One other important reminder: Be sure to note your successes. Because with all the hard work you've done and all your new knowledge and understanding, with all the challenges you've overcome and all your wonderful plans, you're sure to have plenty to celebrate!

Troubleshooting: Controlled Breathing

At times, people have difficulty using controlled breathing to achieve reductions in physical symptoms. This appendix describes common dilemmas you may encounter and suggests remedies for them. Even if you're doing well with your breathing practice, reading through the examples is worth your time, since it can give you good ideas to improve your success.

Dilemma #1: "I just can't seem to do controlled breathing."

Occasionally, chronic overbreathers find it difficult to get air into the lower 25 percent of their lungs. Shallow breathing has simply become such an entrenched style that it's difficult to change. If this is true for you, there are several remedies to try.

First, spend ten minutes twice a day for a few days practicing controlled breathing, lying on the floor face down with both hands under your head. This position in and of itself results in abdominal breathing for most people.

Next, try controlled breathing while lying flat on your back. Continue to focus on "ballooning" your stomach as you inhale and to lace your hands over your abdomen as a check that the air is going down into the lower portion of your lungs.

You might also try adding some imagery to help you. Imagine, for example, that your body is a hollow cavity and imagine yourself slowly drawing the air down through your chest into your stomach, then farther down into the pelvic area, and down farther yet into your thighs and ultimately down to your very toes. Or imagine that you want to fill your belly with helium almost to the point of bursting, till you nearly "lift off" the floor and rise up into the air. Experiment with images of your own invention that help you to pull air deep down into your abdominal cavity. (Your imagination could have fun with this!)

As you focus on your *manner* of breathing with the above strategies, don't forget also to continue *timing* your inhalations and exhalations, taking four full seconds to inhale, four to exhale. On rare occasions, in their efforts to achieve abdominal breathing, people find themselves taking large breaths, but from the *upper* chest —thoracic breathing. If at the same time they unintentionally *speed* their breathing, they may end up taking huge, rapid, gasping breaths and overbreathing even more than usual — the exact reverse of their goal. Remember, it's important *both* that the breathing be slow *and* that it extend to the bottom of the lungs; remember to monitor both position and timing of your breathing during your practices.

Many studies of people with medical problems affecting their lungs do suggest that, oftentimes, slowing the breathing will deepen it somewhat automatically. So some extra attention to "slowing down" as you practice your controlled breathing may solve the "deep" problem without any additional efforts on your part.

If continued practice on your own doesn't seem to help, finding someone to assist you is a good idea. Physical therapists typically are skilled at teaching breathing strategies, as are mental health professionals who frequently treat anxiety disorders. You can call your physician, a medical clinic, or a mental health center to inquire about resources available in your area. Or you can contact the Anxiety Disorders Association of America (ADAA), using the address provided in Appendix V, to get names of professional members in your area who specialize in the treatment of anxiety.

Finally, you may decide to learn an alternative strategy for reducing physical arousal level, an option discussed in Appendix II.

Above all, remember that learning controlled breathing is like learning any new skill, whether it's riding a bicycle, keyboarding or driving a manual-transmission car. It may feel foreign and difficult at the outset but, with practice, can become almost second nature.

So keep practicing, try to resist discouragement and, by all means, seek outside help if you need it. The results will be well worth it.

Dilemma #2: "I tune into my body and that frightens me."

Occasionally, people become anxious when they first try controlled breathing because the reduction in "background noise" makes internal events more noticeable to them, raising their anxiety level. Joe consulted a therapist for help overcoming his long-standing panic attacks. In addition to the attacks themselves, Joe, like many panic sufferers, struggled with multiple worries about his health — the combined legacy of a nervous, overprotective mother, a somewhat sensitive temperament, the symptoms of the attacks themselves, and a painful loss during his youth. (A beloved uncle's sudden death had taught Joe just how disastrous the results of serious medical problems could be.)

The first few attempts Joe made to practice controlled breathing were quite difficult for him. The problem: When Joe stretched out in his recliner and lay quietly, he suddenly became aware of "extra" heartbeats (physicians call these preventricular contractions — PVCs).

Joe had been to his physician — several times in fact. She'd assured him of his good health and sound heart. She told him that his occasional PVCs were no cause for alarm. They might be happening slightly more often when he lay quietly because of a slower heart rate at that time, or because of his heightened anxiety just then. But chances were best, she felt, that they were happening at the same frequency as usual for Joe, but were simply more noticeable and striking because he *was* so quiet and still. Had he been active and occupied, he might not have even realized when they occurred.

It took much courage and persistence, but Joe forced himself to continue his practice sessions. Despite his anxieties, he soon was able to master the technique and eventually even to become comfortable with it. Ultimately he overcame his panic attacks and felt calmer on a day-to-day basis.

Joe's PVCs are only one example of the physical events and sensations that happen in our bodies all the time. A sudden pain shoots through the temple, then disappears; your stomach gurgles or "drops" with a sudden, swooping sensation; you feel a dull ache in your chest; your face flushes; your hands tingle briefly. You usually don't know the reason for the events, and you may think nothing of them — if you even notice them in the first place.

At times when you're quiet and more "tuned in" to your body, though, these events are more noticeable. They capture your attention because there's so little else to override it. If you then respond to them with instant alarm and further spiraling of symptoms — as panic sufferers are prone to do — increased anxiety can easily be the result.

In fact, this reaction to controlled breathing, though not typical, is a perfect example of how physical sensation can lead to panic if the process is not interrupted. Controlled breathing is one central element of an effective interruption strategy.

But what do you do if, like Joe, you find that the cure makes the disease worse? What if controlled breathing actually *increases* feelings of anxiety, due to heightened awareness of internal events?

First off, if you haven't seen a physician and you have specific concerns about physical symptoms, by all means, consult your doctor. It's probably safe to assume you've already done so, right? And he or she has assured you that you're in good health? In that case, the *single very best strategy to follow is to persist in the breathing practice,* realizing that your tolerance will increase rapidly, and you'll soon be comfortable with (and receiving benefits from) the procedure.

In fact, as you'll learn in Session nine and again in Session ten, it's doubly important that you practice every day, twice a day, and for at least four minutes at a stretch. Practicing only intermittently or breaking off practice *because* you feel uncomfortable is *not* helpful.

Consider whether there are slight modifications that can help you to feel more comfortable with the practice. Practicing when someone else is in the house may be helpful, since it addresses worries about experiencing genuine health problems while alone. After you've become comfortable in the presence of another person, be sure to take the next step and begin to practice when you're alone, till you're equally comfortable with that.

Another modification that can help is to select a specific relaxing image to use during your practices. Make the image as detailed and vivid as you can and engage all your senses. An image of yourself lying on a beach, for example, could include the sensation of warmth from the sun on your skin, the sound of waves in the background, the smell of the water, feelings of heaviness in your body — everything you can imagine.

Each time you practice the controlled breathing, fix the image in your mind. Whenever your attention wanders to a physical symptom, pull it firmly back to the image. This refocusing of attention, incidentally, is an extremely useful skill that will be used more directly in Session six, so building up your "attention-focusing muscles" will help you later as well.

If you continue to feel anxious during the breathing practice and you're skeptical about the wisdom of continuing it, try this experiment: Practice the breathing conscientiously for ten days, twice a day. Keep track of your practices in your journal and rate your overall anxiety level on a scale of 1 to 10 at the end of every practice session. You should see the anxiety drop quite reliably by the end of the ten days.

It's hard to force yourself, true. But remember: Your doctor assures you that you're healthy; the anxiety about physical symptoms is an integral part of your anxiety disorder; and you want desperately to overcome the agony of panic attacks. This is the way to do it.

Finally, if you ever encounter any unforeseen difficulty in following the program, consider contacting a qualified professional to guide you through it. The more you feel your progression through the program is atypically rocky, the more valuable such outside help can be.

Dilemma #3: "I need to be in control."

Sometimes people feel fearful of "losing control" when they become relaxed during controlled breathing practice. The solution is similar to that for Dilemma #2: In essence, hang in there, tolerate the feeling, and discover for yourself that *it won't happen.* In Session eight, you learned about other strategies (challenging your self-talk) to help moderate those fears. But the best way is simply to do it and do it and do it again. The anxiety *will* diminish.

Someone who's been sexually abused is particularly likely to experience this dilemma. For them, relaxation can raise frightening feelings of vulnerability. Generally speaking, controlled breathing as a relaxation strategy is less likely to arouse these feelings than some of the more meditation-like methods. Oftentimes, using the method while sitting up with eyes open is enough to minimize the negative reactions and allow the method to diminish anxiety as intended.

There are other strategies that can help, too: Assure yourself that conditions are safe *before* you begin your practice each time. You can do this verbally, reminding yourself that you're in charge of the practice session and that you're doing something positive for yourself. You might also attend to any external features to help you feel safe. (Some people feel safer practicing in the presence of others, for example, while others feel safer alone; some women find that locking the doors helps their sense of security.).

While it can be tremendously difficult at first, you'll gradually discover that it's possible to relax and *not* have bad things happen. And in fact, breaking the connection between relaxation and vulnerability can be extremely therapeutic *and* helpful in your ultimate aim of overcoming panic.

If your history has been especially difficult and injurious, going through the program in partnership with a therapist whom you trust is highly recommended.

Dilemma #4: "Emotions are getting in the way."

Some panic sufferers experience an increase in anxiety when they relax, but it's not associated with a specific experience they can identify — no heightened awareness of alarming physical sensations and no specific fear such as losing control. The experience might be termed a surge of emotion, often sadness, that occurs when they become quiet. Often, their style of dealing with inner unhappiness or uncomfortable feelings has been to keep intensely busy to avoid thinking about the issues that trouble them. To pause and relax can be upsetting or anxiety-producing because it suddenly allows all those submerged feelings to come rushing in.

Do you find that when you pause to relax, tears sometimes come to your eyes for no reason? Do you sometimes find yourself, during lulls, feeling a welling of emotion you can't identify and becoming somewhat anxious at that point?

If this description characterizes you, there are a couple of things to do. One is to continue practicing and, during the practice sessions, to try focusing on a specific relaxing image — floating in a hot air balloon, curling up in an easy chair in front of a fire, walking in the woods. The particular image most relaxing to a given person is quite individual, so *you* pick your image. With continued practice, you'll become better at focusing your attention at will.

Along with that, start using your journal in the following manner: Some time after a breathing session, take twenty minutes to write down any feelings that occurred during the session and/or any feelings that arise while writing. Open your mind to any thoughts or memories that float to the surface and record them, no matter how unimportant they seem. Sometimes one "unimportant" idea will lead to another and then another, and you'll end up realizing something that's not unimportant at all.

Sally found she became deeply sad whenever she used controlled breathing. At first, she didn't understand the source of her sadness. Once she began freewriting in her journal, though, she identified her worry and sorrow about a sister's ongoing difficulties — something she tried not to think about *because* it made her so sad. Her sorrow led her to think about her sister's difficult early life, a consequence of severe alcoholism in the family. And these thoughts took her ultimately to the deepest, most profoundly sad place of all — her pain at the way she *herself* was neglected and mistreated when she was young.

Sally's realizations led to some relief, at least to the point that she could practice controlled breathing and work on her panic attacks. But they also led her to begin work in parallel, through psychotherapy, on resolving the early pain that still influenced her life. She ultimately mastered her panic *and* made peace with the truth about all that she'd suffered in her young life.

Feelings are funny. The more you try to push them away, perhaps because they're painful or frightening, the more insistently they hammer at the door, demanding to be admitted. Sometimes they disguise themselves so cleverly that you aren't fully aware of the nature of the feeling; you may think it's anxiety when it's really anger or sadness. (And the scarier the feeling, the cleverer its disguise.) But you can be sure that any feelings you're trying to keep at bay will continue to make you uncomfortable in some subtle way *until you face them head-on and deal with them.*

It's often a good idea to write only for a specified amount of time and then to put away your paper and pencil, realizing you'll take time to write the following day. Limiting the time allows you to address important issues without becoming overwhelmed by them; after all, you *do* have to go on with your life. And at the same time, the writing helps you to stop avoiding the feelings that keep kicking up trouble for you as long as you keep denying them.

And once again, if you aren't in any sort of counseling or therapy, give it some consideration; it's an excellent way to find relief from feelings that are interfering in your life and a useful adjunct to your own self-guided work on panic.

Dilemma #5: "Controlled breathing just isn't helping my anxiety when I need it the most."

Sometimes, people feel able to conduct controlled breathing adequately, but it doesn't seem to have much impact on their anxiety level. At times, in fact, it may even seem to make anxiety worse. But that may be a misinterpretation. It was in Lori's case.

Lori found that whenever she responded to anxiety with controlled breathing, it actually seemed to bring on panic — not at all the result she sought. To determine the source of the problem, for a week she kept close track of all her experiences with controlled breathing, recording the times she practiced the method formally or informally and its effects on her. After a week, Lori realized that whenever she practiced the breathing techniques at home, they did, in fact, reduce her level of tension. But her records showed that she was practicing her controlled breathing so rarely, she hadn't really developed much skill with it. When she began to feel anxious, she wasn't able to use it effectively despite her efforts, and her anxiety continued to mount — as panic does unless interrupted. She then concluded, mistakenly, that the controlled breathing was *causing* the increased anxiety.

Once she'd analyzed the situation, Lori herself could see the source of her problems. She vowed to practice controlled breathing regularly and began using it several times a day in non-anxious situations, soon developing her skills much more solidly. When she then used it during times of mounting anxiety, it did indeed reduce her symptoms.

Summary

In short, strategies to consider if you're having difficulty using controlled breathing effectively include further practice, the addition of imagery, attention to potentially interfering emotional issues, modification of practice conditions, and consultation with a professional. Once you've begun to achieve some success with controlled breathing, you'll be ready to use it as part of a more comprehensive strategy to halt panic in its tracks.

Dilemma #6: "I've practiced and practiced but controlled breathing just doesn't seem to help me."

Occasionally people try controlled breathing, use the method accurately (do indeed achieve slow and abdominal breathing), and practice faithfully (twice daily for at least four minutes), but they simply don't feel the method has much impact on their level of arousal. Perhaps for these people, overbreathing doesn't play as significant a role in their anxiety picture as it does for most panic sufferers. If this is your situation, you may want to focus your time and energy on moving forward to learn the other strategies in the book, which simply may have greater usefulness to you for overcoming your panic.

Alternatives to Controlled Breathing

You learned in Session five that, for those seeking a more comprehensive strategy for reducing physical stress and tension, *mindfulness meditation* — though certainly not the only method available — might offer special advantages for those with panic disorder. First, although the goal of mindfulness meditation is not relaxation *per se*, its focus on breathing does help to reduce physical arousal levels, and most people find it a relaxing practice. In fact, the method has been shown to result in improvements in a variety of problems related to stress and anxiety (described in the books referenced below.)

Perhaps more important, the emphasis placed by mindfulness meditation on moment-to-moment awareness can be a huge help to you, as you work toward becoming more aware of emotions and feelings *as they arise*. As you'll learn in Session seven, these feelings, which you've all too often learned to ignore, can frequently serve as triggers for panic. Simply becoming more aware of feelings the moment they develop can diminish the likelihood of panic arising in response to them.

The method's emphasis on the *present* can also be a useful antidote to panic sufferers' characteristic tendency to catastrophize about the *future*. And learning and practicing mindfulness meditation in a group format, as it's typically taught, can offer a supportive group experience which, while not specific to those with panic, can still be of much benefit to you.

Methods for locating courses in your area include checking the Internet and contacting mental health agencies and medical programs known for emphasizing prevention and well-being (e.g., cardiac rehabilitation programs, especially those located in university medical centers)

* * * * *

Another strategy worth mentioning, commonly termed the *relaxation response*, is a method developed by Dr. Herbert Benson and described in his books, some of which are referenced below. While one of these should be consulted for a full description, briefly, the method involves breathing naturally, pairing each exhalation with the silent (inward) repetition of a self-chosen word or simple phrase, perhaps the line of a poem or prayer. After multiple inhalation-exhalation cycles, a state of decreased physical arousal — for some, almost a trance-like state — is achieved.

As you can see, the method is somewhat comparable to controlled breathing in that it can be employed "on the spot" and is capable of reducing physical arousal in a relatively short time. It can, in fact, be used as a substitute for controlled breathing in the SRB method for interrupting panic taught in Session six. And many panic sufferers find this an especially helpful strategy for reducing overall levels of stress, perhaps because it can incorporate a belief that is especially meaningful to them.

* * * * *

Finally, of course, stress reduction classes, which generally involve training in some form of physical reduction of tension, are widely available in most communities. These can often be located through medical and mental health clinics, health clubs, university extension offices, community centers and ads in area newspapers.

Recommended Resources for Further Reading

Benson, H., & Klipper, M.Z. (2000) *The Relaxation Response*. New York: Morrow-Avon.

Benson, H. & Stark, M. (1997). *Timeless Healing: The Power and Biology of Belief*. New York: Fireside.

Kabat-Zinn, J. (1994). *Wherever You Go, There You Are: Mindfulness Meditation in Everyday Life*. New York: Hyperion.

Kabat-Zinn, J. (1990). *Full Catastrophe Living: Using the Wisdom of Your Body and Mind to Face Stress, Pain and Illness*. New York: Dell.

Kabat-Zinn, J. (2004). *Coming to Our Senses: Mindfulness, Dharma, & Living Life as if it Really Mattered*. New York: Hyperion.

Troubleshooting: Exposure

This appendix describes various dilemmas people might encounter in the use of the exposure method and suggests strategies to overcome them. Even if your exposure program is going well, the appendix is useful to read since it highlights various principles that can enhance your own use of the method.

Dilemma #1: "My anxiety across exposures isn't declining as it should"

What if you follow the plan laid out at the beginning of this session and you don't see the predictable drop in anxiety after several exposures to an item? Chances are, you need to make the item you've selected less difficult by breaking it down into more manageable steps.

Perhaps you've been trying to drive around the block by yourself, and six tries later, you still rate the anxiety you feel in the situation at 9 or 10. In this case, "back up" to something much easier: Get into the car, start the engine and sit in the driver's seat for ten minutes while looking at a magazine.

Even if this item seems too easy to you, start here and continue for at least *four repetitions during which your anxiety remains low* before moving to the next item, which might involve driving around the block with a companion in the car.

It's also possible that your exposure practices are occurring too infrequently to be effective. Are you conducting exposures on a daily or near-daily basis? You should be. After all, if you were anxious about public speaking and you only gave one speech a year, your anxiety wouldn't decline as a result of the yearly practices. But if you gave a speech every day for a month, you can be certain that by the thirtieth day, you'd be significantly less anxious in the situation. To be effective, exposures need to occur on a frequent, regular basis — daily whenever possible.

Be sure, too, that you're still practicing controlled breathing and SRB daily in the manner described in Sessions five and six. Even if you feel the techniques are quite simple for you at home (under *optimal* conditions), the repeated practice will ensure that they become *overlearned* skills — more likely to be effective even under the most *difficult* conditions. That will give you the added confidence you need to continue practicing exposures on a regular basis, which is necessary for *habituation* to occur, that is, for anxiety to decline across repeated exposures to a situation.

Remember, in addition, that when you're actually conducting an exposure, you should use SRB when you experience any sensations associated with anxiety. Doing so reduces your anxiety significantly *before you leave* the situation. In fact, if necessary, modify your item to *require* that you stay until anxiety declines (e.g., "I'll go into the store and stand near the doorway till I feel calmer.") And remember that while in the situation, you should attend to the situation itself, so you'll be aware of cues that bring forth anxiety and can break their hold over you.

In short, if you're not witnessing a drop in anxiety across exposures, you should do four things to reverse the situation:

1. Develop "easier" items and "back up" to master those before again tackling the item that gave you difficulty.

2. Be sure to practice your anxiety-reduction skills of controlled breathing and SRB every single day.

3. Practice exposures on a daily or near-daily basis.

4. Remember to use SRB during your exposure to ensure that you experience the situation fully and that your anxiety drops before you leave the situation. Make this required drop in anxiety an integral part of the item itself.

Dilemma # 2: "One of the items in my hierarchy is too scary to tackle." What if you sail through several items in your exposure hierarchy and *then* you reach one that seems too scary to tackle? By now, you probably know exactly what to do: If there's too big a gap between the item you just mastered and the next one on the list (or if you reach one, tackle it repeatedly and don't see your anxiety dropping the way it should), you need to narrow the gap by creating several additional items that fall between the two.

Perhaps you've readily mastered trips alone to the grocery store and now you want to go to the mall alone, but it seems too frightening. Consider adding some items to "bridge the gap": Enter a much *busier* grocery store by yourself; enter unfamiliar stores *outside* the mall; go to the mall first *with a friend* at a time when the stores are *closed*; then include a friend again in your first few trips to the mall when it's *open*. There are myriad ways to alter the difficulty level of items.

Each of the items suggested can also be made into more items with even finer variations in difficulty. Going to the mall with a friend could involve simply strolling the mall, without entering stores; or it could require you to enter individual stores in the mall, first with your friend, then by yourself while she waits outside. The item can specify different times of the day, different days of the week, different locations in the mall, different tasks — any of the dimensions that influence your ease in the situation. Remember: It's better to have "too many" items in a hierarchy than too few; better a few extra successes than unnecessary setbacks in your confidence.

Once in a while, you may encounter an item you didn't expect to be all that difficult, but you can't seem to get past it. If that occurs, ponder briefly what might account for its higher-than-expected difficulty level. Does it involve different people — perhaps people who cause you to feel "on the spot" in some way? Does the situation involve substantially different expectations of you, expectations you perhaps feel ill-equipped to handle? Does the item symbolize or remind you of an especially difficult time in your history?

If there are emotional reasons for unexpected difficulty of an item, identifying them can help you to understand and tackle the relevant issues directly. This knowledge can also guide your efforts to create additional, more manageable items for your hierarchy.

But sometimes, creating appropriate items for an exposure hierarchy isn't a straightforward task. The next and final section will consider this topic.

Dilemma #3: "There's no way to practice my feared situation."
As you're well aware, you can develop items of gradually increasing difficulty more easily for some situations than for others. If you're anxious about being alone, for example, you can easily create items to produce the "desired" amount of anxiety to be practiced on a daily basis. You simply set up a series of items in which you vary the length of time you're alone and how many "supports" you allow yourself during those times. You might begin by staying alone in one room of your house for increasing amounts of time, then move to staying alone in the entire house, again for gradually increasing periods of time. You could then adjust the difficulty level of the task by initially allowing yourself regular phone calls to a support person to diminish your feelings of aloneness, then gradually "thinning" the frequency of calls as you move up your hierarchy.

Anxiety about going into stores is another situation that lends itself easily to developing good items for an exposure hierarchy. The situation is readily accessible and the dimensions that affect difficulty level can be varied across a wide range. But as you well know, developing hierarchy items for other situations can be considerably more difficult. If you're having trouble developing appropriate items for your feared situations, several strategies can help.

First, as you learned in Session nine, using imagery — creating a feared situation in *imagination* — is one effective means for developing good hierarchy items. Another approach involves finding ways to duplicate certain aspects of a feared situation. For example, what if you've successfully mastered your avoidance of all sorts of "everyday" situations, but you remain anxious about parties and large social events? What items might you develop for exposures in this case? After all, large parties don't happen that often, and you can't exactly throw a party for yourself every day just to provide a good exposure opportunity.

But you can create situations that gradually *approximate* a party situation more and more closely, that expose you to the *elements* of a party situation without recreating the total experience. The specific items you develop will depend on the dimensions of parties that create difficulty for *you*. Is it the need to small talk?

One possible practice item might be to approach one person every day at work and make three "small-talk" comments, continuing the practice till you've become noticeably more comfortable. Is it tough being in a room full of relative strangers? An appropriate item for practice might involve entering a public place alone to sit down, drink a beverage, and read the newspaper. Again, the specific dimensions involved, the particular items you generate, and the order in which you arrange them will vary according to the details of your own anxiety and avoidance. The task, as always, is to create a scenario related to your feared situation that will be somewhat anxiety-producing but achievable.

In a similar vein, perhaps you can use sensory elements from a situation — cues associated with it — for a few exposure items. Are there particular smells, sounds or sensations connected with the situation you've been avoiding? If so, try to find ways to recreate those and use exposure to eliminate your anxiety in response to the cues. After you've done so, entering the actual situation should be at least slightly easier for you.

Some items might need a combination of imagery and "real-life" elements. Perhaps one of your panic situations involves medical appointments. You might create an item requiring that you sit in the doctor's waiting room or the hospital emergency room for fifteen minutes to imagine you're awaiting an actual appointment. In essence, this experience exposes you to important cues related to the situation — the sights, the smells, and your own feelings of heightened anxiety in the setting. For a later item, you might request an appointment in which you only talk with the doctor and defer an actual exam till a later date. You might also invite a companion to accompany you to the first few appointments.

Be imaginative. Brainstorm about all the things you could do to approximate a feared situation. Use a combination of imagery, "pieces" of the real situation, situations that replicate important elements of the situation, invented tasks — whatever you can come up with. Expose yourself to *real-life elements* of the situation and *imagined versions* of it. The rules are the same: Items should proceed from easiest to most difficult and should progress in measured "steps" of slightly increasing difficulty level.

Summary

In short, if you're having difficulty seeing the benefits of your exposure work, first review whether you're conducting it based on the principles outlined in Session nine and reviewed in this appendix. Evaluate the items in your hierarchy for appropriateness, and if you need to modify some or create new ones, consider the ideas offered here and in Session nine. Ask yourself if you've given your efforts enough time to produce results. And *after following all these suggestions, if you're still having problems, contact a qualified therapist* who can help out; when problems arise, two heads are better than one.

Troubleshooting: Unsatisfying Outcomes

What if you've followed the program conscientiously, but you're just not happy with your results? This appendix describes different problematic outcomes you might experience and suggests remedies for them. All readers will benefit from reading the appendix since it offers a review of important principles and steps toward a panic-free life.

Dilemma #1: "I'm still having lots of panic attacks."
If this statement characterizes your situation, first, ask yourself these questions:

-Are you practicing controlled breathing and the SRB method on a *daily* basis at home, as well as "out in the world"?

-Are you able to use controlled breathing in different bodily positions and while engaged in different activities (while walking, watching TV, brushing your teeth)?

-Are you able to use SRB well during at-home practices, producing vivid feelings of anxiety, then reducing them effectively?

-Are you able to "catch" impending attacks early in the panic cycle?

-During your attempts to use SRB to halt panic, do you have difficulty refocusing on the present because your catastrophic fears are so intense?

-Do you still harbor deep fears of danger from a particular physical symptom (e.g., still worry that a rapid heart rate means an impending heart attack), even though your doctor tells you there's no reason for alarm?

-Are you so anxious you've been unable to force yourself to undertake exposures, either to external places or internal sensations? This is a particularly important question, since, for most people, exposure is an absolutely crucial element in overcoming their panic and agoraphobia.

-Do you have a "life problem" that is unresolved and troubling you?

Did asking the questions above help you to pinpoint more specifically some difficulty that may be responsible for your continued panic? If so, that realization may well show you the way to a solution, indicating where you should concentrate your practice efforts. For example, if you're not practicing the SRB method regularly at home on a daily basis as described in Session six, beginning to do so should, in time, help with the problem of persistent attacks. Even if you aren't sure where your difficulty lies, reviewing the chapters on controlled breathing and on the SRB method, including the exercises that follow the chapters, will be helpful.

Difficulty practicing controlled breathing often enough or regularly enough may be a problem if you're not having success with it, making practice sessions a frustrating, unpleasant undertaking. If so, consider seeking a therapist's help to use it more effectively. If the problem is simply one of making the time for regular practices, page 182 offers some suggestions that may be of help.

What if you're not "catching" impending attacks early enough? In that case, scan the pertinent portions of Session six and reread Session seven about the triggers of panic attacks. In addition, review your journal to analyze the specific situations and symptoms that usually pave the way for your attacks. Recognizing these will help you to intervene more quickly and, thus, more effectively.

If you still experience deep fears based on the belief that your physical symptoms may mean impending catastrophe; or if you know intellectually those fears aren't realistic but you're still deeply affected by them; or if physical sensation remains difficult for you to tolerate, there are several approaches to try. First, review Sessions nine and ten and follow the program of external or internal exposures as described. If you're too frightened to undertake this process, or if you practice the methods described for some time but still feel fearful, consider contacting a therapist, particularly one with a cognitive-behavioral approach who can help you to address your anxiety-producing beliefs more systematically. Or join a therapy or support group.

If you're having difficulty even sorting out the nature of the problem, consult a therapist to help you clarify the problem and explore solutions. A therapist may be of help as well if you feel there's a broader life problem contributing to your panic or interfering with your efforts to overcome it.

Finally, if you aren't on medication, you might consider that option more seriously. Medication can help control your symptoms and allow you to tolerate the increased anxiety involved with some of the treatment strategies — which, in turn, will reduce anxiety even further in the long run. Session eleven outlines information and guidelines about medication use.

Dilemma #2: "I'm not having many outright attacks, but I'm a little bit anxious all the time."

If this is your situation, you might consider first learning an adjunctive stress-management technique to use on a daily basis. You might start the process by consulting Appendix II, which discusses mindfulness meditation as one very useful anxiety-reduction strategy. Or, as before, you might consider consulting a professional who teaches relaxation.

Again, ask yourself whether there are life issues contributing to your chronic anxiety — perhaps an overly hectic, anxiety-producing lifestyle or conflict within an important relationship or maybe a general dissatisfaction with yourself or your life. Consider possible methods of attack on any issues you identify (e.g., stress management classes, assertiveness training, grief work, couples' counseling or whatever other strategy best fits the specific situation).

The special section that follows Session twelve explores more fully various strategies for addressing chronic anxiety. Reading the section carefully and adopting some of the methods best suited to your circumstances can have a marked, positive effect on your overall level of tension and anxiety.

Keep in mind that you must be doing beautifully at panic control if your panic attack frequency has declined despite chronic anxiety. Perhaps what you need most is simply more time (all the while continuing your daily practices).

It may be that your difficulties represent an anxiety problem other than panic disorder *per se*. Panic attacks commonly occur not only with panic disorder but also with social phobia, simple phobias, obsessive-compulsive disorder and generalized anxiety disorder, as well as with port-traumatic stress disorder. While the methods provided in the book are useful for controlling panic attacks whatever their source, if you suspect that you may be suffering from an anxiety disorder other than panic, it's best to be evaluated by a qualified mental health professional who can provide appropriate treatment recommendations.

Finally, consider the option of medication or psychotherapy to add power to your program.

Dilemma #3: "I'm not having panic attacks, but I still have lots of physical symptoms like dizziness or a rapid heart rate or just "weird" feelings.

This is in some ways a variant of Dilemma #2, but here the problem is less the awareness of chronic tension than the awareness of physical symptoms that *reflect* tension. First, pursue the recommendations given following Dilemma #2 to help reduce overall arousal. If part of the problem is that the sensations are still *worrisome* to you, check the guidelines for dilemmas #6 and #7; they may be helpful to you as well.

Finally, consider Jody's experience. Jody first developed panic at a time when her marriage was on somewhat shaky ground — though this was not a factor she identified initially. Jody did report a history of factors that might suggest a vulnerability to panic: Her mother had suffered from multiple anxieties and panic and Jody herself had been a rather sensitive, anxious child. For several years, she had been in an unfortunate school situation characterized by unpredictability and harsh punishment, diminishing her already tenuous feelings of safety and security. And finally, she'd seen a high school friend die in a sudden and shocking manner, further increasing her fears about unpredictable and unavoidable disaster.

Jody's initial panic attack seemed related to an episode of physical illness, and once she entered a behavioral treatment program, she progressed rapidly, mastering the techniques to identify and halt impending attacks with relative ease. She also worked hard at understanding what "lowered her threshold" to attacks in hopes of strengthening her resistance and intervening sooner.

But despite her success in controlling outright panic and, over time, her recognition that intermittent physical symptoms (dizziness, rapid heart rate) didn't signal danger, Jody was troubled because the symptoms continued to arise. Each time she experienced a bout with the symptoms, she saw her therapist for a session or two; and each time, she was able to identify something troubling or worrisome in her life — a co-worker who annoyed her, concerns about an ailing grandfather, or questions about whether she and her husband were "truly suited to one another." In fact, Jody began to suspect, looking back, that unspoken concerns about her marriage may have contributed to her first outbreak of panic.

One day, after several very good months, Jody announced to her therapist that she'd come to understand an important connection that seemed central to her continued emotional well-being. As Jody phrased it, "I've figured out that whenever I don't feel good physically, it almost always means I'm upset about something. So now instead of just feeling crummy or trying to get rid of the physical symptoms or trying to lower my anxiety by deep breathing and reassuring myself, *I look for what's bothering me.* I try to figure out how I feel and what I want to do about it *and that usually takes care of the physical problem.*" She went on to say, somewhat humorously, that her realization had also decreased her underlying fears about some undetected physical problem. "I figure it can't be a brain tumor causing my headache if it's because I'm furious with my mother-in-law!"

Remember, physical sensation occurs in all our bodies and is generally benign. *In addition, it may reflect underlying anxiety* and in that sense, can be a signal not of something *physically wrong,* but of something *emotionally* troubling to you, a message telling you to look deeper, as Jody learned to do, and to figure out just what your body is trying to tell you.

Dilemma #4: "I'm not having many panic attacks, but I'm still avoiding; I simply can't bring myself to go back to certain places or situations."

If this is your dilemma, review the troubleshooting guidelines in Appendix III. The most important remedy for you, assuming you're willing to conduct exposure practices to overcome the problem, is to develop an exposure hierarchy for those situations which starts with the easiest item you can generate and which involves the narrowest possible "distance" between items. It's also important, of course, to conduct exposures every day and to be certain to stay in the situation long enough for your anxiety to diminish. Medications may be worth considering, and though you must be tired of hearing so by now, finding a qualified therapist to assist you might be a good start to a solution.

Dilemma #5: "I'm doing everything now that I used to avoid, but I'm not enjoying it."

Remember Joan, from Session nine? This was her experience too, at one point in treatment; you may want to review what she had to say. It's true that the reduction in fear must come first; the enjoyment will follow eventually. You also may want to ask yourself if other issues, not panic, relate to the absence of joy in your life. If you conclude this is true, consider the remedies proposed for Dilemma #8.

Dilemma #6: "Physical sensations still alarm me, although I do interrupt the panic cycle."

The best solution to this very common dilemma is to redouble your efforts at following the recommendations and strategies described in Sessions nine and ten. You should also recognize that emotional changes often lag behind changes in behavior; it can take time for changes in your level of fear to "catch up" with the impressive changes in your panic symptoms per se. Also reread Session seven and explore very seriously how your fears arose. And you may want to think about joining (or starting) a support group with others who are conquering anxieties. Talking about the fears and getting input from others who understand your situation in a most intimate way can be immensely helpful and reassuring.

Dilemma #7: "I still worry a lot about my body."
Consider your history, both the experiences that may have brought about your anxieties about your health and also how long you've carried these anxieties with you. It's been a major accomplishment to overcome panic attacks in the face of those worries! To address them, you might consider more intense work on your attitudes, beliefs, and "automatic thoughts." Perhaps, depending on your particular situation, psychotherapy may be appropriate to explore specific emotional issues such as fears of death or loss.

Dilemma #8: "My panic attacks are gone but I'm still unhappy."
While overcoming panic can cause wonderful "ripple" effects in other areas of your life, solving your panic problem will not necessarily solve everything. If there were other sources of unhappiness in your life when you began the program, sources the program didn't address, chances are, those problems still remain. Try to evaluate the "sore spots." What *is* the nature of your recurrent unhappiness or dissatisfaction? Do you understand it? Can it be changed?

This is one of the dilemmas that argues most strongly for consultation with a therapist. In working with a therapist, you can identify the problem more precisely and explore what can be done — what you *want* to do — about it. You can then tackle the problem directly, whether that involves changing something about yourself or your life or perhaps finding ways to feel more comfortable with your circumstances.

Reference Notes

Numerous sources, both research studies and clinical reports, contributed over time to the development of this program and this book. Though these original sources could have been included in reference notes throughout the text, it was felt that the notes would be an unwelcome distraction to most readers. Instead, they have been placed in this separate appendix, organized by session. New references added to this edition are, in virtually all cases, placed at the beginning of the references for that session, for the ease of readers seeking to locate the newest additions.

Naturally, certain areas of investigation, for example, medication research, have spawned a great deal of new research, and others, scarcely any, and this is reflected in the number of new references added per session. While an effort was made to review as much of the research as possible, only those studies deemed pertinent to self-directed therapy *per se,* and to the interests of a largely consumer population were included.

Principles and techniques that are widely known and generally accepted in the field are not referenced specifically. However, where a finding is quite new or controversial; where there may be some question regarding reasons for a particular recommendation; where one individual or research team was responsible for originating a valuable, new technique or approach; or where results of a specific study are described, original references are provided. Where needed, additional explanatory notes are also provided.

The average reader probably will not feel a need to review this material. Professionals using the book may wish to locate original sources or pursue more detailed information on a particular question, and will find the Appendix of use for that purpose.

Session One: What is Panic?

Dammen, T., Arnesen, H., Edeberg, O., Husebye, T. and Friis, S. (1999). Panic disorder in chest pain patients referred for cardiological outpatient investigation. *Journal of Internal Medicine*, 245 (5), 497-507.

American Psychiatric Association. 2000. Diagnostic and Statistical Manual of Mental Disorders. 4th ed., Text Revision. Washington, D.C.: APA.

Beckfield, D.F. (1997). Understanding and addressing susceptibility to panic, in L. VandeCreek, S. Knapp, and T.L. Jackson (Eds.), *Innovations in Clinical Practice: A Sourcebook* (Vol. 16). Sarasota, FL: Professional Resource Exchange, Inc.

Coyle, P.K. and Sterman, A.B. (1986). Focal neurologic symptoms in panic attacks. *American Journal of Psychiatry*, 143, 648-49.

DeJong, G.M., and Bouman, T.K. (1995). Panic disorder: A baseline period. Predictability to agoraphobic behavior. *Journal of Anxiety Disorders*, 9, 185-199.
This study is packed with facts and findings about symptoms of panic attacks and the characteristics of those who develop avoidance behaviors (that is, most panic sufferers). It also describes the sequence many panic sufferers follow as they overcome attacks.

DuPont, R.L., Rice, D.P., Miller, L.S., Shiraki, S.S., Rowland, C.R., and Harwood, H.J. (1996). The economic costs of anxiety disorders. *Anxiety*, 2, 167-172.

Mullaney, J.S. and Trippett, C.J. (1979). Alcohol dependence and phobias: Clinical description and relevance. *British Journal of Psychiatry*, 135, 565-73.
This report found that a substantial percentage of the alcoholic sample studied also suffered from agoraphobia and/or social phobias; that men with both alcohol and anxiety disorders were more likely to be in treatment for the alcohol problems; and thus,

that the percentage of men with phobias (including panic disorder with agoraphobia) is likely to be underestimated.

Noyes, R. Jr. and Kletti, R. (1977). Depersonalisation response to life threatening danger. *Comprehensive Psychiatry*, 18, 375-84.

Regier, D.A., et al. (1988). One-month prevalence of mental disorders in the United States. *Archives of General Psychiatry*, 45, 977-986.

Rosenbaum, J.F. (1996). Panic disorder in the emergency room. *Emergency Medicine*. 1996 (Aug.), 54-69.

Weissman, M.M. Panic disorder is a family affair. (1991). Keynote address presented at the Eleventh National Conference on Anxiety Disorders. Anxiety Disorders Association of America.

Session Two: The Roots of Panic

Breier, A., Charney, D.S., and Heninger, G.R. (1986). Agoraphobia with panic attacks: Development, diagnostic stability and course of illness. *Archives of General Psychiatry*, 43, 1029-36.
This comprehensive study found that a sizeable percentage of adult agoraphobics had been reared in chaotic or abusive homes in their early years.

Crowe, R.R., Noyes, R., Pauls, D.L., and Slymen, D. A family study of panic disorder. (1983). *Archives of General Psychiatry*, 40, 1065-69.2.

Faravelli, C., Webb, T., Ambonetti, A., Fonnesu, F., and Sessarego, A. (1985). Prevalence of traumatic early life events in 31 agoraphobic patients with panic attacks. *American Journal of Psychiatry*, 142, 1493-94.

Judd, L.J. (1992). The future: Our understanding of panic disorder. Panic Disorder: Consensus for the '90s. Washington, DC, 3 May.

Klein, D.F. and Gorman, J.M. (1987). A model of panic and agoraphobic development. *Acta Psychiatrica Scandinavica*, 76 (suppl. 335), 87-95.

Laraia, M.T., Stuart, G.W., Frye, L.H., Lydiard, R.B., and Ballenger, J.C. (1994). Childhood environment of women having panic disorder with agoraphobia. *Journal of Anxiety Disorders*, 8, 1-17.

This study reported a high incidence of particular kinds of separation in the histories of females who later developed panic disorder. These included many more parental separations (based on a strong trend in the findings) and some likelihood of deaths in the household. The women were also far more likely, compared to those without panic, to come from families in which there was a chronically ill family member or a member with substance abuse problems.

Leckman, J.F., Weissman, M.M., Merikangas, K.R., Pauls, D.L., and Prusoff, B.A. (1983). Panic disorder and major depression: Increased risk of depression, alcoholism, panic and phobic disorders in families of depressed probands with panic disorder. *Archives of General Psychiatry*, 40, 1055-60.

Raskin, M., Nurberg, G., Prince, R., Fine, J., Levine, P., and Seigel, O. (1989) Abuse of the child and anxiety in the adult. *New York State Journal of Medicine*, 89, 138-140.

Rosenbaum, J.F., Biederman, J., Gersten, M., Hirsheld, D.R., Meminger, S.R., Herman, J.B., Kagan, J., Reznick, J.S., and Snidman, N. (1988). Behavioral inhibition in children of parents with panic disorder and agoraphobia. *Archives of General Psychiatry*, 45, 463-70.

Torgerson, S. (1983). Genetic factors in anxiety disorders. *Archives of General Psychiatry*, 40, 1086-89.

The notion of a lifelong vulnerability to separation in those who develop panic disorder as adults continues to be controversial but, in this author's view, quite compelling. The following sources, as well as Laraia et al., 1994, offer strong support for the argument that separation anxiety is especially prominent in the histories of adults with agoraphobia and panic:

Deltito, J.A., Perugi, G., Maremmimi, I., Mignani, V., and Cassano, G. (1986). The importance of separation anxiety in the differentiation of panic anxiety from agoraphobia. *Psychiatric Developments*, 4, 227-36.

Gittelman, R. and Klein, D.F. (1985). Childhood separation anxiety and adult agoraphobia. In *Anxiety and the Anxiety Disorders*, edited by Tuma, A.H. and Maser, J.D., Hillsdale, NJ: Lawrence Erlbaum Associates.

Klein, D.F. (1964). Delineation of two drug-responsive anxiety syndromes. *Psychopharmacologia*, 5, 397-408.

This study, mentioned specifically on page 35, found an especially high percentage of childhood separation anxiety in individuals who developed severe panic disorder and agoraphobia as adults.

Liebowitz, M.R. and Klein, D.F. (1979). Clinical psychiatric conferences: Assessment and treatment of phobic anxiety. *Journal of Clinical Psychiatry*, 40, 486-92.

McGennis, A., Nolan, G., and Hartman, M. (1977). The role of a self-help association in agoraphobia: One year's experience with Out and About. *Journal of the Irish Medical Association*, 70, 10-13.

Raskin, M., Peeke, H.V.S., Dickman. W., and Pinsker, H. (1982). Panic and generalized anxiety disorders: Developmental antecedents and precipitants. *Archives of General Psychiatry*, 39, 687-89.

Weissman, M.M., Leckman, J.F., and Merikangas, K.R. (1984). Depression and anxiety disorders in parents and children: Results from the Yale family study. *Archives of General Psychiatry*, 41, 845-52.

Session Three: Panic and Personality

Beckfield, D.F. (1987). Importance of altering global response style in the treatment of agoraphobia. *Psychotherapy*. 24, 752-758.

Chambless, D.L. Characteristics of agoraphobics. (1982). In *Agorophobia: Multiple Perspectives on Theory and Treatment*. Edited by Chambless, D.L. and Goldstein, A.J. New York: John Wiley and Sons.

Mavissakalian, M. and Hamann, M.S. (1987). DSM-III personality disorder in agoraphobia. II. Changes with treatment. *Comprehensive Psychiatry*, 28, 356-61.

This study examined personality features of patients with panic disorder and how some of these changed as the panic symptoms improved. Of particular interest, there was a striking improvement in the self-confidence levels of agoraphobics once they were able to successfully overcome their symptoms.

Noyes, R., Jr., Reich, J.H., Suelzer, M., and Christiansen, J. (1991). Personality traits associated with panic disorder: Change associated with treatment. *Comprehensive Psychiatry*, 32, 283-94.

Breier, A., Charney, D.S., and Heninger, G.R. (1986). Agoraphobia with panic attacks: Development, diagnostic stability and course of illness. *Archives of General Psychiatry*, 43, 1029-36.

This study, described on page 36, included a tabulation of panic sufferers' theories of what was happening to them at the time of their first panic attack.

Shear, M.K., Cooper, A.M., Klerman, G.L., Busch, F.N., and Shapiro, T. (1993). A Psychodynamic Model of Panic Disorder. *American Journal of Psychiatry.* 150, 6.

Session Four: The Timing of Panic

Shear, K.S., Houck, M.S.H., Greeno, C., and Masters, B.S. (2001). Emotion-focused psychotherapy for patients with panic disorder. *American Journal of Psychiatry,* 158, 1993-1998.

Anxiety Disorders Association of America. (1997). Pregnancy and panic disorder. *ADAA Reporter,* 8 (Spring), 1, 22-24.

Breier, A., Charney, D..S, and Heninger, G.R. (1986). Agoraphobia with panic attacks: Development, diagnostic stability and course of illness. *Archives of General Psychiatry,* 43, 1029-36.

This study (pages 50-51) found a high percentage of women with panic who experienced an increase in their attacks during the one to two weeks before their menstrual periods.

Chambless, D.L. and Goldstein, A.J. (1981). Clinical treatment of agoraphobia. In *Phobia: Psychological and Pharmacological Treatment.* Edited by Mavissakalian, M. and Barlow, D.H. New York: Guilford.

This source is one of several that highlight the role of interpersonal conflict in precipitating outbreaks of panic and agoraphobia.

Last, C.G., Barlow, D.H., and O'Brien, G.T. (1984). Precipitants of agoraphobia: Role of stressful life events. *Psychological Reports,* 54, 567-570.

Leibowitz, M.R. and Klein, D.F. (1979). Clinical psychiatric conferences: Assessment and treatment of phobic anxiety. *Journal of Clinical Psychiatry,* 40, 486-92.

These investigators reported an increased onset of panic attacks following various physically disruptive events such as surgery or serious illness.

Stein, M.B. (1986). Panic disorder and medical illness. *Psychosomatics,* 27, 833-838.

Tearnan, B.H., Telch, M.J., and Keefe, P. (1984). Etiology and onset of agoraphobia: A critical review. *Comprehensive Psychiatry*, 25, 51-62.

This review confirms the findings of both earlier and later work on the high frequency with which panic arises initially in the wake of background stress or a specific event — a loss or separation, interpersonal conflicts, physiological upheaval or other significant life changes.

Zal, H.M. (1987). Panic disorder: Is it emotional or physical? *Psychiatric Annals*, 17 (7), 497-505.

Session Five: Take a Deep Breath...

Abelson, J.L., Weg, J.G., Nesse, R.M. and Curtis, G.C. (2001). Persistent respiratory irregularity in patients with panic disorder. *Biological Psychiatry*, 49, 588-595.

Meuret, A.E., Wilhelm, F.H. and Roth, W.T. (2001). Respiratory biofeedback-assisted therapy in panic disorder. *Behavior Modification*, 25, 584-605.

Schmidt, N.B., Woolaway-Bickel, K., Trakowski, J., Santiago, H., Storey, J., Koselka, M. and Cook, J. (2000). Dismantling cognitive-behavioral treatment for panic disorder: Questioning the utility of breathing retraining. *Journal of Consulting and Clinical Psychology*, 68, 417-424.

Results from this study called into question whether breathing retraining provided any additional benefits for reducing panic beyond those produced by other elements of cognitive-behavior therapy. In the case of *self-directed* therapy, however, it is deemed important as an initial step in treatment due to its indisputable effects on physiology, its cognitive value in demonstrating the relationship of overbreathing to panic symptoms and its impact on self-efficacy, posited to be an important factor in success in overcoming panic disorder.

Breathing retraining also helps to strengthen readers' determination to continue the program through the rapid symptom relief it offers and, if continued beyond completion of the program, may even decrease susceptibility to future recurrences through its role in improving the physiological "buffering" of minor increases in anxiety as discussed in Session five. Most important of all, it offers readers the confidence and encouragement they will need to engage in the later task of exposure therapy which, in the absence of therapist support, is especially critical.

Both clinical experience and the following controlled research studies support the value of controlled breathing techniques for reducing panic symptoms.

Bonn, J.A., Readhead, C.P.A., and Timmons, B.H. (1984). Enhanced adaptive behavioural response in agoraphobic patients pretreated with breathing retraining. *Lancet, 2,* 665-69.

Clark, D.M., Salkovskis, P.M., and Chalkley, A.J. (1985). Respiratory control as a treatment for panic attacks. *Journal of Behavioral Therapy and Experimental Psychiatry,* 16, 23-30.

Franklin, J.A. (1989). A 6-year follow-up of the effectiveness of respiratory retraining, in-situ isometric relaxation and cognitive modification in the treatment of agoraphobia. *Behavior Modification,* 13, 139-1671.

In this study, the respiratory retraining was especially effective for reducing panic attacks, while the cognitive modification and relaxation training were better for reducing avoidance.

Salkovskis, P.M., Jones, D.R.O., and Clark, D.M. (1986). Respiratory control in the treatment of panic attacks: replication and extension with concurrent measurement of behaviour and pCO2. *British Journal of Psychiatry,* 148, 526-32.

The following sources, as well as Franklin, 1989, and Salkovkis et al., 1986, discuss the relationship of acute and chronic hyperventilation in panic disorder. The Munjack et al., 1993, reference, in particular, provides a thorough review and analysis of the topic.

Ley, R. (1989) Dyspneic fear and catastrophic cognitions in hyperventilatory panic attacks. *Behaviour Research and Therapy,* 1989, 549-554.

Lum, L.C. (1976). The syndrome of habitual chronic hyperventilation. In *Modern Trends in Psychosomatic Medicine 3.* Edited by Hill, O.W. London: Butterworths.

Munjack, D.J., Brown, R.A., and McDowell, D.E. (1993). Existence of hyperventilation in panic disorder with and without agoraphobia, GAD, and normals: Implications for the cognitive theory of panic. *Journal of Anxiety Disorders,* 7, 37-48.

Rapee, R. (1986). Differential response to hyperventilation in panic disorder and generalized anxiety disorder. *Journal of Abnormal Psychology*, 95, 24-8.

Hodgkin, J.E., Connors, G.L. and Bell, C.W. (Eds.). (1993). *Pulmonary Rehabilitation: Guidelines to Success* (2nd Ed.). Philadelphia: J.B. Lippincott.
Three chapters in this book are highly recommended for their guidelines pertinent to breathing strategies:
Bergren, D.R. Respiratory physiology in health and disease, 444-477.
Certo, C. Chest physical therapy, 222-245.
Weiser, P.C., Mahler, D.A., Ryan, K.P. Hill, K.L., and Greenspon, L.W. Dyspnea: Symptom assessment and management, 478-511.

Padesky, C.A. (1992). Brief Treatment for the Highly Anxious Client. Institute for the Advancement of Human Behavior Workshop, Chicago, IL.
Dr. Padesky has drawn attention to the importance of continuing controlled breathing for four minutes or more in order for full benefit of the method to be achieved.

I'd like to specifically acknowledge Emily Hauck, Ph.D., of Dean Medical Center for helping to improve this chapter by generously sharing her resources and expertise in pulmonary physiology and rebreathing strategies.

Session Six: When Panic Hits
Bouton, M.E., Mineka, S. and Barlow, D.H. (2001). A modern learning theory perspective on the etiology of panic disorder, *Psychological Review*, 108, 4-32.

As noted, the SRB method taught in this program was developed over time based on methods described originally in Goldstein, A. and Stainback, B. (1987). *Overcoming Agoraphobia.* New York: Viking Penguin.

It should be noted that the SRB method is not an end in itself, but a method that achieves several goals important in overcoming panic attacks. While it does, in fact, interrupt catastrophic thinking and decrease physiological arousal (which, in turn, halts impending panic), it also offers users a coping strategy which decreases their fear of panic and, thereby, the likelihood of attacks; it provides relief early on, which furthers readers' ability and willingness to approach feared situations (i.e., to engage in exposure); it provides a repeated demonstration that much of their anxiety and symptomotology arises from their own thinking in a highly predictable relationship — a crucial understanding for successful cognitive restructuring; it increases their sense of self-efficacy (which Bouton, Mineka, and Barlow posit are important in overcoming panic); and, finally, it increases their ability to identify early triggers for symptoms, which increases awareness of emotional themes related to their panic attacks.

It should be noted that the descriptions on pages 75-76 are extreme oversimplifications; during panic, there are of course a whole host of interactions among systems with one reaction influencing another and, in turn, being influenced by others. It was felt, however, that a streamlined explanation would be most useful for a panic sufferer whose primary aim is to understand panic sufficiently to achieve control over his or her symptoms.

While various clinicians and researchers have articulated and further extended our understanding of the panic cycle (in essence, that a physical sensation prompts a catastrophic misinterpretation, leading to spiraling of the two and to eventual, full-blown panic), the two researchers who follow were among the very first to outline this notion:

Ley, R. (1985). Agoraphobia, the panic attack and the hyperventilation syndrome. *Behaviour Research and Therapy*, 23, 79-81.

Ley, R. (1985). Blood, breath and fears: A hyperventilatory theory of panic and agoraphobia. *Clinical Psychology Review*, 5, 271-285.

Clark, D.M. (1986). A cognitive approach to panic. *Behaviour Research and Therapy*, 24, 461-47.

Session Seven: The Triggers of Panic

While there's often reference in the popular press to low blood sugar (or *hypoglycemia*) as a possible trigger for panic attacks, in fact, research has repeatedly failed to find any genuine connection between them.

Beckfield, D.F. (1997). Understanding and addressing susceptibility to panic, in L. VandeCreek, S. Knapp, and T.L. Jackson (Eds.), *Innovations in Clinical Practice: A Sourcebook* (Vol. 16). Sarasota, FL: Professional Resource Exchange, Inc.

Liebman, S.E., and Allen, G.J. (1995). Anxiety sensitivity, state anxiety, and perceptions of facial emotions. *Journal of Anxiety Disorders,* 9, 257-267.

This study suggests that a chronic state of vigilance (typical among those with panic, as well as other anxiety disorders) triggers heightened anxiety in ambiguous situations. Thus it's easy to see how readily panic might be triggered in different social situations.

Shear, M.K. and Weiner, K. (1997). Psychotherapy for panic disorder. *Journal of Clinical Psychiatry,* 58, supp. 2, 38-43.

Stein, M.B. (1995). Irregular breathing during sleep in patients with panic disorder. *American Journal of Psychiatry,* 152, 1168-1173.

Telch, M.J., Silverman, A., and Schmidt, N.B. (1996). Effects of anxiety sensitivity and perceived control on emotional responding to caffeine challenge. *Journal of Anxiety Disorders,* 10 (1), 21-35.

This research confirms that, indeed, when those with panic disorder understand the *reason* for their symptoms, they automatically experience far less tendency to generate catastrophic explanations and to panic — hence the importance of understanding sources and triggers, including in the emotional realm.

The paper also discusses the various ways in which caffeine influences panic symptoms.

Session Eight: Challenging Catastrophic Beliefs

Craske, M.G., and Pontillo, D.C. (2001). Cognitive biases in anxiety disorders and their effect on cognitive-behavioral treatment. *Bulletin of the Menninger Clinic,* 65, 58-77.

Hedley, L.M., Hoffart, A., Dammen, T., Ekeberg, O. and Friis, S. (2000). The relationship between cognitions and panic attack intensity. *Acta Psychiatrica Scandinavica,* 102, 300-302.

The Dammen et al. (1999) study referenced in Session one surveyed patients referred to a cardiology outpatient clinic for evaluation of chest pain and found that *thirty-eight percent* of them, in fact had diagnosable panic disorder and no underlying cardiac disease. This may help panic sufferers to realize that physical symptoms, no matter how powerful and specific, truly can represent an aspect of their panic, and not an indicant of underlying, catastrophic physical illness.

Beck, A.T., Sokal, L., Clark, D.A., Berchick, R., and Wright, F. (1992). A crossover study of focused cognitive therapy for panic disorder. *American Journal of Psychiatry, 149,* 778-783.

Borkovec, T.D. and Whisman, M.A. (1996). Psychosocial treatment for generalized anxiety disorder. In M. Mavissakalian and R. Prien (Eds.), *Long-term Treatments of Anxiety Disorders.* Washington, D.C.: American Psychiatric Association.

Brown, G.K., Beck, A.T., Newman, C.F., Beck, J.S., and Tran, G.Q. (1997). A comparison of focused and standard cognitive therapy for panic disorder. *Journal of Anxiety Disorders, 11,* 329-345.
This study is one of the huge volume suggesting the central importance of cognitive restructuring for overcoming panic in an enduring way.

Chambless, D.L., Caputo, G.C., Bright, P. and Gallagher, R. (1984). Assessment of fear of fear in agoraphobics: The Body Sensations Questionnaire and the Agoraphobic Cognitions Questionnaire. *Journal of Clinical and Consulting Psychology, 52,* 1090-1097.

Clark, D.M., Salkovskis, P.M., Gelder, M., Koehler, C., Martin, M., Anastasiades, P., Hackmann, A., Middleton, H., and Jeavons, A. (1988). Tests of a cognitive theory of panic. In I. Hand and H.U. Wittchen (Eds.), *Panic and Phobias II.* Berlin: Springer-Verlag.

Greenberger, D., and Padesky, C.A. (1995). *Mind Over Mood: A Cognitive Therapy Treatment Manual for Clients.* New York: Guilford.
This reference is an excellent self-guide to challenging unwanted thought patterns.

Harvey, J.M., Richards, J.C., Dziadosz, T., and Swindell, A (1993). Misinterpretation of ambiguous stimuli in panic disorder. *Cognitive Therapy and Research, 17,* 235-247.

Michelson, L., Marchione, K., Greenwald, M., Glanz, L., Testa, S., and Marchione, N. (1990). Panic disorder: Cognitive-behavioral treatment. *Behaviour Research and Therapy, 28,* 141-51.
This paper offers a brief, yet clear, description of some of the important strategies of cognitive restructuring for panic, such as Socratic questioning by the therapist and client-generated "tests" of their beliefs about their symptoms.

Michelson, L., Marchione, K., Greenwald, M., Testa, S., and Marchione, N. (1996). A comparative outcome and follow-up investigation of panic disorder with agoraphobia: The relative and combined efficacy of cognitive therapy, relaxation training, and therapist-assisted exposure. *Journal of Anxiety Disorders, 10,* 297-330.
This reference indicates clearly that, to eliminate panic attacks in an enduring way, cognitions must be addressed.

Ottaviani, R., and Beck, A.T. (1987). Cognitive aspects of panic disorder. *Journal of Anxiety Disorders, 1,* 15-28.

Rapee, R.M. (1995) Psychological factors influencing the affective response to biological challenge procedures in panic disorder. *Journal of Anxiety Disorders, 9,* 59-74.

Rapee, R., Mattick, R., and Murrell, E. (1986). Cognitive mediation in the affective component of spontaneous panic attacks. *Journal of Behavioural Therapy and Experimental Psychiatry,* 17, 245-253.

Reiss, S., Peterson, R.A., and Gursky, D.M. (1988). Anxiety sensitivity, injury sensitivity, and individual differences in fearfulness. *Behaviour Research and Therapy, 26,* 341-45.

Salkovskis, P.M., and Clark, D.M. (1991). Cognitive treatment of panic disorder. *Journal of Cognitive Psychotherapy, 3,* 215-226.

Van Den Hout, M.A., Van Der Molen, M., Griez, E., and Lousberg, H. (1987). Specificity of interoceptive fears to panic disorders. *Journal of Psychopathology and Behavioral Assessment, 9,* 99-106.

Westling, B.E. and Ost, L. (1993). Relationship between panic attack symptoms and cognitions in panic disorder patients. *Journal of Anxiety Disorders, 7,* 181-94.
This study, described on page 106, found that panic attacks accompanied by catastrophic thoughts (e.g., "I'm having a heart attack!") are likely to be more severe than those that are not.

Session Nine: Taking Back Your Life

Park, J.M., Mataix-Cols, D., Marks, I.M., Ngamthipwatthana, T., Marks, M., Araya, R., and Al-Kubaisy, T. (2001)
Two-year follow-up after a randomised controlled trial of self- and clinician-accompanied exposure for phobia/panic disorders. *British Journal of Psychiatry, 178,* 543-548.

This study is particularly meaningful to those following the program outlined in this book, since it shows not only the effectiveness of self-directed exposure in overcoming panic and agoraphobic symptoms, but also the resilience of gains made.

Acierno, R.E., Hersen, M., and Van Hasselt, V.B. (1993). Interventions for panic disorder: A critical review of the literature. Clinical Psychology Review, 13, 561-578.

Wittchen, H.V., and Essau, C.A. (1991). The epidemiology of panic attacks, panic disorder, and agoraphobia. In J.R. Walker, G.R. Norton and C.A. Ross (Eds.). *Panic Disorder and Agoraphobia: A Comprehensive Guide for the Practitioner* (pp. 103-149). CA: Brooks/Cole Publishing Co.

A note to therapists: When someone appears to have panic disorder but symptoms do not improve as expected with appropriate intervention, including exposure therapy; and where a history of serious trauma exists, it may be that the person is suffering not from panic disorder but from post-traumatic stress disorder. This requires more specialized understanding and treatment techniques, outside the scope of this book. One resource that is highly recommended is this one:

Winston, S. (1996). Identifying and treating phobias following a trauma. In Lindemann, C. (Ed.), *The Handbook of the Treatment of the Anxiety Disorders* (2nd Ed., PP. 367-398).

Session Ten: Internal Affairs

Ito, L.M., De Araujo, L.A., Tess, V.L.C., De Barros-Neto, T.P., Asbahr, F.R., and Marks, I. (2001). Self-exposure therapy for panic disorder with agoraphobia: Randomised controlled study of external v. interoceptive self-exposure. *British Journal of Psychiatry*, 178, 331-336.

Rudd, M.D. and Joiner, T. (1998). The role of symptom induction in the treatment of panic. *Behavior Modification*, 22(1), 96-107.

As noted in the chapter, primary credit for the development of the method of exposure to somatic sensations in the treatment of panic disorder belongs to David Barlow, Michelle Craske and associates, though aspects of it have also been included in a number of other well-researched treatment programs for panic disorder.

A variety of modifications were made in the method to maximize its applicability to a wholly self-directed program such as this one. First, the method was altered somewhat to parallel more closely the exposure method that readers have already mastered. Second, gradations in difficulty level for each sensation were introduced, such that exposures commence at a fairly non-threatening level but still culminate in full-intensity exposure to feared sensations. Finally, the method is presented late in the program, at a juncture at which readers have already experienced both a decline in anxiety regarding internal sensation and an increased confidence in their abilities to manage anxiety and tolerate sensation.

These modifications were made in the interest of improving readers' understanding of the technique, their ability to apply it on their own without professional guidance, and their comfort and willingness to do so. It is likely that any potential sacrifice in efficacy is outweighed by improved accessibility and, thereby, both compliance and success with the method.

Many of the methods for producing sensation provided in this chapter were adapted from strategies used successfully by former colleagues at Dean Medical Center (Madison, WI), in particular, Emily Hauck, Ph.D., John Martin, Ph.D., and Bill Stewart, Ph.D., all three with postdoctoral training in Behavioral Medicine.

Other sources included numerous published and verbal reports of the technique, most prominently the following two references:

Barlow, D.H. and Craske, M.G. (1989). Producing the panic sensations. In *Mastery of Your Anxiety and Panic*. Albany, NY: Graywind Publications.

Padesky, C.A. (1992). Brief Treatment for the Highly Anxious Client. Institute for the Advancement of Human Behavior Workshop, Chicago, IL.

The following are two of an increasing number that demonstrate very positive outcomes of a treatment program which includes interoceptive exposure (direct exposure to internal sensation):

Klosko, J.S., Barlow, D.H., Tassinari, R., and Cerny, J.A. (1990). A comparison of alprazolam and behavior therapy in treatment of panic disorder. *Journal of Consulting and Clinical Psychology, 58*, 77-84.

Telch, M.G. (1991, November). Group-administered panic inoculation training in the treatment of panic disorder: A controlled trial. Paper presented at the 25th annual meeting of the Association for the Advancement of Behavior Therapy. New York.

Some researchers and clinicians have begun to speculate that the primary mechanisms of interoceptive conditioning treatment packages may be the cognitive components, the self-monitoring, the physiologic relaxation and the nonspecific treatment effects incorporated into it, more so than the inductions of sensations per se. The following study, which recorded the physical changes during panic induction procedures, is one whose results could be interpreted in this way:

Riley, W.T., McCormick, M.G.F., Simon, E.M, Stack, K., Pushkin, Y, Overstreet, M.M., Carmona, J.J., and Magakian, C. (1995). Effects of alprazolam dose on the inducation and habituation processes during behavioral panic induction treatment. *Journal of Anxiety Disorders*, 9, 217-227.

The following two references, as well as Sharp et al. (1996), referenced in Session 11, and Ito et al. (2001), referenced in this Session, are provided in support of the discussion on pages 151-152 (Which is Better? External or Internal Exposure?) They all include reports of success rates for CBT indicating that those utilizing *in vivo* exposure methods rival those using interoceptive methods:

Margraf, J., Barlow, D.H., Clark, D.M., and Telch, M.J. (1993). Psychological treatment of panic: Work in progress on outcome, active ingredients, and follow-up. *Behaviour Research and Therapy.* 31, 1-8.

Michelson, L.K., and Marchione, K. (1991). Behavioral, cognitive, and pharmacological treatments of panic disorder with agoraphobia: Critique and synthesis. *Journal of Consulting and Clinical Psychology.* 59, 100-114.

Session Eleven: The Question of Medications

Space does not permit inclusion of the myriad of studies evaluating the impact of specific medications on panic disorder. Studies referenced here are primarily overviews of medication usage in panic disorder, studies that examine the combination of medications with cognitive-behavioral therapy and those that convey general principles of importance in the use of medications for panic.

Barlow, D.H., Gorman, J.M., Shear, M.K., and Woods, S.W. (2000). Cognitive-behavior therapy, imipramine, or their combination for panic disorder: A randomized controlled trial. *Journal of the American Medical Association, 283,* 2529-2536

Biondi, M. and Picardi, A. (2003). Increased probability of remaining in remission from panic disorder with agoraphobia after drug treatment in patients who received concurrent cognitive-behavioural therapy: A follow-up study. *Psychotherapy & Psychosomatics, 72,* 34-42.

Davidson, J.R. (1998). The long-term treatment of panic disorder. *Journal of Clinical Psychiatry, 57,* 17-23.

Davidson, J.R. and Moroz, G. (1998). Pivotal studies of clonazepam in panic disorder. *Psychopharmacology Bulletin, 34,* 169-174.

Foa, E.B., Franklin, M.E., and Moser, J. (2002). Context in the clinic: How well do cognitive-behavioral therapies and medication work in combination? *Biological Psychiatry, 51,* 987-997.

Kampman, M., Keijsers, G.P., Hoogdvin, C.A., and Hendriks, G.J. (2002). A randomized, double-blind, placebo-controlled study of the effect of adjunctive paroxetine in panic disorder patients unsuccessfully treated with cognitive-behavioral therapy alone. *Journal of Clinical Psychiatry, 63,* 772-777.

Kasper, S., and Resinger, E. (2001). Panic disorder: The place of benzodiazepines and selective serotonin reuptake inhibitors. *European Neuropsychopharmacology, 11,* 307-321.

Moroz, G., and Rosenbaum, J.F. (1999). Efficacy, safety, and gradual discontinuation of clonazepam in panic disorder: a placebo-controlled, multicenter study using optimized doses. *Journal of Clinical Psychiatry, 60-604-61:*
This study found no evidence of a rebound effect following the discontinuation of clonazepam (Klonopin), which distinguishes it from the other benzodiazepines used most commonly to treat panic disorder (e.g., alprazolam, or xanax.).

Pollack, M.H., and Marzol, P.C. (2000). Panic: course, complications and treatment of panic disorder. *Journal of Psychopharmacology, 14,* 25-30.

262 Master Your Panic

Rapaport, M.H., Wolkow, R., Rubin, A., Hackett, E., Pollack, M., and Ota, K.Y. (2001). Sertraline treatment of panic disorder: results of a long-term study. *Acta Psychiatrica Scandinavica*, 104, 289-298.
This study confirmed the widely-held clinical impression that the side effects of SSRIs generally decrease quite markedly over time, and also demonstrated the efficacy and safety of one of them, sertraline (Zoloft), over a 2-year period.

Sheehan, D.V. (1999). Current concepts in the treatment of panic disorder. *Journal of Clinical Psychiatry*, 60, 16-21.

Slaap, B.R., and den Boer, J.A. (2001). The prediction of nonresponse to pharmacotherapy in panic disorder: a review. *Depression and Anxiety*, 14, 112-122.

Spiegel, D.A. (1999). Psychological strategies for discontinuing benzodiazepine treatment. *Journal of Clinical Psychopharmocology*, 19, 17-22.

Stein, M.B., Norton, G.R., Walker, J.R., Chartier, M.J. and Graham, R. (2000). Do selective serotonin re-uptake inhibitors enhance the efficacy of very brief cognitive behavioral therapy for panic disorder? A pilot study. *Psychiatry Research*, 94, 191-200.

Westra, H.A., Stewart, S.H., and Conrad, B.E. (2002). Naturalistic manner of benzodiazepine use and cognitive behavioral therapy outcome in panic disorder with agoraphobia. *Journal of Anxiety Disorders*, 16, 233-246.

Abelson, J.L. and Curtis, G.C. (1993). Discontinuation of alprazolam after successful treatment of panic disorder: A naturalistic follow-up study. *Journal of Anxiety Disorders*, 7, 107-17.

Breier, A., Charney, D.S., and Heninger, G.R. (1984). Major depression in patients with agoraphobia and panic disorder. *Archives of General Psychiatry*, 41, 1129-35.

Klerman, G.L. (1988). Overview of the cross-national collaborative panic study. *Archives of General Psychiatry*, 45, 407-12.

Lesser, I.M., Rubin, R.T., Pecknold, J.C., Rifkin, A., Swinson, R.P., Lydiard, R.B., Burrows, G.D., Noyes, R., and DuPont, R.L. (1988). Secondary depression in panic disorder and agoraphobia:

Frequency, severity and response to treatment. *Archives of General Psychiatry*, 45, 437-43.

Pollack, M.H., and Otto, M.W. (1997). Long-term course and outcome of panic disorder. *Journal of Clinical Psychiatry*, 58 (suppl. 2), 57-60.

Sharp, D.M., Power, K.G., Simpson, R.J., Swanson, V., Moodie, E., Anstee, J.A., and Ashford, J.J. (1996). Fluvoxamine, placebo, and cognitive behaviour therapy used alone and in combination in the treatment of panic disorder and agoraphobia. *Journal of Anxiety Disorders*, 10, 219-242.
This study is a very well-controlled comparison of the effects of medication, cognitive-behavior, and their combination for treating panic.

Smoller, J.W., and Pollack, M.H. (1997). Recent developments in the pharmacotherapy of anxiety disorders. *ADAA Reporter*, VIII-1, 1 and 23-24.

Session Twelve: Where Have You Been? Where Are You Going?

Goldstein, A.J., deBeurs, E., Chambless, D.L., and Wilson, K.A. (2000). EMDR for panic disorder with agoraphobia; Comparison with waiting list and credible attention-placebo control conditions. *Journal of Consulting and Clinical Psychology*, 283, 2529-2536.
Given the popularity, even trendiness, of EMDR (Eye movement desensitization and reprocessing), it's important to note that, prior to this study, it had never been adequately tested for effectiveness; its purported efficacy has been based solely on anecdotal reports or on comparisons with a no-treatment control condition. This study, however, compared EMDR to a credible attention-placebo control condition and found no evidence of EMDR's effectiveness as a treatment for panic disorder.

Wright, J., Clum, G.A., Roodman, A., and Febbraro, G.A.M., (2000). A bibliotherapy approach to relapse prevention in individuals with panic attacks. *Journal of Anxiety Disorders*, 14, 483-419.

Beckfield, D.F. (1997). Understanding and addressing susceptibility to panic, in L. VandeCreek, S. Knapp, and T.L. Jackson (Eds.), *Innovations in Clinical Practice: A Sourcebook* (Vol. 16), Sarasota, FL: Professional Resource Exchange, Inc.

Barlow, D.B. (1997). Cognitive-behavioral therapy for panic disorder: Current status. *Journal of Clinical Psychiatry*, 32-37.

Craske, M.G., Brown, T.A., and Barlow, D.H. (1991). Behavioral treatment of panic disorder: A two-year follow-up. *Behavior Therapy*, 22, 289-304.

Fava, G.A., Zielezny, M., Savron, G., and Grandi, S. (1995). Long-term effects of behavioural treatment for panic disorder with agoraphobia. *British Journal of Psychiatry*. 166, 87-92.

Gould, R.A., Clum, G.A., and Shapiro, D. (1993). The use of bibiotherapy in the treatment of panic: A preliminary investigation. *Behavior Therapy*, 24, 241-252.

In this study, 73 percent of those with panic disorder were able to overcome their panic attacks through reading a self-help book on coping with panic (plus follow-up phone calls to the participants to be certain the book was being read).

The two studies that follow continued this work; and the research by Hecker, et al., evaluated and further extended the work on bibliotherapy for the treatment of panic.

Gould, R.A., and Clum, G.A., (1995). Self-help plus minimal therapist contact in the treatment of panic disorder: A replication and extension. *Behavior Therapy*, 26, 533-546.

Lidren, D.M., Watkins, P.L., Gould, R.A., Clum, G.A., Asterino, M., and Tulloch, H.L. (1994). A comparison of bibliotherapy and group therapy in the treatment of panic disorder. *Journal of Consulting and Clinical Psychology*, 62, 865-869.

Hecker, J.E., Losee, M.C., Fritzler, B.K., and Fink, C.M. (1997). Self-directed versus therapist-directed cognitive-behavioral treatment for panic disorder. *Journal of Anxiety Disorders*, 10, 253-265.

Self-Help Resources. There are many books available on overcoming panic, some of them very good. Each book has special strengths and, invariably, teaches something new. Once you've mastered the techniques in this book, and have had a chance for the ideas to "settle" in your mind, and for the techniques to become a part of your regular routines, you may choose to read others as well, with much benefit.

While it's beyond the scope of this book to evaluate all the other self-help books available, a good source of books on panic disorder and agoraphobia, and on the other anxiety disorders as well, is available from the catalog published by the Anxiety Disorders Association of America, and also available on their website, www.adaa.org. The website also lists self-help support groups available in every state, and is a useful all-around resource.

The organization is composed of both professional and consumer members, and promotes research and education for the prevention and treatment of anxiety disorders. Consumer members receive a self-help newsletter at regular intervals, state listings of health care professionals and self-help groups, other informational materials, and discounts on the various publications available through their bookstore.

In addition to accessing the ADAA through their website, you can write to them at 8730 Georgia Ave., Suite 600, Silver Spring, MD, 20910 or phone (240) 485-1001 for information on becoming a consumer member at a very modest fee, and for a free copy of the bookstore catalog.

Additionally, a majority of those with panic and other anxiety disorders find self-help groups a great support. Even those unable to locate or attend a group can benefit by subscribing to the newsletters published y several organizations that promote and assist self-help groups. The ADAA, as described above, provides a comprehensive listing of those available in various areas of the country.

A particularly useful organization, due to its excellent newsletter and the geographically widespread number of support groups it sponsors, is A.B.I.L. (Agoraphobics Building Independent Lives), located at 400 West 32nd St., Richmond, VA, 23225-3428, (804) 353-3964; www.anxietysupport.org.

Finally, the Madison Institute of Medicine is an enormously helpful resource, both for professionals and for individuals suffering from anxiety disorders. The nonprofit organization's Information Centers offer literature searches on mental health topics, answers to quick reference questions by phone, referrals to support groups and specialists, CME courses and inexpensive patient information booklets on topics including panic disorder and agoraphobia, social anxiety, posttraumatic stress disorder, fearful flyers, obsessive-compulsive disorder in adults and children, and trichotillomania. The information and services provided represent the latest in expert, authoritative knowledge in the field.

Madison Institute of Medicine, 7617 Mineral Point Road, Suite 300, Madison, WI 53717; (608) 827-2470; www.miminc.org.

Appendix VI

Record-keeping forms
to duplicate and carry with you.

Panic Episodes Log

Use daily to record episodes of panic and near-panic. (Detailed instructions for use can be found on pages 56-58.)

Time / place / companions present during attack:

Severity of attack from 1 to 10:
1 _____10
No anxiety noticeable   Worst anxiety ever felt

First signs (e.g., racing heart, uneasy feeling):

Activities / thoughts / feelings just before attack:

Other ideas re: precipitants of attack:

Major activities / overall mood of the day:

Coping strategies used / effects of:

_____

_____

Remember the following points in completing the log:
    -Be sure to record every episode in any case, whether or not it progresses to a full-blown attack.
    -If you judge an episode of anxiety to be anticipatory anxiety, remember to label it AA and note what situation you were feeling anxious about entering.
    (In that case, you'll have no entries for first signs, activities just before attack, or other ideas about precipitants.)
    -If you have no panic attacks or near-panic episodes to record at the end of the day, note only the main activities and overall mood of the day.
    -If you experience mild anxiety that progresses no further, note the experience briefly.

Planned Practice of SRB

Note that if you use SRB as a coping strategy, which you should do anytime you notice sensations of anxiety, you'll record that use in your daily log; this record is for your formal, planned practices:

What situation did I use to produce anxiety?

How vividly was I able to imagine (or recall) the situation I selected?* (You need to make it feel as "real" as possible.)

1 _____10

How much did my anxiety level increase over normal?

1 _____10

Did I begin using SRB the moment my anxiety began to develop?

1 _____10

How well was I able to stop any catastrophic thinking?

1 _____10

How well did I refocus my thinking on the present?

1 _____10

What did I notice in the present that absorbed by attention?

How well was I able to alter my breathing (that is, use controlled breathing as taught in Session #5)?

1 _____10

*All the rating scales should be rated from least (1) to most or greatest (10)

Overall, how well did the practice session go:

How well was I able to apply the method according to Session Six instructions?

1 _10

How much did my anxiety decrease as a result?

1 _10

How confident am I feeling of my abilities to conduct SRB during practice sessions?

1 _10

What parts of the practice still need "fine-tuning"?

Any further thoughts about how I might improve my use of the strategy, about the practice session or about SRB in general:

Note: After a few formal practices, you may feel well able to use the method and at that point (not before), you can reduce your record-keeping, simply noting the fact of your practice and anything striking that you noticed.

   If you ever find yourself having difficulties using SRB "in real life," in addition to reviewing Session six, resume the more detailed record-keeping to "catch" any weak areas.

Challenging Catastrophic Cognitions

Anxiety-producing   Challenges
   Self-statements

-Remember to thoroughly evaluate your self-statement before you generate challenges, using the guidelines on pages 116-117 and the "Special Help" Summary, Challenging Catastrophic Cognitions: Questions to Ask Yourself (page 123). Make any notes you find helpful to you.

Recording Exposures

This form will make it easier to record your anxiety level during exposures, as described on page 139.

Along the bottom of the graph (marked Day 1), record the day of the week (or the date) you conduct your first exposure to a given place or situation.

Indicate the level of anxiety you felt during the exposure by placing xxx's above the day, right up to the number that matches your anxiety, where 1 x indicates almost no anxiety and 10 indicates the worst anxiety you've ever felt.

Use the same procedure for subsequent exposures to that same situation or place.

Use a new sheet for each new situation you decide to tackle using exposures, so you have a separate record for every different situation. That way you'll see your progress most clearly!

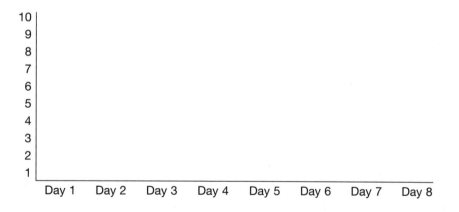

Index

More Books With *IMPACT*

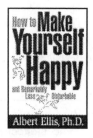

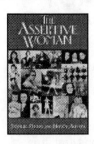

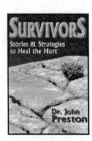